RAISING *my* BROTHER'S CHILD

SCOTT **HILTON**

TMD Publishing

Raising My Brother's Child
99 Real-Life Stories + 290 Practical Insights
to inspire those raising children they didn't bring into the world

ISBN: 978-1-959083-00-9 (Hardcover)
ISBN:978-1-959083-01-6 (Paperback)
ISBN: 978-1-959083-02-3 (eBook)
ISBN: 978-1-959083-03-0 (Audiobook)

Front cover artwork by Taylor Manley
Graphic Design & Book Design by Colin Edwards
www.thatsmydadproject.com

THE

that's my DAD

—— PROJECT ——

breaking cycles of generational fatherlessness
and inspiring fathers to become great dads

- CONTENTS -

THANK YOU

To my parents, Norris and Marilyn Hilton. Thank you for being the best parents a man could have and for teaching me the meaning of true religion, compassion, hospitality and unconditional love.

To my wife, Diana. Thank you for standing by my side and for enduring what many women would not have endured.

To the 300+ boys who lived at Eagle Rock. Many of you endured the misfortune of my many mistakes. I love you all and thank you for enriching my life.

To my children, Danny and Aly. Thank you for never complaining about having to share your dad with 300 others. You were a joy to raise and I'm proud to say I'm your dad.

To Patrick Henry, our first DYS licensing agent. Thank you for your patience and coaching in those early years and for remembering that everyone is a work in progress.

To the thousands of people who entrusted me with financial resources. Thank you. Together, we sought to help those most vulnerable among us.

To Belinda Hiti. I wish to offer you a huge thank you for being the best co-worker I've ever had. Your compassion, selflessness, and tireless work ethic are unmatched. I would not have given leadership of Eagle Rock to anyone else and I appreciate you continuing to carry the torch.

To the dozens of Eagle Rock Houseparents. You quietly loved our boys unconditionally and made untold, sacrificial investments in their lives. You are heroes to many.

To Colin Edwards and Nathan Gallman. Thank you for figuring out a way to get my thoughts off of the paper and into the world.

To Jenny Gallman, my editor. Thank you for making a country boy appear to be a professional writer.

To my friends & family. Thank you to each of you who took the time to read & offer insight on the pre-published versions of this book. It made the difference.

- *PREFACE* -

I am convinced that the most honorable people on the face of the earth are those who take care of children to whom they did not give birth. There is no greater calling. These people, whom I choose to call "Volunteer Parents" (VP's), faithfully and quietly go about doing one of the most important and sometimes most difficult tasks of all humanity - that of caring for children.

Whether you are a foster parent, adoptive parent, house parent, cottage parent, work in a group home, or are for some other reason raising children to whom you did not give birth, you face unique challenges and must have a unique mindset to survive.

This book was originally intended to be a collection of devotional thoughts to encourage VPs. It grew into more than that. I trust it will encourage, inspire, and instruct the real heroes of humanity - those who are raising their brother's child.

It is my deepest desire that, through these pages, helpful insights will be gained to help us all reduce the suffering of hurting children and to break the cycles of dysfunction that so often influence them.

FOUNDATION 1

- *UNDERSTANDING YOUR CALLING* -

A Higher Calling
A Pat on the Back
Failure
Disappointment
Perseverance

CHAPTER 1

- *A HIGHER CALLING* -

My cousin Ric is on staff at a large church. The church is well known for its youth and children's programs as well as for producing a number of sports and music camps for children. Ric, being the creative genius of the family, realized that the church places so much value on music and athletics that it often fails to see real talent when it comes in other forms. He decided to do something that no one had ever thought of doing. He decided to have a "talentless talent show." Actually, it was not talentless. It was to be a show which included all sorts of real talent, but none of it could consist of anything musical or athletic.

Think with me for a moment. Every talent show to which I have ever been consisted of people singing, playing musical instruments, or performing some sort of athletic feat. Ric's show would have none of the above. He decided he should have auditions and was amazed at all the non-musical, non-athletic things people could do. One kid claimed he could put his entire hand inside of his mouth. He auditioned and won a spot in the show. However, he accidentally got his fist stuck inside his mouth and had to receive medical attention. Others performed all sorts of amazing "talents."

A few days before the show, one of the church custodians approached Ric and asked if he could audition to be in his talent show. Roosevelt had been a custodian for many years. Because he seemed to always get his job done, nobody really paid much attention to what he did. Ric was both curious and nervous about the audition. He said he had no idea what "talent" Roosevelt might present, and he did not want to hurt his feelings if it was not entertaining enough for the show. Roosevelt took Ric to a large, empty room in the church. In the corner was a stack of about one hundred chairs. Anyone who has been to a modern church building knows the sort of chair I'm talking about. They are designed to be stacked and moved out of the way when not in use. Roosevelt handed Ric a stopwatch and said "Clock me." What happened next was, according to my cousin, one of the most amazing things he had ever seen. Roosevelt literally ran across the room, began unstacking the chairs at breakneck speed, and within one minute had all the chairs perfectly set up in rows. In less than one minute the room went from being totally empty to being completely ready to seat one hundred people. He then told Ric to restart the timer. To Ric's amazement, Roosevelt restacked the chairs and had them neatly placed in the corner of the room in less than one minute. Ric stood in amazement. Roosevelt earned a spot in the show.

About 500 people attended the Saturday evening "no-talent" talent show, and it turned out to be quite an event. Roosevelt performed his feat and the amazed crowd gave him a standing ovation. The elderly custodian, whom nobody paid much attention to, had a calling on his life and a unique talent. He was an important part of the church.

You, as a VP, have a calling on your life. It may not get much attention, and it may not happen within the walls of a church, but it is still a calling. It has been said that one's calling in life is where his or her greatest joy collides with the world's greatest need. I would add that joy does not always come in the form of warm fuzzies. Sometimes joy comes from simply knowing you are being obedient to God.

My university gave a 20% discount on tuition to anyone who planned to enter full-time ministry. I found it interesting that almost all of the people receiving the discount were planning to be on staff at a church or with a missionary organization. However, I knew it would get some strange looks if I listed my ministry as "want to be a Dad to troubled boys." Therefore, I opted to keep it simple and said I was going into "youth ministry." I got the discount.

My father is a Baptist minister with all the credentials. He has been a pastor for many years. However, I believe his greatest ministry may have been in his daily life outside the church. He has coached little league, served on the school board, was president of the PTA, and most importantly for me, has been just a plain-ole-good Daddy. He and my mother have taken dozens of hurting people into their home where they ministered to them. My mother is not the typical preacher's wife. She cannot sing, play piano, or teach Sunday school, but has always been there for my sister and me. When we went away to college, she began taking care of international students from our local community college. They needed help with everything from learning how to use deodorant to learning how to speak English. Many nights, Momma stayed up all night teaching English and often served as a surrogate mother for homesick kids. One time there was a bad car accident involving a student from another country. His family could not afford to take care of him, so when he was released from the hospital, my mother took him into our home and cared for him for several weeks. She impacted this young man and his family far more in our home than she could have done inside the church walls. On many occasions, the students would become depressed and homesick and my parents would be there to give them a hug and a listening ear. Some of those kids became Christians and are committed to Christ today – partly as a result of what went on at our house – not in our church building.

The same can be said for my grandparents. They were forever taking people into their home, including the child of a relative who had been killed in an accident. My grandmother died at age 99, so when we planned the funeral, we assumed no one would attend. She had outlived all of her friends. However, when the day of the funeral arrived the church was packed with "young" people. Because

I was both amazed and curious, I asked my Dad, "Who are all of these people?" He replied that most of them were people who had lived with my grandparents at one time or another. I don't mean one or two people – I'm talking about dozens of people. My grandparents had a ministry in their home just like you do!

I challenge you to redefine your concept of "ministry." If you think most of God's work is done in the church, think again. God can use a home as much as He can a church. Your opportunity to mold and direct a child and love on him or her is the greatest opportunity in the world. Your calling, like my parents', may not be to go to a foreign land. Your missionary calling may very well be found in your living room and at your dinner table. You, like Roosevelt, may go unnoticed by the multitudes, but you are important. Just imagine how well Roosevelt's church would have functioned if he had not mastered the God-given skill of stacking and unstacking chairs. He helped his church grow from a small home group to a 5,000-member congregation by simply doing his part. While you may or may not be called to help grow a church, you are called to help grow something much more important - a child!

According to UNICEF (the United Nations Children's Emergency Fund), there are roughly 153 million orphans worldwide. Every day an estimated 5,700 more children become orphans. In the United States, there are approximately 437,000 children in the foster care system on any given day. According to the U.S. Department of Health and Human Services, in 2016 (the last year of reported data) there were over 117,000 children waiting for adoption, but only 57,000 placements occurred *(Jones, Jennifer S. "How Many Orphans Worldwide? What to Do." Adoption.org, November 18, 2018).* This, obviously, does not include the thousands of children who are being raised by aunts, uncles, grandparents, friends, and neighbors.

According to the Pew Research Center, in 2015 there were 2.3 billion Christians of all ages living in the world. The Center for the Study of Global Christianity (CSGC) at Gordon-Conwell Theological Seminary reported that the number of Christians in the world edged past 2.5 billion in 2019. About 230 million Americans call themselves Christians (learnreligions.com). If my math is correct, there are 77 million more Christians in America alone than there are orphans in the entire world. You can draw your own conclusion about a group that is instructed at least 36 times in its own scripture to care for orphans.

Whether you are a foster parent, an adoptive parent, a house parent, or are literally raising your brother's child, you are a minister. You may not be seen in the pulpit every Sunday; your name may not be in lights, but to that child living in your home, you are the most influential minister they will ever know. You are in a position to forever change his or her world.

In Matthew 7:18 we read of a time when Simon Peter and his brother Andrew were on a fishing trip when Jesus happened to walk by the Sea of Galilee. This is probably not the first time Jesus had seen these brothers, and it is my guess he had noticed they were hard workers. Jesus spoke twelve words that changed their lives: *"Come, follow me and I will send you out to fish for people."*(NIV) Notice he did not say, "Come follow me and I will make you the pastor at First Baptist of Galilee" or "Follow me and I will help you get a theology degree." He simply wanted them to fish for people. I love pastors and recommend theology degrees, but I do not think either of them is required to be a fisher of people. You, as a VP, have a great and important calling. Go fishing!

TEN PRACTICAL THINGS TO REMEMBER ABOUT YOUR CALLING.

1. Do not get hung up on the idea that ministry only happens inside a church building. Ministry is really more a matter of doing what God calls you to do than it is a matter of where you do it.
2. Understand that being a VP is a high calling, and you will be held to a higher standard than most.
3. Realize when God calls a person to service that call may not

be permanent. He may have different jobs for you to do later. However, your relationship and commitment to a child should be permanent.

4. Realize that not all ministry calling gives us goosebumps. Do not let your calling be based on emotion alone. When God calls you to do something, you should be confident, but that does not mean you are going to stay on "cloud nine" all the time.

5. Be committed. Once you are sure of your calling, stick with it. Being a VP is much like being married; it does not always operate on love – sometimes commitment is the only glue holding you together.

6. Be realistic. You may love the idea of being a houseparent at a home for emotionally disturbed boys but also have biological children who will have to live there as well. Is that realistic? Or, you may love the idea of fostering a baby, but is that a realistic plan if you can barely take care of your own needs?

7. Don't expect God's plan for your life to be revealed all at once. That would probably scare you to death. If He is calling or has called you to be a VP, take the first step. Do not get caught up in the "analysis by paralysis" trap.

8. Get your finances in order. Being a VP should never be a part of a plan to gain financial freedom. Many children's homes have discovered that immature people sometimes see houseparenting as a means of having a "free" place to live while they pay off some bills. These houseparents usually turn out to be miserable. Too many people in our society are fostering children because they come with a check. Remember, being a VP is not a job, it is a calling.

9. Get your health in order. Being a VP requires a tremendous amount of energy. I am not saying you have to be a triathlete, but if you are facing chemotherapy or you are 300 pounds overweight it is probably not the best time to start being a VP.

10. Try not to make decisions based on emotion. Sometimes you have to do what you have to do regardless of how you feel about it. Remember that being a VP is not all fun and games. You may have romantic notions about fostering a baby, but when that

baby starts crying in the middle of the night, you may change your mind. You may feel like you need to raise the children of an irresponsible relative, but don't forget that those children may not be as happy about leaving their birth parents as you expected. Count the cost before you jump into the VP life.

CHAPTER 2

- *A PAT ON THE BACK* -

Gertrude must have been seventy years old when I hired her. She had raised a multitude of children and grandchildren and was well known for her cooking abilities. All over town, I had been told what a great cook she was, so I hired her to help our Houseparents with the evening meal. With three boys going to football practice, two in karate lessons, and the rest looking for mischief, our Houseparents barely had time for taxi service, much less to cook a good meal. Gertrude seemed like the perfect helper. She did not really need the money, but with the grandkids off to college, she was feeling useless and needed something to do with her time.

I thought Gertrude's cooking was pretty good until one of the boys informed me she was using "old fashion recipes." When I asked what he meant, he said, "She never measures anything, she just mixes and tastes until she thinks she got it right." I replied that nothing was wrong with that method. The boy said, "I agree, but she's not using a clean spoon – she just takes it out of her mouth and right back into the soup it goes." I could not help thinking of all the soup I had eaten. Unfortunately, being the boss I had to be the one to reprimand Gertrude and point out a few health department regulations - one of which prohibited tasting with the same spoon used for cooking. She was not happy, but she stayed and we all noticed the soup lost some of its "denture cream" taste.

One day during a staff meeting as the Houseparents, the social worker, a counselor and I sat around a conference table for high-level discussions, a loud knock came to the door. It was Mrs. Gertrude. She was mad, mad, mad! I reluctantly invited her in. She was carrying a knife, a spatula, and a key to the pantry. She stood at the end of the table and, in a most agitated fashion, began a rant that I will never forget. She said nasty things about me, the ranch, the house, the boys, the pots and pans, the air conditioner, the welcome mat, the driveway, and the whole pantry full of donated food. Everyone looked at me as if I should stop her. In my mind, I was thinking, "There is no way I'm getting in front of an angry, elderly, black woman with a spatula in one hand and a knife in the other."

She finally calmed down and I went into counselor mode. "Is something bothering you, Mrs. Gertrude?" I calmly asked. It was pretty funny, but I am glad nobody laughed out loud. I had been stabbed with a knife once before, and it was not fun. She replied, "I have been here cooking in that kitchen for four weeks, and not once has anybody told me "thank you!" Half the time these boys don't eat what I fix and I had to give the dogs a whole pot of soup because these ungrateful boys would not eat it." She slammed her key on the table, resigned from her job as cook and walked out, never to be seen again. The air was tense and nobody said a word so I did what any good Baptist would do when he does not know what to do; I said, "Let's pray."

Mrs. Gertrude had come to work at the ranch for all the wrong reasons. For years, she had found her value in life by serving her family delicious meals. There's nothing wrong with that, but she had also become accustomed to receiving compliments about her home cooking. She deeply enjoyed hearing her children and grandchildren make a big deal about her meals. When the boys and staff at the ranch failed to stroke her in the same way, she took it as a form of rejection and felt her value as a person depreciating. Her natural reaction to the rejection was to blame someone or something. We all feel anger when we are rejected and might be tempted to react in a similar way. Being a VP is not a good place for people who require a lot of pats on the back. It is often a lonely and thankless position.

I remember in the early days of Eagle Rock when I was both Director and Houseparent, doing a television interview in which I was portrayed to be some kind of childcare expert. The interviewer asked me several questions that I answered professionally. As I left the interview, there were lots of handshakes and comments about my expertise. Several people patted me on the back and thanked me for the good work I was doing with the boys. However, when I got home a few minutes later, I found that two boys were in a fight, two were refusing to do chores, and two had sneaked out into the woods to smoke cigarettes. My poor wife was at her wit's end while I was off receiving accolades. Needless to say, I went from a "hero to zero" faster than Carl Lewis ran the 40-yard dash. I walked out of the world of public relations into the world of reality – the reality of being a Houseparent.

One of the reasons I deeply respect foster, adoptive, and Houseparents is that they often quietly perform their daily duties while outsiders rarely notice. As Ranch Director, I was more visible and often received all the pats on the back that my Houseparents really deserved.

We all like to feel appreciated and respected, but if that is what you are looking for as a VP you are in the wrong business. Respect and appreciation can never be your motivation. That is self-serving. Your calling is to provide for the children in your care and not for your own ego. The Bible is full of people who did wonderful things but never heard a "thank you." In fact, most of the people in the Bible whom we now think of as "heroes," were ridiculed, laughed at, mocked, and made fun of during their life on Earth.

One night at the dinner table when my son was about thirteen years old he made an interesting observation that I have never forgotten. He said that the most unappreciated person in the Bible was Adam. "Adam," he said, "gets the blame for a lot of things. He is blamed for men having to work to eat and he is blamed for mothers having the pain of childbirth. He is blamed for giving us our sin nature." My son felt like Adam was getting a lot of unmerited blame so he pointed out something that we all forget – none of us would be here if not for Adam.

Think about it for a moment. As a VP you may never be told thank you and you may never get a pat on the back. Very few people will acknowledge your importance, but the fact remains - the child in your home may have never had a chance if not for you. You can give yourself a pat on the back for that.

TEN PRACTICAL THINGS TO REMEMBER ABOUT BEING APPRECIATED.

1. If you are in the VP business so people can brag on you and give you a pat on the back, you are absolutely in it for the wrong reason.
2. If you expect to get a pat on the back for doing what you are doing, you are going to be very disappointed.
3. Everyone likes to be appreciated and recognized. Don't think you are a bad person if you desire it from time to time. That desire is normal as long as it doesn't control you.
4. Some VPs are going to get more recognition and expression of appreciation than others. Some kids are naturally more grateful than others. This is not always reflective of your effectiveness nor of your efforts. Some children have trouble identifying and expressing their feelings of gratitude.
5. The outside world is going to show more appreciation and praise to some VPs than others. Again, this is not a reflection of your effectiveness. It is usually a reflection of the other person's tendency to self-promote.

6. When a child expresses appreciation to you, acknowledge his/her kindness and let him/her know that you appreciate his/her words. Do not try to appear to be super humble by downplaying the child's gratitude or appreciation. Part of their reward is in knowing that they made you feel good.

7. When an adult gives you a pat on the back because you are a good VP, accept it graciously. Don't try to deflect their kindness. Simply say, "Thanks for saying that. I appreciate your encouragement."

8. Do not expect to be a child's hero just because you have made an effort to give him/her a nurturing home. Remember that many of the children we encounter have hundreds of issues to assimilate. Identifying heroes is usually not at the top of their list of things to think about. It is usually later in life when we realize that our parents (or VPs) are our real heroes.

9. One of the basic human needs is the need to be respected. This need can be, and usually is, a good thing and in most cases contributes to civility. Some people, however, feel that if they are respected they will get lots of pats on the back. That is strangely not true. Some of the people I respect the most have no idea how I feel about them because I don't freely give out thank yous and compliments. You are probably more appreciated than you realize.

10. Remember that the only real "pat on the back" you'll ever need is the one you will receive when you stand before God at the end of your earthly life. No amount of earthly gratitude, respect, or appreciation can ever measure up to that which will come when God says, "Well done, my good and faithful servant, well done!"

CHAPTER 3

- *FAILURE* -

It was a Saturday night at 9:45. I had just finished reviewing my notes for a message I was to deliver the next morning. The phone rang. It was my sister. The tone of her voice let me know something was not right. I feared something had happened to my parents or perhaps my niece or nephew, but her words were even more shocking. "When's the last time you talked with Lamar?" Lamar was twenty-five years old and had been gone from the ranch for several years. He came to us as a malnourished eleven-year-old. For reasons that only God knows, this boy held a special place in my heart.

Several people, including my own family, did not understand why I had been so committed to helping Lamar. After all, he was constantly in trouble. Even after he finished high school and got married, trouble followed him. I went out of my way to help him find a job and become productive. He ended up in prison but phoned me regularly. The day he was released from prison he came directly to my house. At one point, Lamar seemed to have things going in the right direction. His marriage was restored; he was working regularly and he was attending church and growing spiritually. I even had him share his life story at a fundraising event. Few people had any confidence that he would live a productive life, but I was sure he could and would.

When my phone rang that night I was not prepared for the news. A friend at the sheriff's department had called my sister so she could relay the news to me. Lamar had brutally murdered four people! Within minutes, every major news channel broadcast the story and Lamar's photo was aired on every headline. The next day I learned that Lamar had actually confessed to the murders. That morning my phone rang constantly. Those who questioned my sanity prior to the murders certainly questioned it now. It turned out to be a long day for me. That night I found myself standing alone in my front yard staring into space, crying, and questioning God. First of all, I knew Lamar's life was over. He would die in prison. Secondly, I felt I had failed. I did not know how or why, but I knew I had failed.

When I began this book, my main purpose was to encourage people. This chapter is written to encourage those of you who feel like you have failed. I know I am not the only one.

The Bible is filled with stories of people who failed. Adam and Eve failed to do the one simple thing God asked of them. Sarah failed to trust God. Jonah failed to follow God's plan for his life. Moses failed to get the Israelites to obey God. Simon Peter failed to stand up for Jesus. Peter, James, and John failed to stay awake and pray. Paul and Barnabas failed to get along with each other.

We know failure was no stranger to Bible characters, but what about modern man? Issac Newton failed elementary school. F.W. Woolworth initially failed as a salesman. Walt Disney was once fired from a job. Winston Churchill failed sixth grade. Babe Ruth struck out 1,300 times. Henry Ford failed with his first two businesses. Tom Landry holds the worst NFL record in history. R.H. Macy had eight businesses fail. Harland Sanders' first restaurant went out of business and left him a poor man. Dr. Suess' first book was rejected by twenty-seven publishers. By most standards, all of these people were failures at one point in their lives.

You have probably heard of the famous failures mentioned above, but have you heard of these? (I will not mention names). The senior pastor who lost his job because his son declared his homosexuality. The pastor whose daughter became a prostitute. The pastor whose daughter became a homeless drug addict. What about the minister whose marriage ended in divorce after forty-four years? You may be surprised to know that each of these men were otherwise successful. They were famous authors, popular speakers/teachers, or pastors of megachurches; yet, they all experienced the painful failure of real life.

If you think failure is only for non-Christians, I strongly challenge you to rethink your theology. But what does all of this have to do with being a VP? It is simple. If you are a VP for any significant amount of time, you are sure to experience failure. It goes with the territory. Do not let anyone sugar-coat the job or convince you otherwise. Failure happens.

Probably the worst failure of my life occurred one afternoon when a friend of mine pulled into my driveway. I was attempting to leave in my car to go somewhere but he blocked me and insisted that I go back into the house where we could talk. He proceeded to tell me that his marriage had fallen apart and that he had "thought of ending it all." I am a trained professional counselor with a Master's Degree and several years of experience. I often led suicide prevention seminars, so I knew what to do. I asked if he had a plan and he shared with me that he had a gun in his pocket. We talked for a long time and even knelt in my living room and prayed. I felt confident that he was stable and that he would not hurt himself, so I did not take his gun from him. He left my house, drove down the street, parked his car, and shot himself in the head. I was devastated. Rule number one in a potential suicide situation is to remove any potential weapons. I had failed to do what I knew I should have done. Two days later I had to face his parents. I thought it would be the hardest thing I had ever done, but I was wrong. The hardest part was seeing his five-year-old daughter cry as she watched the casket being lowered into the ground. I had failed miserably. I hope this never happens in your life, but you can be sure that if you are a VP long enough you will experience some sort of failure.

That being said, allow me to define what I mean by "failure." Failure is something akin to the word "sin." It simply means we "miss the mark" or we "fall short of perfection." We all have our goals, hopes, and dreams for our children. By nature, these goals, hopes, and dreams are part of our "perfect" world. When they are not reached we very often feel that we have failed. However, let us not forget that when we experience failure it does not necessarily mean we have done something wrong. Many VPs and parents have done all the right things and still experience failure. It is part of living in an imperfect world.

TEN PRACTICAL THINGS TO REMEMBER ABOUT FAILURE.

1. Failure happens! You will fail to make good decisions in life. Your children will fail to make good decisions in life. Failing to make good decisions leads to and is "failure." It happens.
2. It is an imperfect world. If we lived in a perfect world no one would fail. Everyone would always make the right decision about everything. God chose to give us free will to choose. The alternative - never having the ability to choose - might eliminate failure, but it is not a great alternative.
3. God desires our faithfulness more than our perfection. It is not wise to assume you are out of the will of God just because the results of your labor do not yield the fruit you desired.
4. It is normal to feel discouraged. The life of a VP can be very discouraging. Those of us who accept greater challenges in life will increase our chances of experiencing failures.
5. Learn from your failure. When a child turns out to be less than what you had hoped for, take an honest look at the things you did with that child. Could you or should you have done something differently? More importantly, try to determine if there were things you could have done that you did not try. Never quit learning and don't be afraid to admit you have failed.
6. Be careful when comparing yourself to other VPs. Some VPs

(ranches, children's homes, foster homes) have learned to "hedge their bets" by being selective with the type of children they help. Naturally, if you only take low-risk children, your risk of "failure" is going to be lower. You can beat yourself up by comparing yourself with others. Learn from others and be honest in self-evaluation, but remember the life of a VP is not a beauty contest or a race.

7. Let your children learn from the past failure of others. You do not always have to mention names but sometimes it helps. When a child fails to succeed because they are arrogant, prideful, or unwilling to listen to good advice, it is ok to point their failures out to them and use them as examples for others. Being used as an example is part of the consequence of their poor choices.

8. Do not think that failing means you were not called. *The Bible* and history are full of people who had a specific calling but failed to succeed in the short term. In the big picture, they succeeded because they were faithful to their call.

9. Decide who really failed. When we attempt to help hurting children, we are almost always trying to correct a problem that someone else caused. Are you the cause of failure or is our imperfect world the cause? In situations where children and young adults make poor choices, are they doing it because you failed to teach them or because they failed to listen to you? Who really failed? It might not be you after all.

10. Redefine failure. Consider the example of Jesus. By definition, he was a failure. Most people in his time expected the Savior to be a great military leader. Instead, He was crucified on a cross. As a VP, we are expected by our culture to produce happy, successful children with life stories that would make good Hallmark movies. If this is your definition of success you should redefine it. You won't see anybody being crucified in a Hallmark movie.

CHAPTER 4

- *DISAPPOINTMENT* -

Michael was intelligent, artistic, athletic, handsome, and charismatic. At eleven years old he had never known his dad and his mom was very sick. After getting into several fights at school, he was referred to the local juvenile probation office from where I received a call. The day he first came to our house I knew immediately he was both special and unusual. Although his grades did not show it, Michael's aptitude test and IQ scores revealed his intelligence as being far above average. He was also the type of kid who could take a sketchpad and pencil and do an unbelievable drawing without ever having taken an art class.

On the football team, he earned a starting position on the first day of practice despite having never played before. He was so aggressive that a group of parents asked the coach to take him out of practice for fear he would hurt their children. His high school coach once told me he had more raw talent than any kid at the school – including several Division I college prospects. When Michael was eleven his body was sculpted like a Greek god. Although he had never seen a weight room, his muscles were so defined and tight you would have thought he had been a bodybuilder for years.

Perhaps the most impressive characteristic, however, was Michael's charisma. People were drawn to his big smile and his quiet confidence. Everybody wanted to be his friend. This kid would have made his dad so proud if only his dad had only been there for him. A local television producer even invited Michael to his studio just for fun and was amazed when he began to sing for the camera. Adults in our community were forever talking about this multi-talented child with extraordinary leadership ability. Everybody had high hopes for him.

I was privileged to be able to live with this boy and to build a very strong bond. We went through numerous difficulties as well as achievements. I have to admit he brought great joy to my life. I was devastated when he decided to return to his mother. He had become like a son to me during those years and I knew his life would not be the same if he moved back in with his mentally ill mother. At the same time, I understood the mother-son relationship and did not blame him for wanting to be with her.

She had recovered from her illness and was doing well, so Michael went back home during his tenth-grade year. We stayed in touch and I tried to get him involved in some positive activities at home. He did well for about a year, but suddenly he quit answering my phone calls. When I made the one-hour trip to his house I confirmed my greatest fear – he and his mother had once again relocated. I had no idea where they had gone. A few months later, a phone call came from a social worker at the juvenile detention center. Michael was going to be there for a while and he had given my name as his contact person. My wife and I immediately went to visit. Neither of us will forget that day as he walked into the visiting room, head hanging low, dressed in prison attire. At that moment, time seemed to stand still. Michael would not be finishing traditional high school. All football scholarship offers were gone and he would not be able to use his charisma to be elected president of his class. There he stood in prison attire and with little hope left in him.

Michael would eventually be released and get a job. He had a daughter out of wedlock but made an honest attempt to be a good father. Although my hopes and dreams for him were dashed, I still knew God had a plan. As a young adult, he visited me often and I was always impressed with his parenting skills even as a young, single parent. There was hope that he would go to college and we even visited a local university. Some time afterward, however, hope was dashed. Just as before, Michael suddenly disappeared. I have not had contact with him for several years now, but I did manage to find his name listed on a department of corrections website. I have written, but there has been no reply.

I would venture to say my story is familiar to scores of VPs. Things often do not turn out the way we plan. If you plan on becoming a VP for any length of time you best learn how to deal with disappointment.

Disappointment is no stranger to the Christian and it was no stranger to a number of important Biblical figures.

Job and Joseph experienced severe disappointment in people, as well as in circumstances. Elijah was so disappointed that at one time he asked God to let him die. Then there was Moses who gave his life to save his people only to later have them reject him. Perhaps the greatest case of disappointment in the Bible was that of the disciples. They fervently believed Jesus would usher in a messianic Kingdom to rescue Israel from Roman oppression. How do you think they felt when this Savior, to whom they had committed so much time and effort, died a criminal's death on the Roman cross? It took them a few days to figure it out, but God had a much bigger plan than they could have imagined. Disappointment, when left unchecked, often leads to discouragement. Discouragement can lead to disillusionment, which leads to depression and defeat. You are too valuable to your children to allow this to happen.

TEN PRACTICAL THINGS TO KEEP YOUR DISAPPOINTMENT IN CHECK.

1. Accept the fact that it will happen. If you adopt the idea that disappointment should never happen or that it means you are a failure, you will not last long. Understand that disappointment

is as much a part of parenting as noodles are a part of spaghetti.

2. Be realistic. Too many people become VPs because they think they will change the world. While their motives are pure, they have to realize even the best people with the purest motives are often disappointed. Learn that setting high goals is ok if you can deal with the letdown when they are not met.

3. Avoid false ideas. When people ask me what my success rate is at Eagle Rock, I always reply, "100%." That does not mean every child has become a star and fulfilled his potential. It does mean every child has been given a chance. As a VP you cannot evaluate your success on whether or not you have disappointment. Disappointment does not mean you are a failure.

4. Do not be overconfident. Too many VPs think they have all the answers. When things do not go as planned they often point a finger and blame others. Accept the fact that you may not be God's gift to parenting. God does not expect you to be perfect. Learn to live with the fact that you may not be as smart as you thought you were. The act of admittance and confession can be very liberating.

5. Do not be a perfectionist. Perfectionists in general live in their own little imaginary world. This delusion is multiplied if you work with imperfect children. Expect excellence but accept sincere effort in your children. I have never known a perfectionist to last very long as a VP. They usually get mad, point fingers at others, and frustrate themselves out of business. If you are a perfectionist, you must either learn to cope or leave. Being a VP is not easy and might be impossible for the perfectionist. There must be some margin for error.

6. Relish the effort even if you lose the battle. We are not called to win every battle or make every situation turn out the way it "should." Our calling is to give it our best effort. Our greatest satisfaction should come in knowing we have done everything we could do to the best of our ability. We have not tucked our tails and run. We have met challenges head-on. We win some and we lose some, but we never quit some.

7. Be patient. Joe ran away in the middle of the night. He ran as far

as he could go. He became homeless and lived in a car for several months. Was I disappointed? Yes. I prayed, but Joe never seemed to get his act together. Fast forward eight years and we find Joe a happily married man and father. He comes by regularly to check in with me and he always thanks me for sticking with him. He needed to go hungry and homeless to come to his senses. Be patient. Your idea of good timing may be off.

8. Share with a friend. You will soon learn that he/she too has disappointment. My children went to a school where a number of foster children attended. I was always amazed at the conversations at our school's football games. It revolved around our common experiences. Share with another VP and you will surely find that you are not alone.

9. Adjust your expectations. I am a believer in setting high goals and making plans to meet them. In high school this poem was written in my notebook for four years:

    I aimed for the clouds and I got off the ground.
    I aimed for the stars and I reached the clouds.
    I aimed for the heavens and I reached the stars.

    Adjusting your expectations does not mean you settle for less than your best. It means you accept your best even when there is some disappointment. Give it all you've got and leave the results up to God.

10. Analyze and learn. Oftentimes we are disappointed because we cannot get our message through the thick skull of the kids we raise. However, sometimes we are disappointed because we made dumb mistakes. In the latter case, it is best to admit our shortcomings and learn from them. A human makes the same mistake twice. A fool does it a third time.

CHAPTER **5**

- *PERSEVERANCE* -

I was so looking forward to the rare opportunity of taking a much-deserved Sunday afternoon nap when I heard a knock at the door. Those knocks are usually not a good sign, but when I opened the door I was pleasantly surprised to see a familiar face from the past. The young man, dressed in full military attire, hardly looked like the little boy who lived with me years earlier. With a big hug, I invited him into my house. I was thrilled to get an update from the boy I had not seen for several years.

Kevin was fourteen when he arrived at our little ranch. The victim of terrible abuse and rejection, he had been in dozens of ranches, foster homes, and treatment programs before coming to us. I was told from the beginning that he probably would not be with us for long. He had a pattern of trying to get himself kicked out when things didn't go his way. However, I was determined to give him some stability. For the three years that he lived with us, we endured every kind of trial one can imagine.

Most of Kevin's three years with us were not pleasant. On numerous occasions, we were up late at night crying or arguing. However, instead of kicking him out of our home, something he would have been accustomed to, we persevered and tried tirelessly to work through his issues. At seventeen he signed up for military service,

39

and I was thrilled. A few weeks later, following some discipline I had handed down, he ran away. I knew homelessness might be a good teacher but I still wanted him to fulfill his military obligation. His recruiter and I began a search and, to make a long story short, found him a few months later. After we found him, we immediately got him sent to boot camp. Prior to this Sunday afternoon, Kevin had served several years in the army. However, I had not heard from him since he left to go to boot camp.

As I welcomed Kevin into my living room that day, I could not help noticing how much he had grown and matured. I almost wanted to check his ID because he did not seem like the same person. He proceeded to catch me up on the past three years of his life. A wife, a child, and three tours of duty in Iraq were part of the story. A bronze star had also been awarded as a result of a battle in which he had acted heroically during an ambush. As he prepared to leave my house after that long Sunday afternoon visit, he looked me in the eyes, gave me a big hug, and said, "I just want to thank you for all you have done for me."

Life's greatest rewards do not come as a result of quick fixes. Good VPs understand that change does not occur instantly. It takes time - lots of time. Our children are often dealing with emotional strongholds that have taken years to develop. These do not go away instantly. How many times have you heard a well-meaning person say, "All these kids need is love." It sounds good, but any of us who have been VPs can tell you that "love" is only the tip of the iceberg. Blood, sweat, tears, and old-fashioned perseverance is more often what is needed. The desire and stamina to stick with it, to be committed to a child, to love them regardless of their actions, is what is required. Too often I see VPs who expect their children to be instant role models, in spite of the garbage in their past. Sorry, it just does not happen that way. Isaiah 40:31 is one of my favorite verses of scripture:

> *But the people who trust the Lord will become strong again.*
> *They will rise up as an eagle in the sky;*
> *they will run and not need rest;*

they will walk and not become tired. (NCV)

For years, I read this verse and never noticed the word "walk." Could not Isaiah have left out the last phrase and made his point just as well?

I believe he may have intentionally included the word "walk" because so many of life's battles need to be fought at a slower pace. The fundamental difference between walking and running is speed. We always want fast solutions and quick answers, but rarely are life's major problems solved that way. We must hang on, stay the course and persevere.

Winston Churchhill, in his famous 1911 speech said, "Except to convictions of honor and good sense, never give in, never, never, in nothing great or small, large or petty, never give in."

I like to ask my boys to solve this riddle: "What is the major difference between a postage stamp and a Teflon skillet?" The answer: One won't stick to anything and the other sticks to everything. As a VP you must be like the postage stamp. The life of a child hangs in the balance.

Author Irving Stone spent a lifetime studying great people and writing biographies. He is quoted as saying:

"I write about people who sometime in their life....have a vision or dream of something that should be accomplished.. and they go to work. They are beaten over the head, knocked down, vilified and for years they get nowhere. But every time they are knocked down, they stand up. You cannot destroy these people. And at the end of their lives, they have accomplished some modest part of what they set out to do."

Don't quit on your children- instead, persevere.

TEN PRACTICAL THINGS TO REMEMBER ABOUT PERSEVERING.

1. It is not easy. If you are expecting things to be easy, you might as well quit before you go any further. It is better to never invest in a child than to invest a little and then quit when things get difficult.

2. Perseverance is not fun. It is our nature to want fast results. We don't like to wait. Do not expect trials to be full of joy.

3. Do not confuse perseverance with enabling. Sticking with a child does not mean not holding him accountable for his actions. We can persevere without enabling. We do this by loving the doer in spite of the deed. Children always need to be held accountable for their actions.

4. Perseverance doesn't always mean we keep a child in our home regardless of his or her actions. There are times when this can be foolish. However, we can persevere in our commitment to a child whether he is in or out of our home.

5. Do not be too quick to quit on a child. Unfortunately, a number of children's homes have rules and regulations that require children to be removed for certain violations. This is done out of necessity but is often abused. Never misuse these rules and regulations in order to make your life easier.

6. Look at the big picture. In the middle of a crisis or a time when perseverance is required, take a step back and look at a child's life as a whole. Consider what might happen to the child if you quit trying to reach him. Consider the effect it may have on him as a future parent and spouse.

7. Perseverance doesn't mean we try to do the same things over and over even though they are not working. While we have to be consistent and stick with core values, we may also need to try new approaches as part of the perseverance process.

8. Do not feel guilty if you feel like quitting. This is quite normal. Remember that the ability to persevere is not based on emotion. You will seldom feel like persevering and you will often feel like quitting. Perseverance is more a matter of blood, sweat, and tears.

9. Remember - children may have strongholds that are not part of

their awareness. These may be rooted in things that happened years earlier and have taken years to develop. To expect to resolve in six months that which took six years to develop is unrealistic.

10. Remember - God has persevered with you. Has he not given you a second, third, or even fourth chance? What if he gave up on us as easily as we sometimes give up on our children?

FOUNDATION **2**

- *UNDERSTANDING YOUR CHILDREN* -

All They Need is Love - Right?
Delayed Maturity
Going the Extra Mile
Bonding and Attachment
Trauma

CHAPTER **6**

- ALL THEY NEED IS LOVE, RIGHT? -

How do you tell the difference between a long-term, seasoned VP and a brand new one? The brand new one seriously believes that all they need is love.

My wife and I were in our mid-twenties when we opened the boys ranch. Even at a young age, I had a rather extensive background in counseling troubled kids and she had a background in teaching high school. When I say "background," I simply mean to say that each of us had jobs working with young people. However, neither of us had ever shared our home with one. We had each been around a lot of kids with emotional and behavioral issues, but we figured that, with enough time and love, they would come to their senses and go on to be productive and happy citizens. Of course, there were those who didn't end up that way. Even before we opened the ranch I had one child commit suicide and another committed murder. I just assumed if they could have lived at the ranch and we could have loved them the way they needed to be loved, then they, too, would have been okay. Henceforth, as a young couple opening our ranch, we were convinced once everything was in place we would see remarkable improvements. After all, all these kids really needed was love, and we would be there to give it!

People would often come up to me after a speaking engagement and comment on some aspect of a story I had told. They were frequently moved with compassion, many times even in tears after I told them how some kids have been battered and broken. The conversation usually ended with them shaking their head, looking me in the eyes, and saying, "Well, all they need is love, isn't it?" I would humbly reply, "Yes, it is," and they would thank me for my efforts and walk away.

A few years after we opened the ranch and several boys were living in our home 24/7, someone kindly said to Diana, "You know, all these boys need is love, isn't it?" Diana kindly smiled at the lady, but as she walked away Diana whispered to me, "She obviously hasn't met our boys!"

It sort of became a joke through the years, and of course, we were kind to the people who thought all they need is love, but it also became a sort of litmus test. Those who had fostered, adopted, been houseparents, or worked in group homes would actually say, "Well, I don't know about that."

Now, before someone gets defensive, allow me to clarify. It *is* true that all they need is love. The problem is that love was needed long before they came into your life. The love they missed somewhere in their development left them very deeply scarred. Love alone will not remove those scars. I should also clarify that most of the readers of this book are caring for kids who came from less-than-optimal circumstances. If you've adopted a child at birth and you took him or her into your arms on the day of their birth, and you know that the mother was well-nourished, healthy, not under stress, not using drugs, not drinking alcohol, not smoking cigarettes, and happy during pregnancy, then this chapter may not apply to you. For everyone else, please get over your romantic idea that all they need is love. There is a strong chance that your child is going to need some medical and psychological help to go along with your love. Love will heal a lot of emotional damage, but not all. When it does, it takes more time than you might think.

As later explained in more depth, a number of influences help form a child's emotional and psychological health. These influences can be traced to the time of conception, and even before. Believe it or not, some research is suggesting that the emotional well-being of grandparents, even those whom the child has never met, can influence their mental health. As a VP you will have to deal with those issues and sometimes love may not be the complete answer. Love is the foundation on which other interventions can build their walls. In other words, love and other interventions often work most effectively when paired together.

One of the most famous chapters in the Bible, known as the "love chapter," is 1 Corinthians 13.

> *I may speak in different languages of people or even angels. But if I do not have love, I am only a noisy bell or a crashing cymbal.*
> *I may have the gift of prophecy. I may understand all the secret things of God and have all knowledge, and I may have faith so great I can move mountains. But even with all these things, if I do not have love, then I am nothing. I may give away everything I have, and I may even give my body as an offering to be burned. But I gain nothing if I do not have love.*
> (I Cor 13:1-3 NCV)

I have read this passage hundreds of times in my life, but recently I realized something that had never before occurred to me. The writer does not say there is anything wrong with speaking in the tongues of men or angels. He does not say there is anything wrong with prophesying or being able to fathom mysteries or knowledge. He does not say it's wrong to have faith that can move mountains and he does not say it's wrong to give to the poor. Apparently, these things are fine with him, and we can further surmise that they may even have some value. His point, however, is that none of these are worth anything unless there is a foundation of love.

A non-biblical word of advice to VPs written in similar prose to this beautiful passage might go something like this:

> *If my child has the very best counselor who can truly understand what is going on and can help my child heal, but I don't love my child, then that counselor is only a clanging cymbal. If a team of professionals can figure out exactly what my child needs and can fully understand where his problems lie, but I don't love my child, we're*

not accomplishing anything. If I feed my child the most nutritious foods, give him a warm and secure house, and pray for him every day, but I don't love him, I've done nothing.

Love is like the centerpiece of a bicycle wheel. All of the spokes are connected to a centerpiece and the rim is then connected to the spokes. Remove the centerpiece and the rim will collapse because the spokes had nothing to hold them in place. Love is certainly the centerpiece of raising children, but it's not everything. Have you ever seen a bike tire function without a rim or spokes? Remove love and not even the best therapies will yield the desired results in a child's life.

TEN THINGS TO REMEMBER ABOUT LOVE.

1. There will be times when you don't have it within your power to love your children. You will have to let God love them through you.
2. Don't confuse love with warm and fuzzy feelings. When you love someone it may feel warm and fuzzy sometimes, but not necessarily every day.
3. Love is not always an involuntary reflex. Sometimes you will have to make a concerted effort to love a child.
4. Actions speak louder than words. It is more important to demonstrate your love to them than it is to vocalize. Children are very perceptive and can tell when someone is just saying, "I love you," versus when they really mean it.
5. Tell your kids you love them, but be aware that with some kids you can be too loose with these words. The person who says, "I love you" without sincerity cheapens the value.
6. Unconditional love can only come from God. Make every effort to love your child unconditionally, but understand that you

will need God's help to do so.

7. There is something unmatchable about the love between a birth parent and a birth child. It is unexplainable. If you have this same type of love for someone else's child consider yourself fortunate and blessed. If you find it difficult to love someone else's child in the same way you love your birth children, don't feel guilty. It can take time.

8. Love is tough. I think these three words would make a great title for a book. It is true.

9. Sometimes love expresses itself in difficult ways. Sometimes you have to do things you may not want to do but you do them because they are best for your child.

10. Love is always other-centered. In every action and every decision made for or about your child, ask yourself this one question, "Am I doing this to benefit myself or am I doing it to benefit my child?" When you become a VP, your concept of "love" must become more like what Paul describes in I Corinthians 13. It is patient, kind, and not selfish.

CHAPTER 7

- *DELAYED MATURITY* -

If you are a Houseparent or a foster parent, the title of this section has likely caught your attention. If you are an adoptive parent there is a very good chance you will find some comfort in the information I am about to present.

During my years running a boys ranch, there were boys of whom I would say, "He will be just fine if we can get him to age twenty-six without any major setbacks." A major accomplishment for many would be to reach the 26th birthday without going to jail or prison.

For the average parent in a normal situation, we tend to believe that our children should be mature enough to make responsible adult decisions by the time they are eighteen. However, unfortunately, for kids raised in foster care or in congregate care settings, this is rarely the case. In fact, I have seen a lot of eighteen-year-olds with the maturity level of a thirteen-year-old. My experience has been that many kids do not reach the maturity level of an eighteen-year-old until they are around twenty-six. Of course, I am speaking in general terms. There were always those few kids who matured much faster. However, foster care with its inevitable baggage seems to almost always have a way of delaying emotional maturity.

Why is this the case? I believe there are several potential factors that are helpful for a VP to understand.

53

1. BRAIN DEVELOPMENT

The scope of this book is not to explain the biological processes of the brain, but most child development experts agree that brain development is moving at a critical pace during the first few years of life. I personally have always felt that the first eighteen months seem to be the most important. If the structure is not properly developed during these formative years there can be a lifetime of consequences.

I like to think of it in terms of an analogy. Let us suppose you want to build a house. You make your plans, write out the list of materials you will need, place your order at the building supply center, and have everything delivered to the house site. At that point, you have everything you need to build a strong house that will withstand years of cold and heat, rains, and storms. Let's assume all the materials are on the ground waiting to be put together when your contractor calls and says, "Hey, I'm really busy and cannot get to your house right now. Just cover up the materials and I will be back in four years to put it all together." You do as instructed and four years later he shows up and starts construction. Unfortunately, he discovers some problems. Some of the wood was not stacked properly and the changes in humidity have caused warping. It is no longer straight. Some of the wood was also infested with insects, and even though it was usable, it was weakened. The tarp blew off one bundle of wood so it got wet and is badly stained and slightly rotted. Nevertheless, your contractor proceeds with building the house. He tries his best to straighten the warped wood, cut the rotted pieces out, and paint the stained wood. When he's all done, your house looks normal from the outside and you are happy. Everything seems to be going well until one day, eleven or twelve years later, you notice there are a few places where your floor has some uneven spots and the roof has some curves and dips. Cracks are occurring in the sheetrock and the shingles on the roof are beginning to curl up prematurely. You call an expert to look at the problems and after studying your house he comes back to you with a frightening report. He says that some of the wood used to build the walls was apparently warped at the time of construction, so it is trying to return to its warped state. It has a memory. He explains that the lumps in the floor are caused by the glue in the plywood breaking down and allowing the wood to come apart. The breakdown of glue was probably due to hidden moisture in the wood. The shingles are curling because shingles have a natural need to be laid flat upon one another and then heated by the sun. Chemical processes occur in the asphalt that makes the shingles bond together and forms a seamless waterproof layer. Apparently, the chemical process did not occur in a timely manner so the shingles never bonded properly. The walls are buckling because the studs were never completely straight. They probably looked straight to the contractor at construction, but the weight of the house has stressed them and is now revealing some imperfections. The nails throughout the house are losing their grip because prior to construction they had acquired some rust and the gluelike oil they were pre-treated with was gone before they were driven into the wood. Basically, the entire hidden structure of the house is flawed. It is probably not going to fall down, but there are going to be nagging issues for as long as it stands.

You see the analogy. All the right materials were there to begin with, but they were not put together at the right time. The house looks good from the outside but inside it is falling apart. This is what happens to the brains of children who are abused and neglected. In some cases, the same may apply to non-abusive trauma situations. Years later the lack of structural integrity manifests itself in immaturity because these individuals do not have the structure to make mature decisions. Sometimes we have to do a total makeover which involves identifying and removing all the rotten wood. In most cases, we also have to learn to live with some annoyances.

2. SUBCONSCIOUS RETREAT

Immaturity can be the result of a child's subconscious desire to retreat. In a healthy brain, a person develops appropriate means of dealing with stress and challenges. Again, if the structure of the brain is not properly developed there may be a lack of ability to deal with stress. Therefore, our children do not develop the coping mechanisms needed to deal with challenges brought on by life. Most people face an ever-increasing level of stress and challenge with every year that passes. For some children the lack of ability to handle that stress causes them to retreat to a less stressful, less challenging time in their life. This is what we call immaturity.

3. OVER-SYMPATHETIC CAREGIVERS

For some children, immaturity is enhanced when their parents' or caregivers' responses to them are overly sympathetic. This is particularly true for children in foster care. When we read the horror stories of how these children were mistreated, it is our natural tendency to react in sorrow. Because we feel sorry for them, we sometimes fail to challenge them enough. We are worried about overwhelming or hurting them. How many times has it been said, "It is no wonder he acts that way – look at what he's been through." I know I said that a lot, and it is true, but sometimes we can allow the pendulum to swing too far on the side of sympathy. Let me be clear, we all need to be sympathetic and empathetic. However, feeling sorry for kids to the point that you don't prepare them for the real world is hurting them more than it is helping.

4. OVER PROTECTION

Immaturity is sometimes the result of over-protection. In my lifetime, I have known several adults who came from healthy families but turned out to be extremely immature. As I stop to think about these situations it seems to me there is a common theme. These young adults have been over-protected. Why does this happen? There are several reasons. First of all, there are some parents who should have been communist dictators instead of a parent. They just have to be in complete control of everything. However, more often than not, there was an event that made the parent feel insecure. They may have lost another child and therefore feel like they could lose their surviving child – so they overprotect. The child who is overprotected may have been sick as an infant or may have come close to death as a result of an accident. The child may have some sort of disability and the parent feels the need to protect them. Adoptive parents may overprotect because they feel it is their responsibility. After all, they obviously take their commitment seriously. Whatever the case may be, overprotected children are often immature.

5. GENETICS

The apple doesn't fall far from the tree. We all know there is a centuries-old debate over heredity versus environment. I would venture to say that most anyone who has ever fostered or adopted would lean to the side of heredity. I do. I cannot tell you how many times I have seen adopted or fostered kids who never knew their birth parents, but grow up to be just like them. I realize that this statement is not going to win any popularity contests but I am just calling it like I see it. This happens regardless of who raised them. However, I have also seen just the opposite, so don't lose hope.

It then stands to reason that, in most cases concerning foster children and the majority of adoptive children, the birth parents had some maturity deficiencies. As difficult as it may be to acknowledge, immaturity may have a genetic link.

On a side note, I have intentionally chosen to not fully address the topics of *attachment and trauma*. These can certainly contribute to immaturity, but they are discussed more thoroughly in other chapters. The writer of Hebrews seems to be frustrated. Listen to what he says:

We have much to say about this, but it is hard to explain because you are so slow to understand. By now you should be teachers, but you need someone to teach you again the first lessons of God's message. You still need the teaching that is like milk. You are not ready for solid food. Anyone who lives on milk is still a baby and knows nothing about right teaching. But solid food is for those who are grown up. They have practiced in order to know the difference between good and evil.
Hebrews 5:11-14, NCV

A great deal of mystery exists regarding the book of Hebrews. Scholars disagree on who wrote it, to whom it was written, and even when it was written. However, we do have one major clue within the letter itself. Chapter 5 verse 12 says the recipients of the letter should have been more mature. This dates the writing at a time when Christianity had been around for a while - long enough that the believers should have known the basic tenets of the faith. However, they were immature and the writer says he needs to start from scratch – go back and cover the basics – give them milk instead of meat. Therefore, I believe it is fair to say this writer was frustrated then and he would probably be frustrated the same today.

It can be very frustrating to deal with immaturity. It can become even more so when we see children show signs of appropriate maturity only to have them digress. A lot of patience is required. As a VP you are very likely to experience a lot of immaturity-based frustrations. This can be a good thing, and like the writer of Hebrews, you may need an outlet to express some of your feelings. However, keep in mind that feeding raw meat to babies makes them sick (figuratively speaking). Know when to give milk but strive for the day when you can give meat.

TEN PRACTICAL TIPS REGARDING IMMATURITY.

1. Don't take it personally. You may have poured your heart and soul into developing a responsible and mature young adult only to realize that he is still immature and irresponsible. It may not be your fault at all, but a direct result of his or her past experiences.

2. Do your best to understand psychology. This book is not meant to be a psychological masterpiece, but there is some good, well-researched information out there if you really want to understand. Sometimes gaining an understanding of a subject

brings relief.

3. Don't over-sympathize. There is nothing wrong with feeling sorry for a kid because of his past, but never lose sight of the fact that the past is done. The future is what you want to affect.

4. Give yourself an over-protector evaluation. Take a close, honest look at yourself and ask if the reasons for overprotecting are for your benefit or for the child's benefit. If you overprotect in order to fill a personal need, you should re-evaluate.

5. Be patient. As I stated early in the chapter, it may take twenty-six years to reach the maturity level of an average eighteen-year-old. Sweat and pray through these years, but don't give up.

6. Don't underestimate. Sometimes the kids who appear to be the least mature turn out to be the most responsible adults.

7. Expect the norm. We all know that the kids in our care will probably be immature, but it does not hurt to expect maturity. Sometimes they will accidentally live up to your expectations.

8. Don't give them excuses. It is OK to explain to your kids that there may be psychological and developmental reasons for their immaturity. However, always let these explanations come as a point of discussion about catching up and overcoming.

9. Watch closely. Children and young adults with developmental delays (immaturity) will often want to hang out with kids who are much younger and thus vulnerable. Watch them closely to avoid inappropriate behavior perpetrated by the older child or young adult.

10. Be supportive. When they make immature decisions, help them realize and take responsibility for their choices but resist being too tough with them. There is a balance that prevents destroying the child emotionally while bringing them to a proper level of maturity.

CHAPTER **8**

- GOING THE EXTRA MILE -

When I was nineteen years old and beginning to realize God was calling me to work with disadvantaged kids, I did not foresee that seven years later I would be opening a boys ranch. At that time, I figured I would get my degree and find a good place to work where I could help children. I liked the idea of working in a ranch setting, but it did not really seem practical to open my own place. I knew many excellent ranches were already in existence, so I figured I would work for one of them. During college and graduate school, I worked at two hospitals, a runaway shelter, and a boys' ranch. It was during this time I began to realize something that deeply bothered me; time after time I encountered children who had experienced what we call multiple placements. It was not unusual to encounter a fifteen-year-old who had lived in twenty different places. He might have lived with three relatives, four boys' ranches, two psychiatric hospitals, and a dozen foster homes. That was disturbing to me, and that is largely why I went to the trouble of founding Eagle Rock Boys Ranch. We lived by the motto *Going the Extra Mile*. We did not have a *three-strikes-and-you-are-out* policy. We did everything in our power to avoid kicking a kid out of our ranch, thereby making him a part of the carousel of multiple placements. We tolerated a lot of things that most people would not tolerate. We truly went the extra mile because I believed it was absolutely necessary if we planned to reach certain kids.

If we give up too soon we fail to demonstrate the love of God. Yes, we can demonstrate love to a kid, but the demonstration of the love of God is a much more difficult thing. God does *not* tell us, "I will keep you in my family as long as you do not make too many mistakes." For that matter, most parents do not treat their birth children with a three strikes and you're out philosophy. Parents typically keep trying.

At Eagle Rock we let our kids know that if they committed a crime they would do their time, but we would take them back after the appropriate consequence. If one stole my car (which happened on occasion), I sent him to boot camp but, I also visited him every week and brought him back to Eagle Rock when he had done his time in jail.

One of the saddest stories I've ever heard was from a friend who had been a child welfare worker for over thirty years. She maintains a letter-writing correspondence with a man who is now serving a life sentence in prison but was once a child in her caseload. She says that in one of his letters he wrote, "I still wonder why XYZ gave up on me. I think if they had stuck with me a little longer I would not be where I am today."

Going the extra mile requires sacrifice. At Eagle Rock, we once had a boy who was so out of control he almost got himself killed. He ran away one night and walked for miles down a dark and secluded railroad track, spent the night in an abandoned house, and hitched a ride with a total stranger the next day. He did this not once but numerous times. We decided he needed psychiatric help so we sent him to a hospital with the intention of taking him back to the ranch after an evaluation. While at the hospital he jumped out of a second-floor window, ran down the street, and stole a car. For several weeks this thirteen-year-old drove around in a stolen car and ate food from dumpsters. Finally, the police caught him. He was placed in a secure facility for his own safety and so he could receive psychiatric help. Because Eagle Rock placed heavy emphasis on relationship building, we felt it was necessary to continue our relationships with boys who had gone through these situations. I decided to be the person from Eagle Rock to continue our relationship with this particular boy. For the next two years, I made the four-hour trip one Saturday each month to visit with him for a short time. As it turned out I was the only visitor he had. I missed a lot of good college football games and burned a lot of gas just to play horseshoes with the boy for a few hours on visitation Saturday. I would return home exhausted, but I was not alone. At Eagle Rock, this was part of our culture. I am definitely not the only staff member who made such a sacrifice just because we felt like a boy needed someone who would go the extra mile with him. This boy eventually returned to Eagle Rock and graduated from high school before going out on his own and becoming a working citizen. I am convinced had someone not gone the extra mile, that boy would still be in trouble today.

The term *Go The Extra Mile* is commonly used in the English language but has its roots in the Bible. In Matthew 5:41, Jesus is wrapping up his famous Sermon on the Mount when He says, *"If someone forces you to go with him one mile, go with him two miles (NCV)."* We should be careful to consider the context under which this is said. It was the Roman practice in Jesus' time that civilians were required to carry the luggage of military soldiers for one mile when commanded. I seriously doubt anybody really appreciated being forced to serve the Roman soldiers who were charged with keeping them under Roman rule. Consider some poor guy who just got off work and is headed home to his family having to obey when a soldier says, "come here boy and carry my bags." Do you think he would be happy about it? Would he offer to carry them for a mile farther than required? Probably not, but that is what Jesus instructs us to do. I believe Jesus is saying that his followers should always try to go beyond the call of duty. We too often take the easy path when Jesus is telling us that is not the way of the cross.

Our children probably do not deserve to have us go beyond the call of duty to help them. However, we do not exactly deserve to have God go beyond the call of duty for us – do we?

TEN PRACTICAL TIPS ABOUT GOING THE EXTRA MILE.

1. If you are a foster parent, be honest with yourself and your child about what is or is not acceptable in your home. It is heroic to tell a child that you are going to go the extra mile and be committed to him regardless of his behavior. However, heroism is not always realistic. You may have your marriage and your birth children to consider, so do not overcommit yourself. It does no good to go the extra mile to help your foster child while you destroy your marriage and family. Foster kids want your honesty more than your heroic attempts.

2. If you are an adoptive parent accept the fact that you must go the extra mile just like you would if you had given birth to the adopted child. Do not adopt if you are not ready to make that commitment. There is nothing as sad as seeing a kid get un-adopted. Trust me - I have seen it a lot.

3. If you are a group home, children's home, or ranch, establish your identity up front. If you have a *three strikes and you're out* policy, let that be known. If you have boundaries that cannot be crossed, make them clear. It is best to let the kids know your limits. Let them know that life is not fair and that often they will have to work harder to overcome their circumstances.

4. If you are not in a position to go the extra mile you have to accept that the kids in your care are going to have a hard time accepting you. After all, if you are not going to accept them like you would accept your birth children, then don't expect them to accept you like they would their birth parents.

5. If you are one of the ranches like Eagle Rock that prides itself in going the extra mile, it is probably best NOT to tell the kids. They will probably not believe you and the first thing they will do is test you. It is better just to prove yourself through your actions.

6. Going the extra mile does not mean you look the other way every time a kid does something that is unacceptable. It means just the opposite. You acknowledge that he or she has done something unacceptable but you don't end your relationship over the matter.

7. Going the extra mile is not practical in some settings. For example, if your children's home utilizes live-in married couples as Houseparents then you are probably not going to keep those couples very long. I learned this the hard way. I strongly believe that children should have the support of a live-in married Mom and Pop. I recall, though, a kid named Carl who did everything in his power to drive his Houseparents to quit. The final straw was the day he took a jar of pickles out of the fridge, put a handful in his mouth, and put them back into the pickle jar. A few days later, as the family was eating pickles with their hamburgers, he revealed his dirty deed. That was the final straw for those houseparents, and they asked that Carl be removed from the ranch. I asked them to go the extra mile with Carl, but it was more than they could tolerate and they resigned. That really was not fair to this wonderful couple. I am rather certain that the ranches who are fortunate enough to keep Houseparent couples for long periods of time have to set rather tight boundaries with their kids and subsequently must dismiss them when lines are crossed. I suppose you have to decide what is most important based on your personal philosophies.

8. Going the extra mile is not always good for your public relations efforts. If you are a non-profit group home, children's home, or ranch, you have to get donations from the public in order to pay the bills. Unfortunately, the public has a love/hate relationship with the kids who live in these places. They love their innocent faces and they are moved by their sad stories; however, when it comes to a kid misbehaving they are quick to delegate them to the category of *they*. *They* is a pronoun frequently used to describe orphans who misbehave. Somehow they go from being *needy* to *needing to be dealt with*. It can be a little difficult to raise money to support these kids.

9. Going the extra mile is not to be equated with enabling. Enabling is the act of helping children beyond the level of actually helping. If a kid commits a crime he needs to be punished by the criminal justice system. Otherwise, he will not learn his lesson. In less serious matters he needs to be held accountable, too. In neither case does it mean we give up on him. With older kids (around 18) we have to sometimes push them toward responsible behavior. If we do not, they will not be ready for adulthood. If your 18-year-old refuses to get a job and you continue to give him money, you are enabling him. Do not let *going the extra mile* be confused with *enabling*.

10. Going the extra mile is emotionally draining for you as the VP. It means you never give up. It means that no matter how bad it gets you are going to do everything you can to help a kid. I am almost certain that my career would have lasted a few years longer had I not been an *extra miler*. If I had allowed myself to walk away from some of my kids and simply given up, my stress level would have been much lower. I could have taken the easier route, but we are called to do the task God has for us for as long as He wants us to do it. When He no longer gives us the strength to do it, then sometimes that is His way of letting us know our time of service is complete. I may have cared a little too much. I may have gone a few too many extra miles. Nevertheless, that was my calling and God never promised me it would be easy.

- *BONDING + ATTACHMENT* -

It was sometime in the early 2000s after we had operated Eagle Rock Boys Ranch for about ten years when I was invited to be a guest on a television show that would be aired regionally. I figured a few hundred people might see the program. In the interview, the host asked me what I felt was the leading cause of emotional problems in adolescent boys. I did not have to think about it. The answer was easy: "If I can get a good social history of the boy's first 18 months of life," I replied, "I can predict his chances of success and how we should approach his treatment."

I remind you that bonding and attachment disorders were not being discussed at this time in history. I had never heard of Reactive Attachment Disorder and bonding was not a major topic in my graduate training. I was only reporting on what I had experienced. Boys who were severely neglected during the first 18 months of life tended to have emotional problems that were almost impossible to overcome. "Interestingly," I said, "we have had better success with boys who are physically, sexually, or emotionally abused than with boys who are severely neglected."

I was not prepared for the reaction that statement would bring. While I had thought the television program was local, it seemed that my words resonated with people far and wide, and I was contacted by dozens of people who were having difficulties with children who had experienced childhood neglect. To make matters worse, I began receiving numerous calls from couples who had adopted children from other countries.

In the 1990s, international adoption was very popular. It seemed like every time you turned around a friend from church was adopting a child from another country. At one point in the USA, we averaged 20,000 foreign adoptions per year. By the early 2000s, these children were reaching puberty.

The phone calls were all heartbreaking and all too often I could predict exactly what would be said. Typically they came from white, middle-class families in which the husband had a good job so the wife devoted her life to caring for the children. At some point, the couple had gone on a mission trip in which they witnessed the horrors faced by abandoned children in foreign orphanages. Their hearts were moved and subsequently, they spent twenty or thirty thousand dollars to rescue these abandoned children. They brought them home to integrate into their families. Their biological children welcomed them. Grandparents threw big parties. Their church family shared the excitement and the couple looked forward to living the American dream with their *foreign* babies.

Usually about five minutes into the phone call the mother would begin to cry. I often sensed overwhelming feelings of guilt, confusion, and hurt. In some cases, marriages were deeply damaged. In other cases, birth children were at risk. The little angel they adopted had become a little devil and was destroying their family. Sometimes, it was so bad that some of the callers even tried to bribe me to take their adopted children off their hands. In desperation, some would promise financial support for the future care of the child. They simply could not handle their child any longer and desperately needed them out of their home.

Every one of those phone calls broke my heart. Sincere Christians were doing their best to make the world a better place, but because of good intentions, their lives had become dreadful nightmares. I listened to story after story about adopted children who seemed not to care for their new families. The children acted out in aggressive and sometimes violent ways. They seemed not to be able to connect to anyone. I would listen for several minutes, sometimes hours, to adoptive mothers crying through their stories. My first question was always, "Was your child ever left in an orphanage with overworked staff who did not have adequate time to hold the children every day?" Time and time again the answer would be "yes." In many foreign orphanages in the 1990s newborn babies were left to lie in unattended cribs for hours and days at a time with very limited human interaction. There were simply not enough adults to take care of them. The result was often big rooms full of cribs with babies who got very little human touch other than an occasional bottle. Let me be clear, I am not criticizing the people in charge. I definitely know what it is like to have a lack of human resources. Sometimes, I am told, these little babies would go for months, even years, without significant human contact. Many of the babies even developed flat spots on the backs of their heads from lying in the cribs for so long. During my phone conversations when the mother confirmed this had been the case with their child, my heart would drop inside me. I knew exactly what the problem was and I knew I probably would not be able to help the couple or their child.

In this book, I have tried to draw more from my personal experiences rather than from the ideas of others. I try not to point to a lot of research or quote a lot from the experts. I have done that for good reason but I also know there is a lot of good research on the subject of bonding and attachment. What I will be presenting in the following paragraphs is not the result of scientific research. You probably will not find it published in *Psychology Today*. It is nothing more than one man (who happens to have spent 32 years working with hurting children) and his theory regarding the importance of bonding and attachment in children.

I believe that deep within the human species there exists something I will call the *preservation instinct*. The preservation instinct is that piece of human nature that serves to preserve the species. It helps the human species survive generation after generation. Think for a moment about what happens if you are standing under a tree and that tree starts to fall toward you. You don't stand there and wait for it to fall on top of you – you run for cover. Nobody has to teach you that – it just happens because you have a preservation instinct. Even more interestingly, think about what happens when you see a snake in your yard. You naturally put up your guard to protect yourself. Some people think this is a learned behavior but others think it just comes naturally without any teaching or coaching. It does not matter how you know, your reaction is instinctive and is there to protect you from harm. We humans are full of these preservation instincts. If we did not have them the human race would eventually disappear. But how do we develop self-preservation instincts? I believe most of them are passed down genetically but a lot of them are passed down from generation to generation via human teaching (environment).

The very first preservation instinct you experience is that of your mother caring for you as a newborn. This preservation instinct is probably best demonstrated in lower forms (animals) but it is the same instinct. For example, if you go near a momma bear with her baby cubs she will attack. If the cubs are not around she will probably ignore you. In the human mother, the preservation instinct drives her to attend to every need of her child and to protect her child at all costs – just like a momma bear. It is actually a wonderful thing to watch unless you happen to be a husband who accidentally puts your baby in a situation that momma bear perceives to be risky. I believe there is even a chemical reaction in the mother's brain that stimulates her need to be protective. Human mothers, for instance, can identify the various cries of their baby. They seem to have an instinctual code that tells them when the baby is hungry versus when it needs a diaper change. This is all an obvious part of the preservation instinct.

What is not so obvious is the fact that the mother's preservation instinct has two purposes. The first purpose is to protect the baby. The second is to program the baby's own preservation instinct. This is where things get a little harder to comprehend. Scientists typically refer to this programming as neurochemical brain development. The theory is that when a baby interacts with the caretaker, the process itself causes neurological pathways to develop in the brain.

I explain it slightly differently but the principle is the same.

As the mother's preservation instinct is manifesting itself by taking care of the baby, the baby is also learning to preserve itself. It is developing its own preservation instinct by subconsciously figuring out how to get its needs met so that it can survive. For example, it learns that if it needs food in its belly it needs to evoke a particular cry. That cry will evoke a preservation instinct in another human that will result in food being provided. If the baby senses his skin inside his diaper is wet, he evokes a different cry that results in another human cleaning and drying him. The baby is learning his own form of preservation instinct. Remember, at this stage in life he is incapable of providing for or protecting himself. As he grows, the idea takes on new forms. He learns that warmth is needed to keep him alive so he learns to cuddle with his mother and her preservation instinct causes her to cuddle with him. This sort of subconscious communication continues as the caretaker protects and the baby learns how to stimulate the needed responses in the caretaker.

To me, one of the most fascinating preservation instincts is demonstrated when mothers and babies make eye contact. It is fascinating because it is the one thing that can happen without any physical contact. I remember what this was like with my children. I believe that for the parent, the first time your child looks you in the eyes your brain explodes with endorphins. Anyone who has ever experienced it will tell you it is like a million beautiful fireworks going off inside your head. It is even better than your first kiss! (By the way, I still remember my first kiss – at fifteen years old at church camp – awesome!) When you have such an experience it emotionally moves you like nothing else. If you are a parent and your baby looks you in the eyes, you know at that moment you would give your life for that child. I believe that when parents look their babies in the eyes the babies can sense what the parents are thinking. That gives them a sense of security, warmth, and assurance that the world is ok. Sixteen years later your baby boy will have become a teenager. A sweet young lady will look him in the eyes for the first time and he will lose his mind. Just as he was drawn to his mother's eyes he will be drawn to his sweetheart's eyes and the preservation instinct will manifest in a different way, if you know what I mean.

With infants, the whole cycle of back-and-forth subconscious communication is taking place at the same time the brain is being developed. Scientists believe that 90% of brain development occurs in the first five years of life. Therefore, the brain is encoding its own preservation instinct which will eventually help perpetuate the human species.

So the question arises. What happens if the caregiver with all of the preservation instinct is absent during the critical time when the brain is developing? The answer, in my opinion, is that the baby resorts to what I call *secondary preservation instincts*. The purpose of the primary preservation instincts is to make a connection with the caretaker and, in effect, manipulate the caretaker's own preservation instincts in order that the baby's needs are met. However, when the caretaker is absent the baby has to resort to other means of self-preservation. It has to figure out how to survive. Since it has no experience with survival based on bonding with another human being, it resorts to survival by whatever means necessary, sometimes developing ways to survive without human contact. Therefore, it no longer needs to know how to bond and attach with other humans. Much like a muscle that is not exercised will disintegrate, the brain's ability to bond and attach will disappear. When this skill is lost, the person also loses the ability to empathize – or to feel what others are feeling.

Fast forward to age five. The brain is 90% developed, but it has decided that empathy is low on its list of priorities. The ability to exercise empathy has not paid off in the past (it did not help provide any preservation value), so the brain decides that bonding must not be of too much importance.

In my opinion, all of the symptoms we normally associate with a lack of bonding can be traced back to one thing – a lack of empathy. Children who have not bonded properly seem to lose their ability to empathize and therefore are not as aware they are hurting others. I have seen children do some very hurtful things and seem to be unaffected or untroubled by the things they do that hurt others.

I once had an eleven-year-old boy who stomped a kitten to death. You would think he did it in a fit of rage, but that was not the case. For him, it was more like he was experimenting and had no idea he was hurting the cat. Strange, but true. We occasionally had boys start fires. They usually did not mean any harm. They were just fascinated with fire and had no conceptualization that their activity could hurt something or someone.

Over and over during conversations with desperate adoptive parents, they explained how their children seemed void of feelings or did not care who or what they hurt. This makes sense when you consider the idea that they lack the ability to empathize.

Those of us with normal brains find it difficult to understand how an unbonded child thinks. To help you understand, do this little exercise: Assume you were taught that the number three is written as a "4," and the number ten is written as a "5." Now, answer this question: "What is three plus ten?" You answer thirteen and you are correct. However, if you had been taught that three was "4" and ten was "5", you would say that the answer is nine. Are you confused? If so, you know how an unconnected child may feel. Figuratively speaking, children who have not had adequate bonding experiences have not been taught the proper way to write numbers. Therefore, what may seem very simple for you is not for them. No matter how hard they try to process the information they arrive at different outcomes because their brains were not programmed correctly in the first place.

I have noticed that children without adequate bonding experiences do not have a fully developed sense of empathy and this manifests itself in some strange ways. I will name a few:

1. They have no filter in what they say. These children can be brutally honest. You never have to wonder where you stand with them. They say whatever comes to their mind whether or not it may hurt someone else.
2. They have no sense of physical boundaries. They will invade personal space without any hesitation. Ironically, they can be very affectionate. For example, they will hug total strang-

ers. Again, they seem not to know what makes others uncomfortable.

3. They may ask inappropriate questions such as, "Why are you so fat?" or "Don't you think you should cut the ugly mole off your face?"

4. They can be cruel to animals or to younger children. This is not always because they are mean. Sometimes they are just fascinated with the reaction. Again, they are not empathizing. They are not putting themselves into the shoes of those they hurt.

5. They will steal from others. Void of empathy there seems to be no sense of understanding how this may make the other person feel.

6. They tend to destroy property. There seems to be something soothing about this activity without the understanding that it hurts others.

Obviously, there are varying degrees of dysfunction and its correlating behaviors. On the lower end, a child who was neglected but still had some human interaction, even if it was abusive, will often not exhibit extreme behaviors. He will have some remorse for being cruel to animals or weaker humans. On the higher end of the spectrum, a child who was totally deprived of human contact may become a killer. I had one boy who did just that.

There is good news and bad news. The good news is that very few children will be so unattached that they become irreparable. The Reactive Attachment Disorder diagnosis is probably overapplied and most children are not past the point of no return. The bad news is that treating children who are not attached or bonded is an extremely difficult process.

Consider for a moment that you built a new house and five years later discovered the electrician has used faulty wire throughout. If you take no action the house will probably burn down. In order to fix the problem, you have to tear out all of the sheetrock and insulation so you can get to the wires hidden in the walls. After you tear it all out, you discover the wood inside the walls is already scorched and weakened. You can replace all the wire and the electrical boxes, replace the sheetrock, and repaint but the house will probably always be weakened. That is an analogy for the process of rebuilding the brain of a child who has been severely neglected during the first 18 months of life. The problem is that rebuilding a child is ten times more difficult than rebuilding a house. Jesus talks about a man building his house upon the sand. The passage goes like this:

Everyone who hears my words and obeys them is like a wise man who built his house on the rock. It rained hard, the floods came, and the winds blew and hit that house. But it did not fall, because it was built on rock. Everyone who hears my words and does not obey them is like a foolish man who built his house on sand. It rained hard, the floods came, and the winds blew and hit that house, and it fell with a big crash. (Matthew 7:25-27 NCV)

I am fairly certain Jesus was not referring to bonding and attachment in children. However, he is presenting a simple but very important life principle. The foundation is the most important part of a house or a life. We can apply this to our children. If they do not get a good foundation they may fall with a crash. Children who do not learn to bond properly early in life will experience a lifetime of challenges and will almost always be at risk.

However, there is hope and I have seen firsthand that children can overcome severe neglect. One example is a boy named Aaron who came to live with me when he was nine years old. Aaron had spent the first three years of his life strapped in a car seat and parked in front of a television. He had very little meaningful human contact because his parents were strung out on drugs all the time. By the time Aaron was removed from the home by the authorities at the age of three, he was so damaged that he could not speak. In fact, as an adult, he still struggles to make a complete sentence and his speech is slurred. The chronic neglect also contributed to severe learning disabilities which he never overcame. However, Aaron had an uncle who took care of him from age three to age eleven. I took him in when his uncle passed away. A couple of years later his grandfather took him in and gave him a good life. Today Aaron is a productive adult who has learned to interact appropriately with people and holds a regular job. In fact, he even owns a business. Aaron is living proof that children can overcome a childhood of severe neglect.

By the way, I am told that foreign adoptions have gone from 20,000 per year in the year 2000 to under 3,000 per year in 2019. The drop could be largely due to the number of failed adoptions. In the last twenty years, we have learned a lot about the importance of attachment and bonding but we have a long way to go.

TEN PRACTICAL THINGS TO DO IF YOU HAVE A CHILD WITH ATTACHMENT ISSUES.

1. Know the background before you start. This is particularly true if you plan to adopt a child. Always seek to know what really happened with the child in terms of bonding and attachment. Pay particular attention to the first eighteen months of their life. Were they left lying alone in a crib for hours and days at a time without human stimulation? As toddlers were they chronically ignored? Were they left to take care of themselves as small children? Take a look at the chapter I've written on genetic generational curses. Some insight into the life of the birth parents and grandparents may be helpful.

2. Educate yourself regarding bonding and attachment. This book has only scratched the surface. Remember, too, attachment deficiencies can occur on many different levels. On the lower end of the scale, it will manifest itself in social withdrawal or mild social anxiety. On the upper end of the scale, it will manifest itself in violent criminal-type behavior.

3. Count the cost before you start. Most VPs are good-hearted

people with deep desires to help children who are hurting. Sometimes that desire can blind us to reality. Children with severe attachment issues can be extremely difficult to help. They can literally consume all of your time and even all of your financial resources. They can unintentionally destroy family relationships. Sadly, far too many well-meaning couples have taken in children and later discovered they were not equipped to care for them. In desperation, they turn them back in like shelter pets. The children would have been better off if they had not been adopted in the first place. If you plan to adopt or foster a child with severe attachment issues you should know up front that it is likely to drastically change everything about your life.

4. Consider the effect on your family. Whether you are fostering or adopting, caring for a child with severe attachment issues is going to affect everyone in your family. Spouses and children must be on board with you 100%. Prayerfully consider how their presence will affect the children you already have in your home. No matter how badly we want to help those unattached children, it does not make sense to create chaos in the life of your other children just so you can reach one.

5. Get over the *messiah complex*. A lot of VPs, including myself, have fallen into the trap of believing that if they will just persevere and give the child enough second chances, they will be healed. I applaud this attitude and certainly agree we should persevere and never give up on a child. However, I also know that with some children only God can change them. In fact, there are two diagnoses that I am convinced only divine intervention and healing can correct. Those are spiritual oppression/possession and/or a legitimate diagnosis of Reactive Attachment Disorder. It is almost as if these two go hand in hand. I believe that, along with a lot of properly administered therapy, hard work, patience, and sacrifice, a good dose of divine intervention is needed to treat children with either of these diagnoses.

6. Keep life simple. These children do not need to live complicated lives. They need simple routines and predictability. They

typically do not adjust well to sudden changes or a lack of order. They are already dealing with a lot of emotional baggage. Keep things as simple as possible for them. Kids who are on the violent end of the spectrum tend to have some bizarre survival skills. These children have developed a way to compensate for not having the normal empathy-based preservation instinct discussed previously. Therefore, when they feel threatened or when life is complicated or unpredictable these bizarre survival skills tend to surface.

7. The fact that you can explain why a child is acting out does not mean the behavior is acceptable. Certainly, there is room for mercy and, believe me, these kids need some mercy. Don't try to fight every battle, but when their behaviors are hurting others they cannot be excused. It can be difficult but remember that the person being hurt does not deserve to be hurt any more than the disconnected child deserved to be hurt. Even disconnected children have to understand the personal consequences of hurting others.

8. Be appreciative of small steps of progress. Children with attachment issues heal very slowly and many will never experience complete healing

9. Consider alternative therapies. Therapists skilled enough to use talk therapy (traditional sit down in the office and talk) to successfully treat disconnected children are rare. Consider alternate methods such as animal therapy in addition to talk therapy. Sometimes children will bond with animals long before they develop the capacity to bond with humans. One word of caution though; children with severe attachment issues can be cruel to animals. Monitor closely.

10. Find a support system. Whether you are an adoptive parent, a foster parent, a Houseparent, or have literally taken in your brother's child, you will need the support of others who can understand the daily challenges you face. Share thoughts and ideas. Learn from one another, but most importantly remind each other that you are not alone in the battle for the lives of hurting children.

CHAPTER **10**

- *TRAUMA* -

It started out as a normal day for me as a seven-year-old. After school, I walked home and prepared to play with my friends in our safe little neighborhood. I was standing under the carport when a neighborhood kid rode his bike out of the driveway, across the street, and directly into the path of a car. Almost fifty years have passed, but I remember that scene as if it were yesterday. The lady never had a chance to hit the brakes. She hit the boy so hard that his bike broke half in two. One half of the bike slid several feet down the road while the other half flew over her car and landed behind it. My little friend hit the asphalt road and his body bounced along for several feet until it stopped. There was a brief moment of silence. I remember the lady driver jumping out of the car and screaming. She was paralyzed with fear. The little boy lay lifeless in the middle of the road.

Eight years later I had moved to another city and developed new friends. Phillip was my classmate, teammate, and hunting buddy. We spent countless hours together romping through the woods, laughing together, playing sports together, and spending nights at each other's houses. When the phone rang on the night of December 9, 1981, at 11:20 PM, it was Phillip's mom calling. Phillip was dead. I remember it as if it happened yesterday. My parents put me in the car and we headed to Phillip's house. Just hours before, he had dropped me off at my house after football practice. Now I was looking at the spot where they had laid his dead body on the road. The image is still clear in my mind- the headlights of a vehicle shining on the scene of the accident.

I had the good fortune to be raised in a very loving and supportive family. My parents did what most would have done. They loved me through the hard times and were always there when I needed them. I came through both of these traumatic events without any permanent scars. I thought about the two events fairly often but understood that such events are a normal part of life. I did not think I had been adversely affected by either event.

Fast forward thirty-two years. I am the father of two teenagers. On a Friday night, I drove them to an out-of-town football game. We took a carload of my daughter's friends and, as usual, had a great time telling stories and laughing as we rode along. Tonight would be different. As we headed home after the game we came upon an accident scene. A teenage driver had driven off the road and was injured. Traffic was stopped and a truck had backed up into a driveway so that his headlights would shine onto the spot of the accident. Without warning, I began to weep uncontrollably. Somehow I managed to keep driving, but for the next forty-five minutes tears rolled down my face and I could not speak.

I tell these stories because they demonstrate the power traumatic events can have in our lives. I don't think we ever get over the trauma, we just learn to adapt. Sometimes those memories catch us by surprise as they did me on the way home from the ballgame that night. The simple image of truck lights shining on the scene of an accident triggered an emotion I thought had been buried long ago. More importantly, though, is the fact that those traumas deeply affect the way we live our lives – usually in ways we don't even realize. In retrospect, I now believe my losses caused me to develop unhealthy coping mechanisms that remain with me to this day. For many years after Phillip's death, I kept my distance emotionally from all my friends. I had several girlfriends in high school and college but I pushed away when they got too close. It was my way of protecting myself. I was even worse with male friends. Although I have always had a lot of male friends, I kept my distance emotionally. The week after Phillip died I put my hunting rifle in a closet and have not seen it since. I still associate hunting rifles with the death of my friend so I avoid them. Any time I am invited to go hunting I immediately think of excuses not to go. My reasoning is irrational, but somehow I fear I might lose that friend if we go hunting or shoot guns together. The same applies to bike riding. I still enjoy riding several hundred miles per year but quite often I catch myself being hypervigilant about cars and driveways. Our traumas impact us for life.

As a well-adjusted individual from a supportive family, if I have been so negatively affected by traumas in my life imagine how they affect children who have experienced traumas much more intensely.

Chris was close to his dad. He often accompanied him to work, and on Saturdays, they rode four-wheelers together. One Saturday morning Chris woke early and was excited about the day he and his dad had planned. He went to wake his dad but there was no response. After shaking him for several minutes Chris called his mom. She discovered that Chris's dad had died in his sleep. That was only the beginning. In the coming months, Chris's mom struggled financially, so she moved in with her new boyfriend. The boyfriend saw little Chris as a nuisance, so he disciplined him harshly. One day he beat him with a horsewhip so violently that it ripped Chris's clothing. He ran away from home and lived in a forest for ten days. Finally, a rescue team discovered Chris deep in the woods wearing only a pair of underwear.

Jeremy was another boy who experienced severe trauma. His birth father broke into his house, locked Jeremy in a closet, and then killed his mother and grandparents. Jeremy eventually freed himself from the closet and discovered the bodies.

Only eleven years old, Joseph came home from school one day to find all of his clothes piled in the front yard of his trailer. They had been set on fire. When he entered the house trailer, his mom's boyfriend threw him through a plate glass window into the front yard where his burned clothes already lay.

Sam was just eight years old when his mother tied him to a bed and, in exchange for drugs, allowed her boyfriends to rape him. He was so poorly treated that he and his sister, driven by hunger, escaped their house one night, stole a bow and arrow, and went hunting in the neighborhood. He told police he was hoping to see a deer to kill. He almost starved to death.

I could continue, but I suspect the readers of this book are all too familiar with such stories. I have learned to never assume I have seen it all. Often in this business, just when you think you have heard the worst possible trauma a child could face, you hear something worse. My only purpose in sharing is to remind us all that the children we have in our care have most likely experienced horrible things in their brief lives. No matter how much they may frustrate us, there has to be some allowance for mercy and grace. No matter how bizarre or inexplicable their behavior, there is usually a back story that might give us greater understanding to help them more effectively.

Perhaps you are raising a child you adopted at birth and they have no noticeable trauma. You may be thinking they have lived a trauma-free life. I challenge you to re-think that assumption. There is a good chance that child experienced more trauma than you realize. We sometimes forget that trauma can start long before a baby is birthed. I am convinced that many times the bizarre or irrational behaviors we see in children and adolescents are the result of in-utero trauma. I will deal with this more in-depth in the chapters on generational curses. It is now generally accepted that tobacco and alcohol abuse during pregnancy can affect a baby for life. Society is now coming to accept something psychologists have thought for a long time – a mother's trauma is transferred to her baby in utero. Just because a child is adopted at birth and raised in a secure and loving environment does not mean he/she has not experienced trauma. Furthermore, trauma can occur during labor and delivery. You may never be made aware of such traumas, but they can have an effect on a child for life regardless of the environment in which they are raised. Oftentimes, medical traumas at birth and during early infancy can have dramatic effects on children for the rest of their lives. I have seen children born to extremely loving and secure parents who followed all of the pregnancy recommendations and did everything the right way, who live with life-altering emotional problems. They often manage anxiety in peculiar ways and some seem to always be on high alert to potential dangers in their environments, even as adults.

Trauma in the life of an adopted child can take place in many forms. Oftentimes, they are born to malnourished mothers. Sometimes those mothers have abused substances or endured abuse, violence, or rejection during pregnancy. I am convinced that children in utero can sense those things. My wife and I read stories and talked to our children when they were in the womb. Something tells me they sensed our care and that gave them some security. Similarly, parents of unwanted children may talk together about not wanting their baby. I believe the baby may be able to sense these things going on outside the womb. How traumatic would it be to come into a world that we knew did not want us? Obviously, many adopted children also experience trauma after birth. Some are left in adoption agencies, orphanages, or foster care. As we saw in the chapter on attachment and bonding, these experiences can be traumatic. Finally, I believe all adopted children experience some degree of trauma in knowing they have been separated from their birth families. For many, it is not a major issue but for some, it is a very delicate matter. Again, trauma of any degree and under any circumstance has an effect on us in some way. We are fortunate indeed if the effect is a positive one.

Children in foster care experience all sorts of trauma. It is often easier to identify because it is a precedent to their placement. However, just because you know a child's life events prior to their placement into foster care, do not assume that you are fully aware of all traumatic experiences. Foster care alone is traumatic. Children first get removed from the only parents they know. Regardless of the circumstances – they are still the child's parents. Then they get put into homes with people they don't know. They are expected to conform to the rules and values of their foster family – not visa versa. And, unfortunately, sometimes the abuse is repeated. The list of traumas in foster care can go on and on.

Once again, although adopted and foster children might seem to be trauma-free, they are usually not. Oftentimes these children have been abused or neglected. They may have experienced the death or severe illness of a parent. Sometimes they feel unwanted. Sometimes they see themselves as a burden to those who have taken them in. They often face scary court appearances and unwanted sessions with counselors and social workers. They may be the subject of huge family disagreements and more. It can be very traumatic even when their new caretakers deeply love and accept them.

Let us remember, too, that trauma does not have to be the result of a single, identifiable incident. Sometimes trauma is brought on by a series of events. I call this *battle-fatigue trauma*. Although there may have been no single traumatic incident, a series of very unfortunate events can pile up and have a similar effect.

I believe it wise to consider the fact that we live at a very, very unique time in the history of mankind. Medical advances are occurring at a rate faster than any other time. Although psychologists and thinkers for many years have considered the effects of trauma on the individual, only in relatively recent history scientists have been able to quantitatively measure those effects. We can now actually take a look, via modern technology, at a picture of a human brain and identify the effects of trauma on its size and structure. We can also measure body chemistry and identify chemical reactions that take place as a result of trauma. For the purposes of this book, I do not see it necessary to go into detail. However, it is worth noting that trauma no longer has to be addressed from a purely psychological standpoint. It has measurable physical and physiological effects.

For many years psychologists have talked about *fight* or *flight*. Although at one time this was just an abstract concept thought to be credible, it is now validated with measurable scientific evidence. Researchers are now able to see and measure brain activity and chemistry which validates the theory. That makes it even more credible and I believe understanding this is crucial to our understanding of trauma and our efforts to help children who suffer from trauma.

The fight or flight theory is based on the idea that all living beings have a built-in survival instinct. I often refer to it as the preservation instinct. Without this instinct, we would become extinct. It keeps us alive. When we are threatened, this instinct kicks us into survival mode. Those who study the brain believe the lower portion is responsible for matters of survival while the upper portion is responsible for everything else. Therefore, when matters of survival arise, our lower brain kicks into action and our upper brain goes into standby mode. Subsequently, there are two choices available to the brain. We refer to them as fight and flight. We either bow up and fight or we run for our lives. The concept is actually rather easy to understand. Consider, for example, that an intruder breaks into your house in the middle of the night. He has a gun and you realize he could kill you. If your brain chooses flight mode, you have several options. You could jump out a window and run away, hide in a closet or under a bed, or even walk toward the intruder and say, "Shoot me and get this over with." If your brain chooses fight mode you are probably going to call the police, grab a weapon, and wait for your opportunity to do bodily damage to the intruder. In either case, you are going to become what we call hypervigilant. In other words, your brain is going to be super sensitive to everything around you and to every move being made. Remember that word - hypervigilant. Now that we understand the basics of fight or flight, let's apply it to the children in our care and the trauma they experience.

Remember the little boy I mentioned who went hunting for deer in the middle of the night? A year later I took him to live in my home. I noticed that he was hoarding food in his room. He would sneak out of his room at night and go to the kitchen where he would find all sorts of food items to hide in his room. The problem reached a climax one day when I discovered several uneaten pork chops hidden under his bed pillow. Even though this boy had plenty of food available to him, he was still hypervigilant. He wanted to make sure he had plenty of resources. He had lived in hunger for so long that his brain seemed to have gotten stuck in the fight mode.

At our home, we discovered many boys wanted to leave the lights on in their rooms at night. I would go to say goodnight and turn off the lights. This often caused them to jump out of bed and ask a question, or sometimes they would beg me to leave the light on for a while longer. While I thought they were just wanting to stay up later, I now realize some of the boys were actually experiencing anxiety as a result of the dark. It may be that many of those boys had had traumatic experiences in dark rooms prior to coming to our ranch. When the lights went out they became hypervigilant as a means of survival and self-protection. Although it was an irrational way to feel in our home, their brains were locked on previous experiences. They more than likely did not even realize it was happening.

A lot of people who have experienced trauma prefer to go into flight mode rather than fight mode. Using our example above, these are the people who hide in the closet or jump out of a window. Flight mode serves the same purpose – it preserves us. In terms of children, this method of preservation can manifest itself in a variety of ways. Some will withdraw and become anxious or depressed. Others will resort to drugs or alcohol. With boys, pornography and/or masturbation can be the flight mechanism. Remember, early trauma has taught these children to escape. Their pattern for dealing with trauma has trained them to deal with all the other issues they face in life.

In some instances, certain events can trigger reactions to past traumas. We have to watch closely so that we can help our children identify triggers and work through them. One night at the ranch a car caught fire in our driveway. No one was hurt and the fire was extinguished quickly but the emotional aftermath lasted for days. One of the boys who witnessed the fire from a distance went into a state of shock and for several hours was basically an emotional zombie. Some psychologists would add a third response called *freeze*. I stayed up all night trying to bring him back to reality. As it turned out, several years prior to his placement with us his mother had burned to death in a house fire. As a little boy, he had

witnessed a horrible incident. The car fire br
matic images for him. He went into *flight* (ɟ
going into shock. Interestingly, neither I r
previously been aware of the circumstan

Children who have experienced tr
oped some sort of fight-or-flight patterns ᴜ.
These patterns are generalized and after a while, ᴄ
play whether the trauma is present or not. In essence, the ᵖ.
become lifestyle habits.

My great grandfather was a carpenter and had a favorite saying, "Measure twice and cut once." He knew his supplies were limited and that once a board was cut it had to be the right size. If not, there would be a domino effect of complications. The same can be said of children who have experienced severe trauma. The brain does not develop healthy preservation instincts early on, so it later develops a domino effect of complications that affect all areas of life.

Children who have experienced severe trauma often require more specialized care than the average person has the knowledge to provide. That is not to say that average people who are compassionate and loving cannot help a child with severe trauma. It is to say that we often need specialized training to understand the root of the behaviors and how we should deal with them. As a young man who had taken several traumatized boys into my home, I lacked the knowledge or experience to deal with trauma properly. I had plenty of compassion and patience but very little knowledge, even with a Master's Degree and several years of experience in the counseling field. I still regret treating the kid with the pork chop under his pillow as if he were selfish and greedy. In retrospect, I wish I had given him a box of healthy snacks to keep in his room. This would have reduced his hypervigilant state until it could be properly dealt with. I mishandled the matter by putting a lock on the refrigerator which inadvertently contributed to further trauma.

Even today, I recommend that children with severe trauma receive specialized treatment from professionals who are experts on the matter of trauma. Most counselors, including myself, are not qualified as such.

addition to training and knowledge, VPs must have three tools in order to properly help child victims of trauma:

1. **RELATIONSHIP.** I cannot emphasize how important it is for children to have a relationship with an adult who genuinely cares for them. This is the foundation on which trust can be built. Where there is no trust, nothing else is going to matter.
2. **COMPASSION.** It is amazing what a compassionate spirit will do in terms of building relationships and trust. Children are very intuitive, and they know when someone truly cares versus someone who is just doing a job. Compassion also helps us persevere long enough to help the child break cycles that have usually been in development for many years before they manifest.
3. **PATIENCE.** Trauma victims can try your patience like no other. As a VP you may find yourself confused and wondering why your child does things that are so irrational. You will very often feel like you are not making progress and you can even reach the point of giving up. Patience is mandatory. Have you ever tried to untangle a fishing line that has been severely tangled? Most people just cut the line and throw it away. We simply don't have the patience to untangle it. Dealing with traumatized children can make you feel the same way. Don't cut the line and throw them away. They need you.

Chapter 8 of John in the Bible tells a story about Jesus' encounter with a woman who had been accused of adultery. The story has nothing to do with trauma or children, but I find it interesting that Jesus' process for dealing with the matter is the exact process to take when dealing with trauma victims. In the story, the Pharisees bring the woman before Jesus and ask if she should be stoned as punishment for her deed. Jesus replies, *"Anyone here who has never sinned can throw the first stone at her"* (NCV). When no one casts their stones they all walk away. Jesus then tells the woman she is not condemned and to discontinue her life of sin.

Jesus demonstrates four steps that are important to remember:

1. *HE KNEW HER SITUATION*. Jesus knew what the woman had done and he called her to face her situation. Identifying and facing the problem is the first step to follow in dealing with traumatized children. This requires some skill and research on our part, but it is where we have to start.

2. *HE HAD COMPASSION*. Notice that Jesus thought long and hard about the situation. I have to think he felt compassion for the lady and even sorry for her as she encountered the harsh judgment of the Pharisees. I can tell you from experience that if you are lacking compassion for the kids you work with, it might be time to give up your life as a VP.

3. *HE DID NOT CONDEMN THE LADY*. He understood that she was worthy of forgiveness and that she was a work in progress. We should not condemn our kids just because they act irrationally. They cannot afford our condemnation.

4. *HE HELD HER ACCOUNTABLE*. Jesus didn't just identify the problem and exercise compassion and mercy. He also knew it was imperative that she make some changes. While we might understand why and how our kids act, we still have to hold them accountable for change. We cannot allow them to continue with self-defeating lifestyles.

TEN PRACTICAL THINGS TO DO WHEN DEALING WITH CHILDREN WHO HAVE BEEN SEVERELY TRAUMATIZED.

1. Take advantage of professionals who have dedicated their lives to the study and treatment of trauma alone. It has become a highly specialized field of study. Do not assume that a counselor is a trauma specialist just because they say trauma is one of

the things they can help with. Most can offer assistance but a specialist can do some amazing things. By analogy, you might not want your pediatrician to perform open heart surgery.

2. Study hard to know every potential trauma your child could have possibly experienced in utero, birth, infancy, early childhood, and beyond. Based on the information you have, make a list of traumas your child may have experienced. When bizarre, out-of-control behaviors occur, refer to the list and try to determine if those behaviors could possibly be connected to the trauma they have experienced.

3. Before adopting a child, consider the challenges you may face as a result of an unknown trauma. Make sure you are ready for whatever may come your way. There is nothing as sad as reversing an adoption.

4. Deal with trauma-related symptoms compassionately. For example, don't lock the refrigerator on a kid who was starved. Be willing to lose some battles while you are fighting the wars.

5. Be predictable. Lack of predictability can trigger fight-or-flight reactions in children and teens. Consistency and predictability can reduce the effect and allow the brain to come out of preservation mode.

6. Respect personal space. Victims of trauma require time to develop trust which allows them to be touched physically. Even a gentle touch on the arm can be alarming to some.

7. Give your child a designated hiding place where they can escape when needed. Those who have survived by flight need to have safe and healthy ways of doing this while they are developing better coping skills. I used to designate kids a special place where they could go when they felt frightened or needed to calm down. There would be no negative consequences for going there. I knew where they were and I knew they were safe. By doing this we both could calm down before addressing issues without escalating the flight tendency.

8. Don't overload with activities. Too much activity can actually be a bad thing for traumatized children.

9. Be extra sensitive about traumatized children when they are

facing new environments. New environments can be overwhelming and can trigger their fight or flight mechanisms. At our boys ranch, we were required by law to give each boy an orientation and have him sign several papers upon intake. Because moving is so stressful for a child, I would often skip the paperwork to allow the boy time to relax and get settled in. There would be time later for all the scary paperwork.

10. Honor their emotions. Our tendency is to downplay emotions in order to maintain control. This is largely because emotions make us uncomfortable. Instead, honor emotions and let them know their feelings, no matter how irrational they may seem, are important to you. Of course, this does not mean you let them have temper tantrums or express themselves inappropriately. It does mean that if they express themselves with a proper degree of civility, they will not receive your condemnation.

FOUNDATION **3**

- *WHAT IS IMPORTANT TO* -
YOUR CHILDREN

Relationships
Predictability
The Power of Choice
Fairness and Justice
Family

CHAPTER 11

- *RELATIONSHIPS* -

Very early in my career, I began to realize that no amount of psychology, psychiatry, treatment planning, behavioral theory, or therapy was of much use if a child does not have a healthy relationship with a caring adult. In a world promoting science and research as the authority, I began advocating for the notion that what a troubled child really needs is a caring adult in their life. It seemed the world of mental health professionals had ideas different from mine and to this day is largely the case. However, fifteen years into my career I decided to get a certification to teach a parenting class. Honestly, I only did it because I needed the continuing education units and I also thought I might make a few extra dollars teaching the class. I really didn't expect to learn much but I did choose a curriculum that was getting great reviews nationally. In fact, it was considered to be the most successful parenting curriculum in the nation. It was so successful that insurance companies were paying for families to attend the classes on the basis that their attendance might curtail the need for expensive therapy for their troubled children. I will never forget the very first words that came out of my instructor's mouth, "If kids don't have healthy relationships with caring adults, nothing else will matter." Finally, after years of dealing with the psychobabble, I found someone who felt exactly what

I had been feeling for years. The absence of healthy relationships is really the problem. It all boils down to this one critical thing.

How are relationships built? It is very simple. You are just there to be a part of their life. You live in the same house. You go places together. You have meals with them. You talk with them. You share stories with them. You show your interest in the things they are interested in. You do fun things together. You help with homework. You laugh with them. You can even watch television with them. That is really all there is to building relationships. It is not complicated, but if it is missing in a child's life you will see the consequences.

Our youth pastor recently held an event at which there was no sermon, no games, and no announcements. Everybody simply showed up at the same place and sat around a campfire together for three hours. He promoted the event as simply a time to hang out.

My teenage daughter accompanied me to a Ladies Service Sorority meeting where I was to speak. The ladies were very welcoming to my daughter and said they would love for her to join the group when she was old enough. In response, she asked one of the ladies about the purpose of the group. To my pleasant surprise, the lady replied, "We just get together and do community service so we have a good excuse to hang out together." There is nothing like honesty.

The common thread to these scenarios is that each is centered on one thing... relationships.

On the way home from the youth event my children may not have had any deep spiritual insights to share, but they were excited because they had made new friends. Consequently, they were much more eager to go back to church on Sunday.

The ladies in the sorority do a good thing for the community, but they are also filling a need that every member shares – the need for relationships.

At the core of every human soul is the need for a relationship. Our most important relationship is the one with our creator. After that, we all crave an intimate relationship with a soulmate. Finally, we all have a need for relationships with family and friends.

There are thousands of theories, programs, systems, and plans for dealing with children. Any of these that do not have relationship building as their number one priority should be immediately thrown in the trash. They are not worth the paper they are written on.

I am often asked to speak about the formula we use at Eagle Rock. People usually want to know how we manage behavior problems. My speech has three points:

1. We build relationships with our boys.
2. The most important thing we do is build relationships with our boys.
3. A children's home without relationships is little more than a warehouse for children.

Genesis 3 presents an interesting situation. In verse 8 we learn that God Himself took a stroll through the garden and actually stopped and talked with Adam. It is interesting because one might think God, the Creator, would spend his days sitting on a big cloud watching the world go around. Instead, He is pictured strolling through a garden talking to the people He just created. Does that tell us something about God? Does it indicate He actually wants to have a relationship with us? Would it not be easier for Him to sit back, give orders, and watch us obey? I believe this one obscure verse of scripture has profound implications. We were created for relationship!

Just as our life is empty without relationship with God, it is also empty without relationship with others. As children, the first relationship we have is with our caregiver – preferably our birth parents. When we become teenagers, our relationship with peers takes precedence. As young adults and young couples, the relationship with a mate becomes most important and is followed by the unexplainable love and intimacy a parent has with his/her own child. In later years, while our children are forming relationships with their mates, our priorities often shift back to the relationships we have with our own parents, and the cycle continues. However, when we miss the fulfillment of relationships at any stage there are often consequences that follow.

How does this apply to the VP? First of all, it is often the VP who inherits the responsibility of teaching the child how to have appropriate relationships. These skills have a lasting impact throughout the child's life, for better or worse. Secondly, if the child's relationship needs are not met they become frustrated and insecure. Frustrated children often exhibit unhealthy behavior and have a greater chance of becoming dysfunctional adults.

Simply put, building relationships with our children is the absolute most important thing we can do as VPs.

TEN PRACTICAL POINTS ABOUT RELATIONSHIPS.

1. Relationship building takes time. There is no substitute for time.
2. Relationship building is the hardest thing you will ever do. It is not easy work. It often takes sacrifice.
3. Children in foster care of any kind are naturally guarded when it comes to building relationships. Most of them have been hurt in the past and do not want to be hurt again. This does not mean we quit trying.
4. Relationships are often one-sided. You may be the giver and the child may be the taker for a long time before a balance develops. Please be aware that if a VP attempts to use a relationship with a child for self-fulfillment, the child will immediately sense it and build barriers because he/she feels used.
5. Relationship building does not have to be complicated. Doing simple things like attending a child's ball games or asking how their day was are relationship-building activities. Relationships are built simply by people showing interest in one another. In the case of the VP, it may be primarily built by the adult show-

ing interest in the child.

6. It begins with your attitude. Your attitude should be one of sincere interest and concern for the child. You can be taught to use a number of techniques, but if your motivation is not sincere the child will immediately recognize it and will close you out of his/her world.

7. Having a relationship with a child does not mean you have to be his or her "buddy." Children do not need adults to be their buddies. They need same-age peers to fill that role. Do not try to act like a teenager just so you can have a relationship. Not only will this technique backfire on you, but the child will also lose respect for your God-given authority.

8. Do not be disappointed when you get nothing in return. One of the ways I show interest is to attend ball games. That contributes to building relationships. However, many times after a ballgame, a boy will be much more interested in being with his friends than he is interested in acknowledging an adult who attended his game. This is a time to check your motivation. Are you there to be appreciated or are you there to demonstrate your sincere interest in his life? Children somehow figure out the answer to that question intuitively.

9. Do not try to fill a role you were not meant to fill. You may never be able to fill a child's need for a relationship with his birth family. Fill whatever need he will let you fill.

10. Think of the three people who had the most positive influence on you. How did they earn their influence? What did they do to develop a relationship with you? Follow their example.

CHAPTER 12

- *PREDICTABILITY* -

When I opened the ranch as a young man, I believed that structure and routine were two of the things our boys would need the most. I still have the printed daily routine I posted on the wall for the boys. They woke up at 5:30 a.m., took showers from 5:45 to 6:15, ate breakfast as a group at 6:15, and boarded the school bus at 7:00. In the afternoon there was a regimented schedule as well that included study hall, laundry, dinner, daily chores, showers, and bedtime. I even assigned each boy a time to use the washer and dryer. I was, at that time, under the impression that a home should be run like a military boot camp. To some degree I was right. Children do need structure. When you have 12 people living under one roof you have to establish a lot of structure. However, as the years passed I moved away from having such a tight schedule because I felt that it was not normal or homelike. It seemed as if our house-parents had become drill sergeants instead of parents. Eventually, I opted for a plan that allowed the kids to have more control over their own schedules. I announced that breakfast would be served at 6:15 and the bus would leave at 7:00. The details of shower times and eating times were left up to the boys to figure out, and surprisingly most of them did. If not, I would intervene and enforce a regimented schedule again. They learned to self-regulate to avoid being controlled. I always held a level of control, but as long as they got things done and met the objectives I let them manage their own scheduling details. We learned through the years that some groups of kids could handle self-regulation and others could not. I found that being able to bend but not break was key. We also learned that while allowing the kids to self-regulate and work out some details, we could not be unpredictable. They had to know what to expect. For example, if we said breakfast would be served at 6:15, we had to serve it at 6:15. If the school bus was scheduled to arrive at 7:00, it needed to arrive at 7:00. My point is that, as VPs, we need to have some predictable routines in our homes but we also need to allow our kids the opportunity to regulate themselves. When they fail to self-regulate, then step in.

Now to the matter of predictability. At Eagle Rock, we owned and operated two thrift stores. Our boys were not forced to work there, but it did provide a place where they could earn some extra money. From time to time our thrift store would be *slammed*; everyone in town decided to donate their unwanted items at the same time. We decided that the slam times were a good time for the boys to work. When we anticipated we would be busy on a certain day (Saturday afternoons for example), we found it best to give the boys three or four days prior notice. We tried our best to predict the start and finish time for their work as well. This gave the boys plenty of time to think about and become excited about the opportunity. However, on a few occasions, our stores got busy unexpectedly and the staff needed help on short notice. It was on these occasions that we learned the importance of planning and predictability in the life of troubled kids. I can tell you from experience that if you walk into their room on Friday night and say, "We got slammed so we're working all day tomorrow," it will not be received well and you'll have an agitated child. By contrast, if you give them a week's notice, they will be much more pleasant.

I imagine by now you are asking, "What is the big deal?" Most people, regardless of the circumstance, prefer predictability and do not like surprises. "What is different about the child I am raising?"

I am glad you asked! I believe that children who come out of less-than-ideal circumstances have an enhanced sensitivity to unpredictability. Take a child, for example, who has been in foster care. Chances are - one day he slept at home and the next day, without much notice, he was sleeping in the home of a total stranger (maybe your home). Most of the time they don't get much warning. It's not like the social worker says, "Johnny, I know your dad gets drunk and beats the tar out of you every night. Therefore in two weeks, on Saturday at 9:00 AM, you're going to live with the Smiths." More than likely the social worker shows up at 2:00 PM and says, "You're going to live with the Smiths today at 3:00 PM." It is evident how kids in foster care can develop a fear of the unpredictable. The same applies to some adopted children. They may be in the most secure and loving home possible but in the back of their mind, they wonder when they will be removed. Do they secretly think that, because they are adopted, they aren't as secure as birth children in terms of being able to stay in a family? I suspect that a lot of adopted kids have heard stories of others being unadopted. They have reason to have doubts. Adopted children, along with children in ranches and children's homes, are not strangers to unpredictable things happening in their lives. If you've been around these environments there is no need to explain.

As previously stated, children who are victims of trauma or even severe instability often develop a natural sense of heightened alertness. They live in a state of self-preservation. When life experiences are threatening over an extended period of time, the brain adapts. Part of that adaptation is the tendency to take special notice when things are not flowing in a predictable manner.

As an analogy to help us understand what this state of mind feels like, allow me to share a personal story: I love to ride my bicycle on a favorite trail near my home. This trail winds through a forest for several miles, so it is not uncommon to ride for an hour without seeing another human being. I usually enjoy being all alone in the woods. However, a few years ago a mentally deranged person attacked and killed a fellow cyclist in those same woods. The killer was quickly captured, but I recall the next time I rode that particular trail my brain went into high alert status. I noticed everything in my surroundings. If I heard something moving in the woods, my adrenaline pumped more quickly. I was constantly surveying everything. If anything looked the least bit abnormal I immediately took notice. A couple of times I pedaled as fast as I could because I sensed someone was following me. None of my fears or heightened state of mind were really rational. With that one exception, the trail had always been safe and the killer had been captured. However, our brains have a self-preservation mode that does not rely on rationality. As I rode through those woods, I was constantly and irrationally taking notice of anything I might deem unpredictable. My perception of the possibilities in my environment had changed.

The same can happen to children. Their perceptions about the possibilities that exist in their environments can cause them to think irrationally. For some children, the brain gets stuck in that mode and they have little control. They can become frustrated with their irrationality, but that is the reality of their state of mind. Anytime something unpredictable happens their brain programming sends a signal that makes little sense to the non-traumatized person whose brain functions in a rational mode. Furthermore, some children tend to generalize. In other words, if they have legitimate insecurity about one area of their life, they may project that insecurity to other areas as well.

For example, my wife shares a funny story about the day her newborn sister came home from the hospital. Although she is ten years younger, the highchair was placed in the spot at the dinner table where Diana had always sat. Furthermore, her parents spent more time with the baby than they did with the other children. Diana felt abandoned. Twenty-five years later an unexpected consequence arose. Soon after we got married I realized that I had trouble sharing a bed with another person. I lived alone for a long time before we married, so I would get up in the middle of the night and move to the couch. This really bothered my wife. Neither of us fully understood why until one day we discovered she has a deep-seated fear of abandonment. It stemmed from her feeling of being abandoned by her parents when her baby sister was born. No, it was not a debilitating fear nor a psychological abnormality. It was simply a little hidden piece of her personality that was revealed when we married. It makes little sense to me, but it is her reality.

The same can apply to your children in the complexity of their minds. If your child seems to be abnormally sensitive to unpredictability, there may be an underlying cause of which you are not aware. The safest way to avoid such issues is to be predictable.

Proverbs 24:27 (NCV)
*First, finish your outside work
and prepare your fields.
After that, you can build your house.*

The point of this wise proverb is that life should not be lived haphazardly. It is important to think through things ahead of time, to plan, and, perhaps most importantly, to get your mind ready for the task ahead. It is great to be spontaneous and live life on the edge, but if that is the way you build your house, the house is probably going to look more like a squatter village than a beautiful estate. If you want to help your kids become strong and stable, give them predictability.

TEN PRACTICAL TIPS ABOUT PREDICTABILITY.

1. Lay out detailed plans for family functions. I used to do a peculiar thing when I took the boys on vacation. As soon as one of them asked what we were going to do, I would go into a minute-by-minute plan saying, "First, we will load these bags into the truck. Then we will drive to I-59, and we will stay on that road for 3 hours. At about 4:00 PM we will arrive at the campground. Then we will go to McDonald's and buy one hundred $1.00 hamburgers..." Sometimes the kids would just stare

at me with amusement; sometimes they would laugh with me over my peculiar behavior. However, for a lot of kids, I could see that my answer gave them a sense of security and calmed them down. Their need for predictability was irrational but understandable.

2. Avoid surprise work projects if possible. If the grass needs to be mowed on Saturday, do not wait until Saturday morning to tell them.

3. With smaller kids, write out your daily activities on a piece of paper and give it to them each morning. This can be soothing for them to know what activities the day holds.

4. Post a family calendar with all important dates. No teenage boy wants to find out on Friday night that he has to go to a wedding on Saturday. He needs a few weeks to psych himself up for the misery to come.

5. For unexpected trips try to give a fifteen or twenty-minute warning. All of life cannot be thoroughly planned. If you see that you are going to need to go to the grocery store, announce it fifteen or twenty minutes ahead of time instead of making the child leave on the spur of the moment. Try not to frustrate your child with too many surprises. We all know a misbehaving child is a frustrated child.

6. If you feel the need to have a printed daily schedule, allow for some flexibility. Kids need to learn to adapt and this is a good time to teach them that life does not always go exactly as planned.

7. I am a proponent of daily family meals together. Do not run your daily meal like a business meeting, but do realize this is a good time to talk about upcoming events.

8. If you have to go on a trip without your child, sit down with them and let them know when, where, and why. Give them an estimated date and time for your return.

9. If you are a Houseparent at a ranch or children's home, you are probably mandated to spend weekly or monthly time away from your kids. Let these dates and times be known and avoid surprise/secret absences. I realize there is a school of thought

that says to slip away without notice so the kids will not have time to scheme up any mischief in your absence. However, this action can leave them feeling insecure and can be a detriment to relationship building. (I must admit, when I was Administrator of our ranch and not a Houseparent, I slipped away without notice rather often because I knew *when the cat was away the mice would play*. Sometimes, even our staff did not know the boss was out of town!)

10. When you go on a trip together, do yourself a favor: tell the child every detail ahead of time. Tell them what time you will leave, the route you will take, how many miles you will drive and how many hours and minutes it will take. Not only does this give them some predictability, but it will also save you from having to answer the "Are we there yet" question 100 times.

CHAPTER 13

- *THE POWER OF CHOICE* -

One of the most powerful and yet overlooked tools in a parenting toolbox is the practice of allowing children to make some of their own decisions.

I can only imagine the kind of thoughts that arise in the minds of some readers when I say this. I am sure some of you are thinking, *Oh no, another one of those modern, liberal parenting techniques. I'll make the rules around here.* If you are thinking this, just hear me out and know that I am with you. When we finally figure out the proper way to allow our children to make some of their own decisions I believe we will realize what a powerful tool it is.

Before I dig into the concept as it relates to parenting in general, let's look at some of the reasons this tool is particularly powerful in dealing with children who have been adopted, are being fostered, or live in congregate care settings.

Jessie was born into a two-parent home, and things went pretty well until he was about four years old. One day while little Jessie was playing in the backyard at his house, he heard his parents get into a big argument. The next thing Jessie knew, his Dad had moved out of the house and Jessie was left with his mother whom he loved dearly. When Jessie asked about his Dad he was told that he had left and there was nothing anybody could do. He was further told that a judge would decide when and where Jessie could visit his Dad. After several weeks, visitation plans were finalized and Jessie was told that he would be going to his Dad's house every other weekend. He asked the judge why his Dad could not visit him more often, but Jessies's mother interjected, "Because the judge says so." Jessie settled into the new arrangement and things went OK until Dad got a new girlfriend who happened to be off from work on the same weekend Jessie was supposed to visit. She changed the visit weekend so she could have more time alone with Jessie's dad. Jessie was abruptly told that his weekend was changed. A couple of years later, Jessie's mom began abusing alcohol, and Jessie was neglected at home. A school counselor reported the neglect and a social worker visited the school. "Jessie, we are going to your house to get your clothes. You are moving in with your Dad today," she said. Jessie moved in with his Dad and made the mom mad, so she filed a child abuse report against her ex-husband. The social worker, out of an abundance of caution, obtained a court order to have Jessie removed from his father's care. She went to the school a few weeks later and told Jessie he was moving to a foster home that evening. Jessie, of course, asked why and was told a judge and a social worker decided it would be in his best interest. Jessie lived in a foster home for three months, but when the foster mom became pregnant she decided she no longer wanted to foster. The social worker moved Jessie to a group home where he was given a long list of rules, regulations, and daily schedules to follow. He was expected to learn quickly and adjust to yet another new home.

Jessie's story is typical of the boys I worked with at the ranch. I am still haunted by the scared and confused eyes of countless little boys who came to live at our ranch. Many times they had the same look as a stray dog caught on the street and placed into a little cage in the back of the dog-pound truck. He does not know who he is with, where he is going, or why he is where he is. The same could be said for some children who have been adopted. Their entire life has been a series of adjustments they have had to make as a result of someone else's decisions. They often do not even know who is making these decisions. Many times they have no input or choice.

They just have to live with it.

Now to the crux of the matter. When children live a life full of unexpected twists and turns they develop a sense of loss of control which leads to anxiety. In happy and healthy homes, children usually do not feel the need for power and control until they reach their teenage years, and even then they experience a sense of security. Children in foster care, congregate care, or adoption often live with anxiety because they have no control. I think we could all relate to that feeling. Just imagine how you would feel if your car was repossessed, your house went into foreclosure, your job was terminated, and you found out you had cancer all in the same week. You would feel as if your life was spinning out of control. This is similar to how our kids feel. One of the small things you can do to help them is to give them some sense of choice or power to choose. It may seem silly, but my experience indicates that even the smallest things can have a soothing effect on a child's or young adult's emotional well-being.

For the new foster child coming into your home, let her pick out her new bedsheets and decorate her room. Take her to the store and give her a choice of which bath linen set she wants. Look for any opportunity you can to give her the opportunity to choose. I am not thinking here of extreme things like letting them buy a $100.00 pair of tennis shoes. If you are creative you can find lots of things to do without spoiling the child or giving her the idea that she is the boss. Things as simple as choosing their own toothpaste or shampoo can ease some anxieties. For adoptive parents, at some point, you will want to let your children decide about pursuing information concerning their birth family. Do not make this decision for them. I believe it goes without saying that prospective adoptable children need to have some choice regarding who adopts them. Obviously, some will be adopted at an age when this is not feasible, but I would say that children five years old or older should at least have visits with the prospective family and a professional should evaluate their feelings about being adopted by that particular family. Anything we can do, short of overwhelming, spoiling, or giving children the impression that they are adults, should be done to give them some power of choice.

The power of choice, in addition to being a great tool for special populations, can be a great tool for parenting in general. The next few paragraphs will explain.

THE POWER OF CHOICE IN BEHAVIOR MANAGEMENT

I have a friend who taught public school for over twenty-five years. She intentionally chose to work at a school that was known for having children with behavior problems. She and my wife are close friends and together could probably write a book on classroom management. One of her techniques for avoiding power struggles when giving consequences for poor behavior involved allowing students to make choices. For example, she would say, "Johnny, you have three choices. You can write ten sentences, or you can write fifty sentences, or you can write one hundred sentences. Which do you choose?" Every time she tells us this story we laugh because it seems so silly. However, she said she never had a kid choose to write fifty or one hundred. They gladly chose to write the ten sentences and felt like they were getting a good deal. On the contrary, she could have said, "Johnny, write ten sentences," and the kid probably would have gotten mad and refused, setting the stage for a power struggle. I have often wondered why this technique works and my conclusion is that one of three things is happening in the child's mind. First, he may be confused. When we do and say things that do not seem to make sense we create confusion in the minds of our kids. This is not always a bad thing because it can throw them off their game. In other words, they are not quite sure how to respond. Secondly, it creates doubt in their mind. It is sort of like the old TV game show *Who Wants to Be a Millionaire?* The contestants are given a choice between taking a guaranteed amount of money (which is much less than a million) or taking a chance on winning a million. Oftentimes they play it safe. A bird in the hand is worth two in the bush. Finally, I think for some children, the simple act of having a choice is soothing enough to merit some unexplained compliance. They trade off the discomfort of disciplinary action in order to gain the comfort of being able to make a choice. The effect is basically the same regardless of their motivation.

I used this same technique with the boys at our ranch. For example, if a boy was caught smoking cigarettes, I might say, "Johnny, there is nothing wrong with smoking cigarettes – it is the cancer that will kill you. Therefore, I am going to give you a choice of three things to help you learn how bad it is. Option 1 is for you to run five miles. This will help you learn what tobacco does to your lungs. Option 2 is to make a $50.00 donation to the American Cancer Society. They may need the money to treat you one day. Option 3 is to sit down with me and read out loud this three-page booklet. This will teach you about the dangers of tobacco."

Every time they would choose to read the booklet - exactly what I wanted them to do in the first place. I made the first two options very undesirable to manipulate their choice so they would choose the one I really wanted them to choose. Inevitably, they came away feeling like they got a good deal, a power struggle was avoided, and hopefully, they at least had something to think about next time they lit up. By the way, on the second offense, they had to choose two of the three options. Power of choice, when administered properly, can be helpful with behavior management.

THE POWER OF CHOICE WITH CHORES

I am a big believer in the idea that everyone needs to pitch in around the house. We all need chores. There is a lot to say about this but for my current purposes let me just say that everybody needs to play some role in the day-to-day operations of any home. There are stereotypical male and female chores, and there is nothing wrong with that, but at some point, everybody needs to experience and gain an appreciation for every chore. My daughter knows how to mow and weed-eat, while my son knows how to sweep and mop. Some kids like the outdoors and some like indoors. There is nothing wrong with letting our kids make some choices about their chores as long as they are not allowed to avoid work just because they are lazy. We are all more productive when we are doing something we enjoy. I would rather mow grass for two hours than go grocery shopping for thirty minutes. My wife could spend half a day shopping for groceries but five minutes behind a mower, which would drive her crazy. We are just different in that way and your kids are, too. Try to let them grow where God plants them with their own gifts and preferences.

POWER OF CHOICE WITH TEENAGERS

I realize that some parents approach parenting like a dictatorship, and I do believe parents should be the authority in the home. However, parenting should be a benevolent dictatorship and wise parents should start allowing their children some input on major decisions when they reach the age of 12 or 13. Now, I am in no way implying that I believe families should be a democracy or that everything should be up for negotiation. But, there is wisdom in recognizing the power of choice.

Take the issue of curfews for example. Oddly, I do not remember my parents setting a hard and fast curfew for me, and I do not ever recall setting one for my two birth children (although my adult daughter now disputes this assertion). Somehow we avoided curfews, but I think we were just lucky. Parents do need to set curfews. Here is how you might do it: First, Mom and Dad need to privately agree on what the appropriate curfew should be. Second, when adolescent Johnny or Susie asks what their curfew is going to be, this is the magic moment when Mom or Dad can say, "Mmmm. Let's see... What do you think?" Johnny or Susie may come up with any of a wide range of answers depending on their personality and/or negotiation skills. If they provide some crazy answer that is clearly out of the question, an appropriate response might be, "Well, that is not exactly what I had in mind. Be home at ____." End of discussion. However, if they give you a somewhat reasonable answer but still too late then you say, "That is a little later than I expected, but tell me why you think that is a good curfew." Then, give them the opportunity to explain. They may actually have some valid points that you can acknowledge. You can even give up fifteen or twenty minutes teaching them that curfew is not an arbitrary number you pulled out of a hat but a necessary deadline with good reasons for having them. If your kid is one of those who throws out unreasonable suggestions just to test your response, he might eventually figure out that this approach is not working. He will then begin to think of things he can do to be more rational so he can persuade you to be more liberal. It will be entertaining to watch him begin to process like an adult even if his motives are self-centered. That is the goal – you want your teenager to think for himself. He will do this if he thinks he is going to be able to benefit from his good choices.

Allow me to explain this concept from a more worldly viewpoint. For many years while I was operating a boys ranch, I was also a small-time real estate investor. The ranch never paid an extravagant salary, so I knew I better do some smart investing if I expected to retire before I was ninety. As it turned out, I became a decent negotiator. I would be lying if I told you my parents allowed me to negotiate much as a teenager, but I cannot help believing they must have allowed me to make a lot of my own decisions. This experience manifested itself when I began negotiating real estate deals – some of them in the hundreds of thousands of dollars. When I found a piece of property for sale I would intuitively begin asking myself a series of questions: Why is it for sale? What does the seller have to gain? What does the seller really want out of the deal? What will it cost to repair? What kind of rent will it bring? After answering these questions I would develop a strategy for explaining my offer to the seller. I learned that real estate transactions can and should be good for both buyer and seller. I made some really good deals and I made a lot of sellers happy because I had learned that decision-making is based on good reasoning. This is in stark contrast to the approach of many real estate investors. Many of them simply try to lowball their buyer and hope for the best, looking primarily to take advantage of someone else's situation. They are like the teenager who says, "Dad, I think my curfew should be 3 AM," interested only in what benefits himself and earning a negative response from his dad. In that scenario, neither party

Raising My Brother's Child

has done anything constructive. The son is just like the real estate buyer who lowballs everybody until he finally realizes his approach is not working for him.

I had an interesting real estate deal occur when I retired. I had lived on campus at the ranch with the boys for twenty-six years, so when I retired I had to find a house of my own. A foreclosure came on the market for an incredibly low price. I knew it was an absolute steal of a deal. The land alone was worth the asking price – not including the huge house. Unfortunately, a dozen other people knew what I knew and the listing agent's phone blew up within a few hours of listing the property. He had never had so many calls about a house. It was at that point I did something bizarre. While multiple offers were pouring in, I knew that most, if not all, were coming from people who just wanted to *steal* the property – to make the deal of a lifetime. I knew some would offer below asking price and others over asking price, all of them trying to get an unreasonably good deal. I quickly offered $28,000.00 more than the asking price, and the bank immediately accepted. I knew the bank wanted the property off their books. But I also knew that when they received multiple offers it would trigger an impromptu live auction which would drive the price far beyond the amount I had offered. When the bank saw my offer they decided to take it rather than deal with the chaos. I got the deal because, somewhere along the line, somebody (perhaps my parents) taught me how to make good decisions. They taught me how to think through things and to be rational. They never said "my way or the highway," but rather "as long as you are thinking through things and being responsible we will trust you." Every parent's goal should be to have children who think wisely for themselves. However, if we never give our kids an opportunity to make choices they may grow up to be indecisive adults. By the way, my investment tripled in value in spite of the fact that I paid much more than the asking price.

There is a rather unusual story in I Chronicles 21. Someone, who the book refers to as Satan, incited King David to take a census. David commissioned the census and it was reported there were 1.1 million men who could handle a sword. Joab, who was appointed

116

to take the census, was not happy so he fudged the numbers a bit. Even worse, God was upset about the ordeal and decided to punish Israel. David came under conviction and apologized to God for being so foolish, but God had already decided they would be punished. He sent a messenger to David and in verse 22 the messenger gave David the bad news.

This is your choice; three years of famine, three months of being swept away before your enemies with their swords overtaking you, or three days of the sword of the Lord- days of plaque in the land, with the angel of the Lord ravaging every part of Israel. Now then, decide how I should answer the one who sent me (NIV).

As I read this peculiar story I could not help but think how similar it sounded to some of the things I had done with the boys from the ranch. The words of the Lord, this is your choice, jumped off the page at me. God did with David exactly what I had somehow learned to do with my children. I wish I could tell you that this passage makes sense to me and that I know why God gave David a choice, but the truth is I have no idea. I am confident there are scholars with a good explanation, but for me personally, I do not have to know why God does what he does – He is God and I am not meant to understand or explain Him. The one thing I do know is that God gave David a choice of punishment and there must be a reason. Is it possible that God, through this story, was giving us a parenting lesson? I will let you decide.

TEN PRACTICAL THINGS ABOUT THE POWER OF CHOICE.

1. Remember that allowing children to make choices does not mean they have final decision-making authority. That authority belongs to the parent.

2. If you are a foster parent, think ahead about decisions you can allow children to make when placed in your home. Sometimes something as simple as choosing bed linen colors can help tremendously in easing a child's anxiety.

3. Set parameters for children to fall into when making decisions. For example, let them choose their own tennis shoes but put a cap on the price.

4. If you are an adoptive parent, discuss birth families at the appropriate age. Allow children to decide how much information they want to know about their birth families.

5. When allowing choices in behavior management make the easiest choice the one you think will benefit your cause the most. Remember that consequences should be about end results – not punishment.

6. Teach your children how to respectfully challenge your decisions in a way that leads to polite discussion. Also, teach them that you are under no obligation to provide justification.

7. If your children routinely challenge and scrutinize your decisions, make a habit of providing soft-spoken, boring, and long explanations. They will hate it and will quickly tire of challenging you.

8. Have your teenagers take a class in professional negotiation techniques. It will pay off throughout their life and it will help them understand the importance of acknowledging their parent's point of view. Decision-making is often about negotiations, and negotiations can be done in a mutually beneficial manner. Good negotiators find a way for all parties to benefit.

9. Realize that children and teens are not supposed to be allowed to take part in *every* decision. Think ahead and establish when it is acceptable for them to be a part of the decision-making process and when it is not.

10. When planning family vacations allow everyone to have input. Set the parameter of time and expense, but leave the rest up for discussion and negotiation. When it's all said and done, mom will probably make the decision anyway!

CHAPTER 14

- FAIRNESS + JUSTICE -

For much of my career, there was no such thing as free caller ID on a phone. That was a special feature that was added to your phone bill. I suppose it was a good thing in those early days at the ranch because I might not have answered the call if I had known it was the principal from the middle school. Her call rarely signified anything good to come and today was no different. I answered and she proceeded to tell me that Jack had run away from school. He had been called to the office for questioning about an incident that occurred during PE class. When the teacher accused Jack of throwing the volleyball that hit a girl on the head, Jack quietly began to cry. He then stood up, walked out of the office, and proceeded to sprint down the railroad tracks that ran beside the school. By the time I got to the school, three police cars had arrived and two officers were chasing twelve-year-old Jack down the railroad tracks. I encouraged the officers to stop, explaining that Jack would eventually get tired and hungry and would return. Nevertheless, the officers kept chasing him for several blocks and finally tackled him. It was a sad sight to see a grown man escorting a handcuffed twelve-year-old boy down the train tracks. They put him in the car and carried him to the juvenile detention center. All Jack had done was run from the school.

Jack was not an innocent child. He had been in his share of fights at school and had been in trouble for stealing. Jack was also known to tell lies. However, most of the time when Jack was confronted with something, he would readily admit to his misdeed and accept the consequences. It was a mystery to me why Jack had become so upset over the issue of throwing the ball that hit the little girl in the head.

The next day Jack was released from detention and came home. We had a good relationship, so he was anxious to tell me his side of the story. He and several other boys were throwing balls as part of the dodgeball game. Someone came to visit the teacher, temporarily distracting her, so one of the other boys intentionally threw a ball at the girl. Meanwhile, Jack was throwing another ball at a boy who had been giving him a hard time. He had managed to hit the boy in the face and bloody his nose. Jack was forthright with his story and admitted that he had done wrong by hitting the boy. He was willing to serve his consequence for that deed. As a result, I was perplexed as to why Jack got so upset that he ran away from school. When I asked Jack about this he replied, "Because I did not hit the girl! Bobby hit the girl and he blamed it on me, but I didn't do it." He went on to explain that he was willing to serve the consequence for hitting the boy, but it was not fair for him to be blamed for hitting the girl.

As the story unfolded the situation became clear because I had seen this sort of thing happen many times before. The boys would get into trouble for something they had done and they, for the most part, understood that there would be consequences. However, if they were accused of something they had *not* done they would become irate. For example, a boy would admit that he had cheated on a test; that was no big deal. However, if you accused him of making the cheat sheet when, in fact, his friend had made the cheat sheet, he would get very upset. In my mind, it seemed no different, but in the mind of my boys, there was a big difference. I used to wonder why that was the case. I would ask the boys, "What does it matter?" They would reply, "Because the truth is the truth."

None of this made sense to me until I realized one day that there is a unique dynamic about fairness that goes on in all our heads. This dynamic is especially strong in the minds of children who have a background of abuse, neglect, or living in a non-traditional setting. These children/teens have many times been born into a world that is unkind to them. They have most often been on the wrong end of injustice. They know all too well the realities of a cruel world. Even kids who live in the best ranches, foster homes, or adoptive homes often have deeply rooted beliefs that the world is unfair. Therefore, the issue of fairness is often a major issue in their lives. While we, as adults, know and accept the fact that the world is unfair, children often have a hard time accepting this fact and, subconsciously, see it as their mission in life to swing the pendulum in the other direction. In other words, they want so badly for the world to be fair that they become irrational. As well-adjusted adults, we can clearly see their irrationality, but in their minds, it makes perfect sense to overgeneralize and overcompensate.

Take, for example, the riots that occurred in the USA in 2020. Some protestors witnessed a well-publicized, isolated case of police brutality and then reacted as if it was their calling in life to correct all injustice. In their passion for the matter, they protested everything any police officer in the country ever did. They even called for abolishing the police. Many people thought these protestors were simply crazy, but in their minds, they were fighting against injustice.

I could not help comparing their ideology to that of the many boys who have lived under my care. Any hint of injustice is blown out of proportion and gross generalization can occur. Given one single incident of false accusation or other injustice, they interpret the whole world as being against them. No one, regardless of background, wants to be falsely accused. However, for an individual with a victim mentality, the matter is multiplied.

The word *victim* opens a whole can of worms to be discussed later. However, for this chapter, I want to simply point out that false accusations greatly contribute to the development of the *victim mentality* that we all despise. Why? When you falsely accuse a child, you enable his tendency to see himself as a victim. He has already been born into an unfair and unjust world. He already knows that he has been on the wrong side of injustice; therefore, a false accusation reinforces the idea that he is and always will be a victim. The last thing any of us want is for our child to embrace the victim mentality. We want them to be overcomers and to have positive attitudes, but when we falsely accuse we kill the overcomer's spirit, we unintentionally contribute to insecurities already in place. Subsequently, they either give up on life or become irrational about their worldview.

It is for these reasons that I was always extremely careful about accusing a child of anything unless I was 100% sure my accusations were accurate. There were times when I knew in my heart a boy was guilty of something but I would not accuse him because I did not want to kill his spirit. I use the term *kill his spirit* to indicate something so discouraging that a child might even quit trying to do the right thing; to make a child feel as if there is no use trying because he would be blamed for wrongdoing even when he was not guilty.

I remember one incident when one of my older boys stole the battery out of my truck and put it in his own. I knew he did it because I found the battery in his truck. When I questioned him he said he did not know how it happened. I politely, without his knowledge, returned my battery to my car and did not say anything else. I was 99% sure he had done the deed. However, it was possible someone else had done it and I had wrongfully called him a thief. I would have then contributed to his worldview that life is not fair and therefore it doesn't really matter how hard you try. I would have killed his spirit.

Some readers may balk at the idea of kids getting away with a misdeed just because there is no proof. This is valid, but I have already been clear that a child's behavior should certainly have consequences. However, my point is that if and when you are going to accuse a child of doing something, be very, very careful. Do your homework and ask yourself what damage might be done to his emotional well-being, considering his background, if you happen to make the mistake of falsely accusing. When we approach a matter with the mindset of innocent until proven guilty, we help kids rebuild trust in the world around them. They will trust the world only if they feel like it is at least trying to be fair to them. Making false allegations, even when well-intended, will almost always kill their spirit.

As Christians, we sometimes wonder why our Bible includes the Jewish Scripture - the Old Testament. Isn't Christianity predominantly about a man named Jesus who came along hundreds of years after the Old Testament was written? I must confess that I have pondered this thought in my personal private life. However, as I seek to grow as a Christian, I see more and more that the Old Testament contains a lot of relevant information about the heart and character of God. For example, Exodus 14:14 says, *The LORD will fight for you; you need only to be still* (NIV).

Imagine the emotional impact we could have on our children if they knew we would fight for them to be treated fairly, and all they had to do was be still. I am reminded of one incident when one of my black boys dated a white girl. Her father discovered the truth and requested a meeting with me and the boy. In that meeting, the Dad said he would never allow his daughter to date a "black boy." I came unglued and tore into that man like a hungry pack of dogs on a pile of fresh meat. I told him I would be embarrassed if my son ever dated a girl as trashy as his white daughter. The boy remained silent, but I could see in his eyes that something changed inside his heart. He knew that I was going to defend his cause. We know God will defend our cause. This gives us all the more reason to defend our children against any form of injustice.

On another occasion we had a neighbor accuse our boys of breaking glass bottles on the road in front of his house. He claimed that he ran over the glass ruining all four tires on his truck. When I asked if he had actually seen my boys breaking the bottles, he said he had not, but he was sure they had done it. He may or may not have been correct about the accusation. It was possible someone driving by had thrown the bottles out of a car. I was not about to let him accuse my boys of doing something he could not prove. The man let me buy him a brand new set of tires. I was out $400.00 but my conscience was clear and I was certain I had not made a false accusation. If the boys were guilty of the deed, I had at least been fair with my neighbor. If they were not guilty of the deed I had kept myself from contributing to the development of a victim mentality. The man should have been 100% sure before making the accusation, but I figured God could deal with him more effectively than I.

Later, in Exodus 23:7, God gives a very clear rule for the Israelites to follow, *"Keep far from a false charge"* (KJV). It is interesting that it says to "keep far." I interpret that to mean I should not even give it a chance. If I am going to accuse a child or a teen of some wrongdoing there had better be no chance I could be wrong.

Finally, Psalm 103:6 says, *"The Lord works righteousness and Justice for all who are oppressed"* (NIV). While I believe the writer of the Psalm is giving us a clue regarding the character of God, I also believe he wants us to strive to have the character of God in our own lives. We are called to work for righteousness and justice, especially for those not able to do so for themselves.

Be very, very careful when accusing a child/teen of something you believe he/she has done. Always give them the benefit of the doubt.

TEN PRACTICAL THINGS TO KNOW ABOUT FAIRNESS AND JUSTICE.

1. It doesn't matter if your false accusation was intentional or not-it will almost always do emotional damage to your child and your relationship with them.
2. Think before you react. There is always the possibility that you have missed something.
3. It is better to err on the side of mercy than to make a false accusation. However, if you do make a false accusation, always admit your mistake and ask for the child's forgiveness.
4. Children get *defensive* when guilty and rightly accused. They get *angry* when innocently and falsely accused.

5. Let your child know when the circumstantial evidence is stacking up against them. They need to know why you have a suspicion of their wrongdoing.

6. It is ok to tell them, "It really looks like you are guilty but I believe you," even when you are not totally convinced that you do believe them. This could send the message you are easily fooled, but more likely it will send the message that you are always interested in justice.

7. When in doubt, wait a day or two. It is amazing how much can be revealed in a short period of time. It is even possible the child will decide to confess.

8. Play dumb. You may feel certain that your child has done some wrong, but if you are not absolutely certain just play dumb. This allows children to let their guard down and truths/proofs more easily slip out.

9. Always let the child tell his or her side of the story as soon as possible after an incident. He needs to feel that he has a voice.

10. Always defend your child from others who make accusations without proof. Children need to know they have an advocate. Be careful, however, not to be an enabler or communicate a willingness to bail them out of every situation they get themselves into.

CHAPTER **15**

- *FAMILY* -

I was a twenty-year-old college student, serving as a church youth minister at a church on the wrong side of town. Most of the kids were poor and few of their parents attended church. While my youth minister friends on the other side of town were planning the latest great event, I was meeting with probation officers and trying to understand the legal ramifications of reporting child abuse. I will never forget the visit I had to the home of Terry, a thirteen-year-old. After stepping over piles of beer cans left lying in the front yard and finally reaching the front porch, I had to carefully choose which porch boards to step on. I wondered at every step if I would fall through and land under the house. The house smelled worse than my high school locker room and Terry's mother had the hospitality skills of a porcupine. Finally, I made it past piles of dirty clothes to Terry's room where he and his two siblings slept on sofas. The purpose of my visit was nothing more than to let Terry know I cared about him. He was excited that I had visited and we chatted for half an hour. I have little memory of our conversation, but one image sticks in my mind. During our entire visit, Terry walked around the room, thumping roaches off the walls. Roaches were flying all over the place, and if he landed a really solid thump it would kill the roach. Terry would smile with pleasure at each

127

killing. It was as if roach killing had become a family sport.

Through the years I have seen some rather interesting if not disturbing things as I have visited the homes of children. In one kid's trailer house the floor had fallen through in the bathroom. If you hoped to use the toilet you had to balance yourself on the floor joist. On more than one occasion I have seen hose pipes and extension cords running from a neighbor's house through the kitchen window. Nothing like having electricity and running water! You may have heard stories of people *jumping* power from the grid to their house via the use of a car jumper cable. It's true - I have seen it. We once took two boys to our ranch after they were discovered taking a bath in the school restroom. The family was living in a horse barn along with the animals.

Poverty and lack of sanitation are not the only troubling things I have seen. I have observed some of the most morally depraved situations you can imagine. I used to make a habit of taking boys to visit their birth families on Friday nights. Sometimes we arrived unannounced. One night we walked into an adult party. Loud vulgar music blasted from the powerful stereo system and a young female on the front porch thrust her hips at me as if to offer a service that I definitely did not want! Once inside the house, I saw a dozen adults sitting around the smoke-filled room. The ones who were sober enough to see me thought I was a narcotics agent and began hiding their liquor bottles. They tried to block my view of an adjoining bedroom but I saw enough to know they were not having a Bible study. The whole house was shaking.

I have also been in homes where it broke my heart to see how the children were treated. Angry stepmothers discharging frustrations on their stepchildren while pampering their birth children. Stepfathers attempting to toughen up their stepsons by being harsh to them. I even worked with one family who had decided to go back in time. They lived in the woods in a cabin with no running water or power. All their food came from the land. Sounds like a great idea until you discover that the parents spent their days drinking moonshine while the children plowed gardens and hunted deer.

I was nineteen when God began to reveal his calling on my life.

I was to work with disadvantaged children and youth. Like most young people with this calling, I was enthusiastic and certain I could save the world. I think the same can be said for most social workers, counselors, foster parents, adoptive parents, and children's home staff. We are all passionate about our work and most of us would lay down our own lives for the children we serve. We find ourselves appalled by the way some adults treat children. We get angry and sometimes want to take certain adults outside and beat them half to death. I cannot tell you how many times I wanted to bash a man's face in because of something he had done to an innocent child. I am not a cursing man but the "b" word has come to my lips many times when I have seen the hell some women put their children through. The *lock 'em up and throw away the key* mentality is no stranger to my mind.

It was with this mentality that I opened Eagle Rock in 1994. I despised the families of the children I sought to help. I felt it was my job to rescue these poor children from their horrible environments and the people who were responsible.

If there is one thing that has changed about me, it is my position on this matter. Where I once thought it was my calling to rescue children from their families, I now see this position as one of arrogance and pride. I am not God and dismantling families should not be on my agenda! God's laws of nature have instituted the family as one of the foundations for happy and productive living. Our well-intentioned efforts to rescue children from families often lead to more trauma and trouble in their young lives.

John was the first boy to live at Eagle Rock. He was thirteen years old. John's mother had left him when he was a child so his dad raised him and his sister. John was very close to his dad, but just prior to John coming to our ranch his dad had been placed in prison. The little boy was crushed. He was originally placed into a state-approved foster home, but his behavior was out of control and I was asked to take him. John was not a terribly misbehaved child. He was just angry and frustrated with his life situation. One day he was playing his radio too loudly so I asked him to turn the volume down. He did but later turned it back up. I was only twelve years his senior so I needed to establish my authority. While he was at school the next day I went into his room, took his radio, and locked it in a closet. When he got home he asked about it. I explained that he had lost the privilege of having the radio because he could not keep the volume turned down. I could see this infuriated him and he began to cry. He soon began to act out inappropriately in ways that we had not previously seen. Finally, one day, in the midst of a crying and screaming fit, he proclaimed that I was not allowed to take his radio because his dad had given it to him. I had not known this but it did not matter. At the time all I could think about was the fact that his dad was a scoundrel. I even considered throwing the radio away. I don't remember exactly what happened to the radio but I do know that several years later when John was old enough to leave our ranch he did. We had a cordial departure and he promised he would keep in touch. However, Diana and I never heard from John again and that broken relationship became one of a few tragedies in our life. We loved John and he still holds a special place in our hearts, but he apparently wants nothing to do with us. I have to deal with the guilt of knowing I mishandled that situation. I had no right to judge his father and definitely had no wisdom in separating him from something that he cherished because it reminded him of his dad. We were told that his dad eventually got out of prison and the two reunited. I will never forget taking John's radio that day. If I had it to do over again I would do things very differently. At the time, my attitude about families was not what it should have been.

Not long after John left us, we took in another boy named Preston. Preston's dad was an alcoholic and his mom had some issues of her own. Thankfully my understanding of things had changed quite a bit by this time. I realized that the vast majority of the children in foster care need their parents more than they need me. When Preston arrived and I met his mother I determined that we were going to be partners in raising her son who was totally out of control at age eleven. Preston lived with us for many years and finally was able to return to live with his mother. During those years a bond developed between my family and Preston's family. We all literally became like family. Twenty-five years have passed since

Preston lived with us, but we still communicate regularly, encourage one another, and support one another in any way we can. We are still family.

I am convinced that one of the greatest mistakes social services ministries make today is assuming we are God's answer to the world's problems. We step in and disrupt families, condemn parents, take away children, and act like we are heroes when we should be seeking to keep families together. We may need to swallow our pride to do so.

In all of my years working with children, I have discovered children almost always seek out their biological parents at some point in life. It occurs in adoptions all the time. Adopted children, with rare exceptions, are curious about their birth families. Even adopted children/adults who were raised in very supportive adoptive families and consider their adopted parents to be their *only* parents, are still curious about their birth families. For some, this curiosity is based on medical needs, but most are trying to fill an emotional void. The void can range from simple curiosity to a strong longing for attachment.

Kevin was four years old when he was taken away from his mother. She had tried to kill him. For many years he was curious about who she was and what she was like. I knew she had mental health issues but when he turned eighteen he wanted to find her, so I encouraged him to do so. He made the long trip across the country, hoping they might reconcile and be able to live together in the future. A few weeks later he called and I asked how the visit had been. He replied that he was glad he made the trip and the visit answered a lot of questions but he said, "She's absolutely crazy!" For him, and for a lot of children in foster care, group care, and adoption, there is a natural curiosity that has to be answered even when answers are not at all what was desired.

For most of the boys I parented, curiosity was a major roadblock to them moving forward in life. They always held hope that their parents would be the loving and accepting parents they had always dreamed of. I found that children often have a short memory when it comes to abuse. They easily forget how bad things were and they long to be back with their families. I always felt it was best to let the boys at our ranch go back to their parents as soon as it was physically safe to do so. I knew it might not be a good situation, but I also knew there was something the boys had to get out of their system before we could move forward and they would understand my desire was to help them and not destroy their families.

Ryan was sixteen years old and was close to his dad. His dad was a drug addict but Ryan loved him. The state social worker and the court system were emphatic that Ryan not be allowed to live with his father. They did not even want him to have unsupervised visits with him. Ryan was doing his best to make the most of a life separated from his dad, but it was very frustrating. I put my reputation on the line and spoke up against the judge, the social workers, and a host of lawyers on his behalf. I noted that Ryan was not being physically or sexually abused and that he was capable of defending himself if that were to occur. The social worker kept pointing out the failed drug screens and even had his dad take one in my presence just to prove to me that he was not clean. I stood strong and eventually, with the help of some legal wrangling, was able to convince them to let Ryan go home to his dad. I don't think it should be our role to keep families apart unless the children are in imminent danger. It is not our role to pass moral judgments based upon our own set of moral values or to use those values to separate children from their parents. We are not God.

We should do all we can to facilitate the reunification of families – even if we do not like the family members. We had one boy who desperately wanted to live with his father. I did not think his father really wanted him, but he said he had had a religious experience that made him a different man. I still didn't believe him and neither did the state social workers. However, we were willing to give him the benefit of the doubt. When the state said Tim could not have weekend visits because his dad did not have an appropriate house (he was homeless), I offered my camper for him to live in and parked it close to the house where Tim lived on our ranch. His dad spent weekends in the camper which was about 300 yards from the house. He eventually said he wanted to be closer to Tim so we allowed him to pitch a tent in the yard outside Tim's bedroom window. The two became camping buddies and Tim's dad proved he was willing to do whatever was necessary to have a relationship with his son. Tim was later able to live with his Dad. Unfortunately, soon afterward Tim was involved in a crime which resulted in him going to jail for an extended period. The brief time he lived with his Dad would be the only time in his life that he ever got to do so. Tim either concluded that his father was all he dreamed he would be or that his father was never going to be the dad he dreamed of. Either way, Tim may have never been able to settle the issue had he not spent those months with his dad.

Sometimes we have to sacrifice our personal feelings and comforts for the benefit of the child. Alfred and Trevon were two brothers who lived at our ranch. We had been warned about their mother. She was a troublemaker and one of those who liked to play the role of victim. She had caused many problems for her social worker, so no one trusted her. In addition, she led her children to believe all sorts of false things about counselors, lawyers, social workers, and anyone who tried to intervene. I knew she was a problem, but I also knew two more important things. First of all, I knew that her boys loved their mother. That is both normal and understandable. The boys wanted deeply for her to be the mother they dreamed she would be. They both wanted to believe everything she told them and therefore considered their having been taken away from her to be a result of bad social workers and police officers who lied about the family situation. Secondly, I knew that the only way they were going to come to grips with reality was to see it firsthand. There was no way they were going to see the truth about their mother if they were not allowed to spend some time with her. With this in mind, I sought to build a relationship with their mother. I knew how she was and I knew what she was capable of doing. I also knew it was best for the boys to get to be with her. After a great deal of logistical and legal maneuvering, I was able to make arrangements to meet her at a bus station about an hour from my house. I took the boys and together we spent Christmas Eve at the bus station. I treated her with respect and the four of us shared presents, stories, and some laughs. A few years later the boys were old enough to be released from state custody and, of course, they immediately found their mother and went to live with her. Only a few months passed before the younger boy reached out to me and asked for help. It took that long for him to realize the reality of the situation and he moved back home to the ranch. In his words, "I was confused about a lot of things." Our children quite often are confused when we step in between them and their families. Sometimes the only way to help them sort through the confusion is to make every effort to facilitate the relationship between them and their families.

The book of Genesis tells an interesting story that exemplifies the power of family and the importance of forgiving and letting go of past hurts. Joseph's brothers were jealous of him so they conspired to kill him. One of the brothers intervened and saved him from death but they did sell him into slavery. As a result of a series of divinely appointed events, Joseph went from being a slave, to being a prisoner, to being placed in a position of authority in the Pharaoh's administration. Joseph warned the Pharaoh of an impending famine, and as a result, the Egyptians were able to store warehouses full of grain. When the famine hit people came from everywhere to buy food from the Egyptians. One such group who traveled from a faraway land to buy food happened to be Joseph's family. The brothers who sold him into slavery were now at Joseph's mercy. He literally held their lives in his hands. When they approached him to buy food he recognized them but they did not recognize him. They had sold him to a group of Ismaelites and had no idea he had become a leader in Egypt. Joseph did not tell them who he was but asked questions about their family. He specifically wanted to know about his father and little brother. They had not made the trip. Eventually, Joseph tricked his brothers into bringing his little brother Benjamin to Egypt. When Joseph saw Benjamin he began to cry uncontrollably and decided to reveal his identity. His brothers were shocked. In the end, Joseph saved the lives of his brothers who had sold him into slavery, and reunited with his father and little brother. He then took care of them for the rest of his life.

Joseph reminds me of a lot of the children I have worked with throughout my career. Their families treat them terribly, but in the end, the children are willing to forgive and forget. The thing they desire more than anything is to have their family together. We should all remember the story of Joseph and consider the power of the bond between members of a birth family. Those of us who have worked with abused children can tell you that, like Joseph, our children will eventually seek to reunite with family if given any chance at all – regardless of how terribly they have been treated in the past.

I dedicated a large portion of my life to building a boys ranch – a place where I could rescue kids from bad situations and put them in an environment where they could succeed. After years of blood, sweat, and tears I have come to dislike the whole concept. Eagle Rock continues and is under good leadership. They continue to help lots of kids, but I now realize that the best boys ranch in the world is not as good as a real family – even when the real family has lots of shortcomings. In a perfect world, we would close all the ranches and do away with foster care altogether. However, that is not realistic and places like Eagle Rock will always be necessary. Foster care will always be necessary. However, I am pleased with current trends toward keeping children in families and avoiding out-of-home placements. We should continue a focused effort toward realistic movement in that direction. Fortunately, in the last 100 years, we have moved away from large orphanage settings which basically functioned as warehouses for children. Perhaps in the next 100 years, we will become creative enough to protect children and rebuild broken families instead of promoting separation based on our moral judgments about them.

TEN PRACTICAL THINGS ABOUT FAMILIES AND THE CHILDREN WE SEEK TO HELP.

1. Don't take it personally when children readily forgive the parents who abused them but blame you for everything that goes wrong in their lives. Children will usually forgive their birth parents and grandparents. They are less likely to forgive aunts, uncles, and stepparents. Forgiving you will be even less likely.

2. Always remember that you are here to meet the child's needs – not your own.

3. Be sensitive to the attachments kids have to personal belongings that may have a connection to their birth families.

4. Attempt to partner with birth parents when possible. Don't let your children play birth parents against foster or adoptive parents.

5. Talking negatively about birth parents in front of their children should be done with extreme caution. It is more often detrimental than helpful.

6. Sometimes birth parents' actions need to be exposed. Do this by asking questions, not by making accusations, that will help children see the truth for themselves.

7. Don't take it personally when adopted children take interest in finding birth parents. Assist them in doing so. This is filling a need they have and has nothing to do with their feelings toward you.

8. Show kindness to birth parents for the sake of the child. It will give them a sense of security. Your love, compassion, and mercy will help build healthy relationships and will help in holding birth parents accountable.

9. When birth parents need to be corrected because they continue to mistreat the child, it is sometimes ok to confront them in front of the child. That can give the child a sense that he has an advocate who will stand up for him.

10. Always understand that a child will have a natural tendency to defend their birth parents. It may take years of maturity development for them to be able to face reality.

- *MANAGING BEHAVIOR WITHOUT* - *LOSING YOUR MIND*

Choosing Your Battles
Lose the Battle - Win the War
Separating Deed from Doer
Discipline Versus Punishment
Points and Levels

- *CHOOSING YOUR BATTLES* -

This may be the most important topic in the entire book. If you don't have a good grasp of it, your life as a VP will be very stressful for both you and your child. As I write I'm thinking of several readers.

I'm thinking of the couple who has decided to be foster parents. You are compassionate people with a genuine desire to help children. You are firm in your convictions about how a home should be run. You know the value of structure and order, rules and regulations. You have an idealistic outlook about what fostering will be like.

I'm thinking of the Houseparent. You've given your heart to the calling. You believe what you are doing is worthwhile. You are hard-working people and are willing to make personal sacrifices. Most of you could have gotten a job anywhere you wanted but you've chosen to work with kids. You want more than anything to do a good job and please your bosses and the wonderful organization that has hired you. You are humble and want to follow all the rules precisely.

I'm thinking of the adoptive parent. You've gone out of your way to give a child a home and a family. You've probably made a tremendous sacrifice of time and money. You don't expect any more from your adopted child than you would expect from your birth child.

Whether you are an adoptive parent, a foster parent, a house-parent, or you've literally taken in your brother's child, you have a right to expect some law and order around your house. You have every right to expect your children to obey the rules regardless of their background or circumstances. I'm with you 100%. However, take my word for it: raising your brother's child is not necessarily the same as raising the one you brought into the world. There are special considerations and personal expectations you may need to evaluate. Please remember that we do not live in a perfect world. Furthermore, raising someone else's child (even though you claim them as your own) is not exactly the order God established. It will never be the perfect situation, so please get over the idea that your kids are going to be perfect. You may need to learn to bend a little so that you do not break.

My wife would be the first to tell you that house parenting was not her favorite thing to do. In fact, she very much disliked it. Diana is a very structured person. She likes to have a schedule and a plan. When we go on vacation she prints an itinerary with an hour-by-hour schedule. When we go camping she prints a menu for every day of the trip. We post it on the refrigerator door in the camper. She grew up in a Hispanic home where parents didn't have to worry about the department of social services intervening – if you know what I mean. Although she was never abused, she was never assured that it was not within the realm of possibility. About three years into our house parenting venture, Diana was so stressed that her doctor told her she had to take a break. She was killing herself. You can only imagine what it was like to have eight rowdy boys living in a house with a mom who posted menus during vacations. It didn't take her long to realize she could not fight every battle that came her way. It is OK to bend a little, as long as you don't break. Aside from driving yourself insane, you will probably drive your children crazy as well. Learn how to choose your battles.

In another instance, there was a boy who absolutely destroyed his bedroom in our house. He tore the door off the hinges, broke the window out, and punched several holes in the wall. It is a long story, but when I finally subdued him and things were under control I realized he was having an emotional breakdown due to the memories of abuse at the hands of his birth father. I chose not to issue any consequences for his misbehavior. This is not to say consequences were not deserved. He definitely deserved them. However, it was not the right time. We did have a brief conversation about learning to deal with pain more appropriately, and I hinted that destruction of property would not be tolerated in the future, but for the time being, I just hugged him and assured him we would work through things together. I choose my battles carefully knowing some battles can wait and some can be forgotten altogether.

One lesson I have learned after many years of working with children is that some adults are simply not wired to be flexible. This seems to be more prevalent with men who tend to hyperfocus on certain issues. I think it has something to do with making a point and establishing manhood. However, these men usually do not last very long in the field of working with children.

The most important thing you can do as a VP is build genuine relationships with your children. This stands true no matter the situation. Foster children, adopted children, and children in group homes all crave relationships with their parents and caregivers. Unfortunately, some of these children have to deal with multiple behavioral issues. They can have so many inappropriate behaviors it is difficult to know where to start. Even a relationship-oriented parent can spend an exorbitant amount of time dealing with behavior problems so there's very little time or energy left for relationship building. You become a methodical, robotic caretaker instead of a real person much like the automatic fish feeder my friend put at the side of his pond which at a certain time each day throws out some food. You do not want to be that kind of parent. If your parenting style is so rigid that it fails to see the intricate emotional makeup of the child, you will never be much more than a fish feeder. It is important to know some battles need to be fought now, some need to be fought later, and a few even need to be forgotten.

Some rules are meant to be broken. We established a rule at Eagle Rock that the boys were not allowed to wear earrings. I had good reason for my old-fashioned rule. However, this was a rule we sometimes overlooked for a while – especially when a boy first arrived at the ranch. On numerous occasions I found myself sitting around a conference table with a twelve-year-old who thought it was cool to wear an earring. He'd seen all the big boys and many of his professional sports role models with earrings so he thought it must be cool. We would get to the part of the intake process where we went over the handbook and the rules. We would be reading through the rules and there it would be – the earring rule. Often the boy's face would grimace in pain. Many times a boy would simply reach up, remove his earrings, and hand them to me. Other times, they would ask if they could take them out later. Occasionally one would question the rule. Even so, I don't ever recall making a boy remove earrings. We passed over it as gently as we could. Sometimes we would tell them they could wear them for a few days before being required to remove them. Believe it or not, it was never a huge issue. Usually, they waited until they got to school and then put them back on. We knew but didn't make a big deal of it. If, after a few weeks, they blatantly continued to wear the earring in spite of our reminder that it was against the rules, we would sit down with them and explain our reasons for having the rule. It was never really a problem. "Why," you may ask, "would you have a rule that you don't enforce?" The answer is simple. We did enforce it. We just chose the right time. I actually felt sorry for the kids when they came in for their intake session. Most of these boys had just gone through a traumatic experience. They had been removed from their home. They had been dragged before judges. They had endured psychological evaluations. They missed their parents and their friends. They were about to go into a strange place and have to learn to get along with all new people. They were having to learn a whole new set of rules. For me, that would be traumatic. The last thing they needed was for some old, white guy to tell them to take out their earrings. For the moment, the earring issue was just not important. It could wait for another day and time when our relationship was stronger. (As it turned out, the boys who had been at the ranch for a while often warned the new boys that it really was not worth the trouble. If they continued to break the rule, they would eventually have to endure Mr. Scott's long and boring story about earrings. Everybody hated that story and nobody wanted to waste two hours hearing it). Many times, after I had gotten to know the boy for a few weeks and he had adjusted, I would casually say, "Hey you forgot your earring." I never had a case where a boy refused to remove his earring without delay. You see, I had not chosen to ignore that battle; I just chose to save it for another day.

We also had a rule prohibiting nicotine use. We had boys at our ranch who were addicted to nicotine by the time they were twelve. It must be a horrible feeling. They would sneak into the woods and take a draw or two every time they got a chance. Yes, we did have rules against it and we had consequences, but many times I just acted like I did not know what they were doing. After all, these kids were dealing with some major life issues much more serious than nicotine addiction. They were dealing with memories of horrible abuse and neglect. They were dealing with rejection. They were wondering why their dads had never taken them fishing or attended one of their ball games. They were deeply hurting inside and the only self-medication they had was a nicotine high. Sometimes I acted like I did not know and sometimes we dealt with it. The choice depended on the particular kid and his particular situation. As I used to tell my staff, "Act like you don't know. There are bigger fish to fry. Choose your battles."

Some rules were non-negotiable. We had strict rules about chores being done and bedrooms being kept clean and orderly. If you ignored that rule for one boy you had to ignore it for all the others. Failure to enforce it resulted in arguments, hurt feelings, and all sorts of secondary issues related to the clean room chore. However, sometimes I was aware that a kid was having a difficult time with some life issues. I might be the only other person in the house who knew, so nobody was going to be sympathetic if I let the rules slide. For example, I might go into this particular kid's room and find it a mess. The right thing to do would be to issue consequences, right? No, I don't believe so! The right thing to do in this case would be to clean his room for him and let everyone else think he had done it himself. A messy room is a minor thing when you have a kid dealing with deep emotional pain. Choose your battles. If you want to be a great houseparent you could even leave a little note of encouragement under his pillow saying, "Hey, I know you're having a rough time so I cleaned your room for you today."

The issue of choosing battles is complicated if you are in a congregate care or group home setting because all of the other kids are watching every move you make. You have to maintain consistency and set standards if you want to avoid chaos. It can be a tricky issue and to further complicate matters there are usually several people making parenting decisions. You might have a married couple living in the home with the kids, then have a program manager overseeing a couple of homes, a director, a social worker, and a counselor all involved in the decision-making process. It can get very messy and cause a lot of friction between the adults if they are not all following the same set of rules. In some cases, the houseparents who live with the kids daily will be the ones who choose to fight every battle that comes along. They feel it is necessary to maintain order. As a result, the program manager, social worker, counselor, or director may need to intervene and say, "Hey, give the kid a break." This creates friction. In other situations, it might be just the opposite. Sometimes the most seasoned houseparents are skilled in choosing battles and those less closely involved look on critically and determine the houseparents are being too lenient.

I wish I had a solution to this problem, but the fact of the matter is that I have never seen a group home, children's home, or ranch where all the adults agreed all the time. However, I do think I can offer some good advice regarding the resolution of this issue. First, I would say communication is vital. That might mean that the live-in houseparent calls the director and says, "Hey Boss, Johnny is out in the woods smoking a cigarette. He doesn't know I know. We'll deal with it later. We have a lot of turmoil in the house right now. Just letting you know." A wise director will say, "Thanks for letting me know. Let me know when you're ready to deal with the cigarette issue." Sometimes communication means the counselor calls the live-in houseparent and says, "Hey wonderful houseparent whose job I could not do if my life depended on it. I just wanted you to know that Susie had a family visit scheduled for today but nobody showed up. She's pretty upset, so it might be a good time to give her a break. If she refuses to go to church, don't push the issue." Communication can solve a lot of issues. The other thing you should do in a congregate care setting is to rely heavily on the more experienced adult. I'm not talking about the adult with the Ph.D., but rather the one who has fifteen years of experience as a houseparent. It was always my observation that the person with the most experience in direct care is the person who makes the wisest decisions when it comes to choosing battles.

For married couples raising children together the matter of choosing battles can be a point of contention as well. One spouse may tend to be more lenient while the other tends to be more rigid. It can become a great point of contention if not handled carefully. I would offer two pieces of advice. The first may sound a little risky, but I'll offer it anyway. Sometimes the spouse who is less emotional / more rational will better understand the need to ignore or delay a battle while the more rigid spouse will want to enforce all the rules entirely. In these cases, it might be best for the less emotional spouse to deal with the issue discreetly. For example, if you see your spouse is going to make an issue of the child's room not being clean, just clean it yourself instead of trying to argue the point with your spouse. A second word of advice concerning conflicts would be to go the extra mile in communicating with your spouse. Be like a good lawyer and study your case deeply. Be able to explain clearly why you think it's a good idea to avoid a battle rather than fight it. Be open to your spouse's differing opinion and jointly agree that no matter which path you take you both want the same end result. Sometimes, when you discover the ultimate goal together you're more likely to find a solution.

Save yourself some headaches. Get off your high horse. Quit thinking everything has to be perfect. Choose your battles wisely. Don't think you can or are required to fix everything at once. You will one day thank yourself.

I'm thinking about the Apostle Paul in the Bible. Some historians have said Paul had more influence on Western culture than any man in history. Early on, Paul was a member of the Pharisees, a Jewish group well known for their inflexibility and strict adherence to Jewish law. They were highly respected for their understanding of and adherence to oral and written traditions. However, if you know the story of Paul, you know his life was changed by a man named Jesus. Jesus was much more into relationships. In fact, he accused the Pharisees of not having their hearts right. He didn't tell them the law was wrong, but he did tell them following law and traditions without tending to matters of the heart was useless.

It is interesting that in I Corinthians 8, Paul addresses an issue that had arisen in the local church and apparently was causing disagreements. It was a custom at that time to offer animal sacrifices to the gods. Yes, slaughtering animals for this purpose was thought to bring the people to favor in the eyes of their gods. Ironically, they then took the meat from the sacrificed animals and sold it in the markets. Some of the new Christians thought it was wrong for them to eat such meat because it had been offered to false gods. They thought this was an insult to their new god – Jesus. Other new believers, on the other hand, didn't see any problem with the idea of eating meat offered to idols. Their thought was that if the idols were fake in the first place, no harm was done. (I would have probably sided with the latter because I like to eat meat – but that is beside the point). Paul was in the position of trying to settle the issue. His solution was interesting. He said, "If it's wrong for you, then it's wrong for you. If it's right for you, then it's right for you. Just don't be a stumbling block for someone else." At least that's my version of what he said. You can read it from the Bible if you want the correct wording. Nevertheless, it is very interesting that Paul, a former Pharisee and therefore stickler for the rules, is basically declaring that relationships are much more important than rules. It is truly amazing that Jesus transformed Paul's thinking so dramatically in such a short period of time.

I would submit to you, the VP, that rules and regulations are good but keep them in perspective. Your relationships with your children are much more important. Some battles can be dealt with leniency. Some battles can be dealt with later. Some battles may just need to be ignored.

TEN PRACTICAL THINGS ABOUT CHOOSING BATTLES.

1. Get over the idea that ignoring a thing or two is going to ruin your children.
2. Take some time to think through and decide what is really important in the life of each of your children. With that information decide which battles are worth fighting. It may be different for each child.
3. Remember it is better to fight and win a few battles than to fight all of them and only win a few.
4. Understand we live in an imperfect world and the things your children have been through may very well affect them for the rest of their life. Accept the fact that you are not going to be a miracle worker.
5. For a child with multiple issues, it might be wise to focus on one or two at a time. You can overload the child with challenges if you try to tackle too much at one time.
6. The reality is - you need your own sanity as well. Fighting every little battle will wear you out and you will be gone.
7. It is ok to include the child in the conversation about which challenges you plan to deal with now and which ones you plan to deal with in the future. This prepares them for future consequences for behavior not currently corrected.
8. It is OK to cheat a little on your child's behalf. For example, do their chore for them on a short-term basis if they are having a particularly difficult time with a life issue. It's better to do that than to force your will at the wrong time.
9. Remember there are some battles that you have to fight imme-

diately. For example, you can't let a kid drive a car recklessly. They might hurt someone. You can't let suicidal gestures pass without notice. Use your common sense.

10. Always remember that raising your brother's child is more complicated than raising one you brought into the world. Learn to accept some exceptionalities. Learn to bend a little to avoid breaking,

CHAPTER 17

- *LOSE THE BATTLE, WIN THE WAR* -

Buttercup was one of my favorite dogs of all time. He was about five inches tall and two feet long - a wiener dog. Buttercup was famous for working his way into people's laps. If one of the boys was upset about something, he seemed to have a way of knowing. He would ease his way into their lap and lay his little head over on their chest as if to say, "Don't worry, I'll be your friend." Had he been a licensed counselor, Buttercup would have made a lot of money because there were many times when Buttercup's TLC was all the therapy a person needed.

However, Buttercup had a bit of a split personality. He was gentle and kind to the boys when they were upset, but he became a vicious guard dog whenever an animal of another species entered his territory. We witnessed him kill cats, snakes, raccoons, possums, rats, and birds on a regular basis. On one occasion he killed about twenty of our chickens. Usually, there was a scuffle of some sort, and sometimes he would get a little beaten up. It also didn't fare well when he tried to have an affair with the neighbor's Rottweiler, but he gave it a good fight!

It was the skunk we all remember most. Late one evening following a counseling session, Buttercup assumed his normal position on the back porch overseeing his large backyard. I happened to be watching when a little black and white skunk cautiously strolled across the yard. Buttercup watched intensely but didn't flinch until he knew he had his prey. The little skunk wandered just far enough into the yard that he could not escape when the fifteen-pound weiner went into attack mode. I believe he thought the black and white skunk was a cat because he used one of his favorite techniques – trap them in the corner of the fence. Just as planned, the little skunk ran exactly where Buttercup had intended and then he went for the kill. It was comical because when he got about ten feet from the skunk he suddenly stopped dead in his tracks. It was as if he thought to himself, "Oops, that ain't no cat." Buttercup had dealt with skunks before and he knew their game, so he stayed just far enough away to avoid being sprayed. There was a long standoff and lots of intimidating barking, but Buttercup finally mustered up the courage to go for the attack. He ran straight for the skunk when, of course, the skunk stood straight up and raised his tail. From a distance I yelled, "Buttercup, don't do it!" but it was too late. He got sprayed with the nastiest smelling skunk perfume you could ever imagine. Nevertheless, Buttercup continued his charge and in no time had the skunk by the neck and was slinging him violently. Finally, the commotion stopped and Buttercup let go of his prey. The little skunk lay dead but that would not be the end of the story.

For the next five weeks, we bathed our little warrior wiener in everything imaginable to try to get rid of the skunk smell. Tomato juice, orange juice, baking soda, dawn dish detergent, peroxide, tea tree oil, toothpaste, and the list continues. I can tell you from experience, that despite what the internet says, nothing gets rid of skunk spray. It just has to wear off.

Buttercup dealt with the consequence, and in time things went back to normal. For the skunk, however, this was the end of the road. He may have won the battle, but he lost the war. Buttercup, on the other hand, lost a battle but won the war.

When it comes to parenting there are two skills related to battles. Skill number one is learning to choose our battles carefully. Skill number two is knowing we sometimes lose the battles but that does not mean we will lose the war.

Matt was probably one of the laziest and most disrespectful kids we had during our tenure at the ranch. He came by his problems honestly. He was just like his father, a career criminal. He was a narcissist, not caring about anybody but himself. He was also a rebel, not willing to do anything anybody told him to do. To make matters worse, he had a state social worker who defended every bad move he made. She was part of the reason he had been in fifteen group homes before he came to us. Her pattern was to blame the poor behavior on the foster parents or the group home and then move him to a *better* place. By the time we got Matt, he was a monster. At the time, I was the director of the ranch and not serving as a houseparent. Matt was extremely disrespectful to the houseparents and disrupted everything. The houseparents' frustration level was leading them toward a nervous breakdown, so I offered to intervene. I never wanted to undermine the houseparent's authority, but in this case, they were begging me to intervene, so I did. I instructed them to avoid all confrontation and not ask anything of Matt. As long as he was not hurting himself or anyone else he was allowed to be as lazy and disrespectful as he wanted to be. We privately asked the other boys to just watch carefully for a couple of weeks. We also cautioned that although Matt was going to get by with a lot of stuff, they should not follow his example and in the end, it would all make sense to them. Once the decision was made and all had been informed, the plan began. Everyone basically ignored Matt. He was allowed to do almost whatever he wanted as long as nobody was hurt. The only person allowed to confront him or give him any direction was me – the ranch director. At first, Matt was suspicious of the arrangement and I think it concerned him a little. His behavior improved for a couple of weeks probably because he was confused that no one was confronting him. This had never happened to him before. However, Matt soon got comfortable and decided it was a pretty good arrangement. He went back to his old ways of cursing at houseparents and refusing to do anything he was asked to do. I knew this was not sustainable, so one morning I loaded all the boys up and took them to a work project. Matt went along because he thought I was going to take everyone to McDonald's. At the work site, he got out of the van and pretended to work, but his laziness soon took over. When I confronted him he gave me a dirty look and walked away. In defiance, he went to the van and just sat there. Interestingly, it was much hotter in the van than it was in the building where the other boys were working, but that is beside the point. I've always been amazed at how dumb stubborn people can be. He would rather prove his point by sitting in a scorching van than do a little work in an air-conditioned building. I just let him sit there while the rest of us finished the work project. We then loaded the van and went to McDonald's as planned. I bought everyone but Matt a combo number three. When he asked where his meal was I explained that the houseparents were waiting for him at the house where they had prepared a nutritionally balanced green salad for his lunch. He fumed for a few minutes as we rode home. He gave me his meanest look and shot me a bird. The other boys just ignored him and continued devouring their burgers. We arrived at the house where everyone jumped out of the van. They were happy and ready to go inside to rest under the air-conditioner. I explained to Matt that he would be eating his salad outside on the non-air-conditioned patio and when he decided he could cooperate with me he would be allowed inside. That's when all "you know what" broke loose! Matt had had enough of me and he let me know it. In so many words he accused me of incest and said my mother had four legs and a tail. He also let me know that I would never get by with telling him what he could or could not do. If Matt had done this forty years ago, I could have taken him out behind the woodshed and won this battle the old-fashioned way. However, he knew my hands were tied and he had won. He just didn't realize that winning a battle does not always mean you've won the war. The next week some illegal drugs mysteriously showed up in his bedroom and I had him arrested and sent to jail.

I would like to tell you that I'm a sweet, forgiving, forgetting, non-vengeful person, but the truth is I have a mean streak. On the day the police came to pick up Matt to take him to jail, I was ready with a camera in hand. He did not know they were coming and was still reveling in the fact that he had gotten by cursing out and flipping off the director. The look on his face was priceless when the officer slapped the cuffs on his wrist. He yelled, "You don't have a right to do this. You haven't read me my rights." The officer calmly said, "Tell the judge, son, tell the judge." I video-recorded the whole thing, and as he walked past me I just smiled. I may have lost some battles with this boy, but I had won the war and both of us knew it.

As a VP you can count on having some battles and you can count on losing some of them. It's ok. Don't worry. You don't have to win all of them. You just need to win the war.

The problem is that most of us don't know the difference between a battle and a war. For Matt, the war was to teach him that poor life choices such as being disrespectful have consequences. Even though he made me angry, deep inside I loved him and my true desire was that he would not become another statistic – either dead or incarcerated. That was my real war. The little confrontations we had along the way were battles and I knew we could lose a few and still convey our message. The look on his face as he was hauled out in cuffs was priceless, not because I'm mean and revengeful, but because he was learning the lesson I wanted him to learn – being lazy and disrespectful has its consequences. I did not have to win all the battles to teach that truth.

Not all battles and wars are as extreme as the one Matt and I had. If your five-year-old refuses to pick up his toys, you can lose that battle. Pick them up yourself and put them in the attic. Your objective is not to make him pick up his toys. Your objective is to teach him to be clean and orderly. When you get them out of the attic a week later, give him another try. If he refuses, then repeat the process until your objective is met. You may have to lose that battle several times by picking up the toys for him, but eventually, you will win the war when he decides it is better to pick up the toys himself.

If your twelve-year-old disrespectfully rolls her eyes at you when you tell her to get off the phone, don't feel like you have to punish her right then and there. She will eventually want you to take her to her friend's house and that will be a good time to bring up the matter of eye-rolling. She'll win the first little battle, but you'll win the war.

When your seventeen-year-old shows up thirty minutes past curfew, you've lost that battle already. When you take the battery out of the car the next morning you'll win the war. Get the picture?

In my office there hangs a display case housing my grandfather's World War II medals. I look at it every day. I'm reminded that on December 7, 1941, the Japanese Naval Air Service bombed a US navy base in Honolulu, Hawaii. This led to the United State's formal entry into World War II. A brutal four years followed but on August 15, 1945, Japanese Emperor Hirohito surrendered. I can remember my grandfather telling me about "Pearl Harbor Day" and about "D-day." He told me about his time in Holland and about the night he almost lost his life. It was a horrible time that left a scar on everyone involved. I can only imagine the fear and defeat the US citizens must have felt on December 7 when word came of their loss in Pearl Harbor. It must have been a horrible feeling. I certainly don't want to put parenting on the same level as war. We are talking *apples and oranges* here. However, for the sake of analogy, I think we can apply this World War to the war we often feel in our homes. Sometimes it can feel like we are quickly losing ground. It can feel like the tail is wagging the dog and we are losing battles left and right. I say to you to be strong and don't give up. Keep pressing on. The U.S. may have lost Pearl Harbor but they didn't lose the war. You may lose a few battles with your child. That's ok as long as you figure out how to win the war.

In II Corinthians 11:24-28 the Apostle Paul writes about some of his adventures:

Five times the Jews have given me their punishment of thirty-nine lashes with a whip. Three different times I was beaten with rods. One time I was almost stoned to death. Three times I was in ships that wrecked, and one of those times I spent a night and a day in the sea. I have gone on many travels and have been in danger from rivers, thieves, my own people, the Jews, and those who are not Jews. I have been in danger in cities, in places where no one lives, and on the sea. And I have been in danger with false Christians. I have done hard and tiring work, and many times I did not sleep. I have been hungry and thirsty, and many times I have been without food. I have been cold and without clothes (NCV).

Does this sound like a guy who had to win every battle? To me, it sounds like a guy who lost a lot of battles. Have you ever wondered what kept Paul going? My guess is Paul understood his objective in life was not to win every battle that came his way. Instead, his objective was to spread the good news about Jesus Christ. In the same way, our job as parents is not to win every battle we have with our kids. Instead, our objective is to somehow help them grow up to be responsible adults. If we keep this objective in mind, we will remember winning is not everything.

Those of us who parent children we did not bring into the world know, all too well, that our strategies have to be a little different. When we have children from birth, we get a lot of opportunities to invest in them. Sometimes with children in foster care, congregate care, or via adoption, we do not have the luxury of having as much time to invest. I like to use the analogy of putting a little change in our pockets. Every experience we have with our child allows us to drop a nickel or dime into our pocket. When we come across a battle, we can reach into that pocket and take out a nickel or dime. When we don't have our children from birth, we don't have as much time to collect spare change and we don't have as many nickels and dimes to draw from. Therefore, we have to choose to lose a few more battles than we normally would. That may seem problematic, but again, it does not mean we've lost the war.

TEN PRACTICAL TIPS WHEN YOU LOSE A BATTLE.

1. Keep calm. It's bad enough to lose the battle, don't lose your cool, too. This empowers your child in the wrong way

2. Take some time to cool down before you analyze your situation. When our kids get the best of us we tend to be emotional. Being emotional causes us to think without turning our brain on. When we lose our cool with a child we lose a whole lot more than just our temper. We lose their respect and our relationship with them weakens.

3. Analyze the situation. Define what your *battles* are and what your *war* is.

4. Don't beat yourself up. With our birth children, it is more realistic to expect compliance. With others, there can be real complications that are not our fault.

5. Determine what is really important.

6. Always be open to the fact that natural and logical consequences are the most powerful teachers.

7. Try not to do any permanent damage to your relationship with the child. A harsh word or harsh physical punishment is probably not going to win the battle, but it could certainly damage your ability to influence for good in the future.

8. Remember you are the parent. Every child is full of foolishness (Proverbs 22:15). Don't stoop to their level.

9. Maintain an air of confidence even if you don't feel you have it. It's ok to lose a battle, but recovering from confidence loss in front of your child is hard to overcome.

10. Always keep as much *change* in your pocket as you possibly can.

CHAPTER 18

- *SEPARATING DEED FROM DOER* -

I once worked with an eleven-year-old boy who had sexually abused his two-year-old sister. He was subsequently placed in a psychiatric hospital and was labeled a *predator*. When he was released from the hospital, the Department of Human Resources refused to allow him to go home and could not find a foster home to take him. I was outraged when I learned the director of another social service agency referred to the boy and his brother as a *bunch of perverts*. That agency refused to offer services to the boy.

Let us be honest. Stories about two-year-old girls being raped are sad and make you angry. Our emotions get stirred to the point that we really do not care about the age of the perpetrator. We would be fine if they locked him up and threw away the key. We are often happy to pin a lifetime label on anyone who does such a despicable thing.

Such was the case with this eleven-year-old, but God moved on my heart to reach out to him and serve as his therapist. For those of you who have never sat face-to-face with a child rapist, you may think it is a difficult thing to do. However, I can tell you by separating the deed from the doer I was able to see the rest of the story of this boy's tragic life. I was able to dig down to the core of who he was as a person. When I removed all the bad scenes from my mind, I could see that deep inside this eleven-year-old had a really good heart. Deep inside he was just like an average boy - he wanted to love and be loved. He had tremendous confusion and guilt about what he had done. He thought his behavior was normal. His home had been rampant with pornography and when he acted upon his sister he was emulating what he had seen in the pornography. He felt genuine guilt when he understood his behavior was abnormal and despicable. When he was labeled a *perpetrator* he began to see himself as such and the self-fulfilling prophecy crept into his life. The downward spiral had begun and, in the eyes of most, he was destined to be a rapist or pedophile in adulthood.

I chose a therapeutic approach centered around helping him re-identify himself. I will explain this approach in the next paragraph but let me first say that counseling with victims and perpetrators of childhood sexual abuse is both serious and difficult. Some kids need much more than I offered so please don't assume this approach works for everyone.

The approach – we dismantled his perception of himself. This meant we separated the deed from the doer. I did not apply any Freudian practices of unearthing pent-up emotions. People say kids need to talk about their abuse and get it out of their system, but the truth is abuse memories are almost always held for a lifetime. Talking about them can help but is not always necessary. He did have an opportunity to tell me exactly what happened but only after we had built a rapport and he trusted me. I exhibited no shock, and I was empathetic and gentle. The counseling was a little more complex than I am prepared to write about, but the bottom line was he came to understand he is not defined by pedophilia and it is NOT true that he will almost surely re-offend (as it is commonly taught). I reminded him of the many good traits he had and together we talked about the harm he had done. I kept a check on him for several years, and he always knew he could come to me if he had inappropriate thoughts or desires. We clearly defined what those were. I assured him that God and I would always love him for who he is and not for what he had done. Today he is a grown man, a good husband, father, employee, and citizen. This would never have happened had he not learned God always separates the deed from the doer – what we call unconditional love.

I once received a call from a family court judge who inquired about placing a fourteen-year-old boy at our ranch. Typically, when the judge personally calls, it means one of two things. Either the judge is desperate to find a place for the child or he/ she has taken a personal interest in the child. In this case, the judge explained to me that the boy had been caught selling marijuana at school on several occasions. He had also broken into a house and stolen some guns. Finally, the boy had stolen an ATV. In my mind, as the judge detailed the boy's rap sheet I developed a picture of what this young man must look like and how he must carry himself. I pictured him to be some sort of gangster-type kid with a thug mentality. The judge insisted that I meet the boy personally, so we set up an interview. I was pleasantly surprised when the boy walked into my office. He was well dressed, well groomed, and well mannered. He was pleasant to talk with and I immediately realized this boy had a high IQ. His appearance and demeanor did not match his rap sheet. I had to separate the deed from the doer in order to get a clear picture of who this boy really was. As it turned out, his marijuana sales were his way of helping support his family. The gun theft was a means to go hunting. The theft of the ATV was necessary for his hunting venture. After this boy finished his detention sentence, he came to live at our ranch and did very well. He is now a grown man with a successful career and is a great husband and father. Sometimes the things we do are not a clear reflection of who we really are deep inside. Children develop survivor skills for a lot of reasons. Sometimes these skills are developed as a means of physical self-preservation. Other times they are a means of emotional self-preservation. Survivor skills are not normally manifested in an appropriate manner. Always remember that the deed is not necessarily representative of the doer, and the truth usually resides somewhere below the surface.

If you read about King David in Acts 13:22 and I Samuel 13:24 you will find that the Bible has some flattering things to say about David. He is commonly referred to as a man after God's own heart and he is the hero of many great stories in the Bible. If you didn't know better, you would think David was a saint. He probably never cursed, drank, chewed tobacco, or went with women who did, right? I don't think so. David was a scoundrel! He threw rocks at people and spied on showering, naked women. Even worse, he carried adultery to a whole new level by killing the girl's husband. Not exactly a candidate for man-of-the-year is he? Nevertheless, God saw through all the clutter to where, deep down inside, David had some exceptionally appealing qualities. God separated the deed from the doer. It is our duty to do the same with our children.

TEN PRACTICAL THINGS TO REMEMBER ABOUT SEPARATING THE DEED FROM THE DOER.

1. Think of a time in your life when you did something inappropriate. Now ask yourself, "Does that define who I am today?" If you got in a fight with your sister at the age of thirteen are you now a *fighter*? If you stole a chocolate chip cookie from your cousin in high school, are you now a *thief*? Not necessarily, and when your children do horrible things it does not mean they will continue the habit. We all make mistakes and often we move on.

2. Look at your children as real human beings- not little destroyers. Know that someday you will have an adult-to-adult relationship with them and the bad deeds will be a thing of the past.

3. If your child does something really stupid don't say, to them, "You stupid kid!" Say instead, "You did something really stupid, kid!" There is a difference.

4. If a child steals something, it is tempting to refer to or think of him as a little thief. If he gets into lots of fights we tend to think of him as violent. While this may be the thought inside your head, it is not wise to say it out loud. Whether we like it or not, our words can become prophetic and sometimes kids become

what they think you expect them to become. It is often better to keep your thoughts to yourself.

5. The reality is that labels such as *thief, liar,* and *troublemaker* are earned labels. Your child has to earn them by stealing, lying, and causing trouble. At some point, you, as a parent, may have to say to them, "I'm sorry everybody calls you a troublemaker but I have no control over that. When you consistently cause trouble you get labeled. However, you have it within your power to change that. It is never too late."

6. Try to put yourself in the shoes of your child. Children who have been mistreated and misguided will naturally have undesirable characteristics. When a child misbehaves, ask yourself, "Would he have acted this way if he had been born into a better circumstance?" The answer is probably "no." The child himself is not flawed – his circumstances were flawed.

7. When a child does something that is inappropriate remember that your objective is to see the child change from the *inside out* instead of from the *outside in.* Labeling a child is an outside-in approach to change.

8. It used to bother me when people referred to the kids from our ranch as *ranch kids.* That title unfairly put them in a box that very often carried negative connotations. The fact that a kid lives on a ranch should not make him any different from others. We don't say a kid is a *single-mom* kid or *two-parent* kid. The deed and the doer are related but not the same. The place of residence should not be a defining characteristic.

9. By separating the deed from the doer, we can preserve in our minds the good qualities of a child. When you see him as a thief it is hard to remember that he can also be generous. When you see him as a troublemaker it is hard to remember that sometimes he is very pleasant to be around.

10. Remember, children do grow up, and one day you both will be adults. Hopefully, the bad deeds will pass and you will have a great adult/adult relationship. While this young person has to be held accountable for his wrongdoings, he does not have to be defined by them.

CHAPTER 19

- DISCIPLINE VERSUS PUNISHMENT -

One of my favorite college professors was Dr. W.T. Edwards. Dr. Edwards was my Greek teacher, but more importantly, he taught us about the practical matters of life and ministry. Dr. Edwards always had a way with words. One time a classmate asked him for advice on handling a situation with some difficult people. Dr. Edwards told the boy to pin a mistletoe to his coat tail. That was a valuable lesson I have used often. During my senior year, I was asked to speak at a weekend youth camp. This would require me to leave class early on Friday afternoon in order to travel to the camp. I explained the situation to Dr. Edwards. He thanked me for letting him know and then he said something I will never forget: *Never let school get in the way of your education.* I contemplated those words for the next five hours as I traveled to the camp. What in the world did he mean by that? After a few hours, I finally realized what he meant. Most of the guys in the Greek class were preparing to go into ministry and he was saying that the lessons we learned in life would always teach us more than the lessons we learned in the classroom. It did not really matter if we could read Greek or Hebrew if we did not know how to apply our knowledge to daily living. An education is not what we get by going to class. It is what we get by living life. School was just a tool to help in our education. Dr. Edwards was not aware at the time, but he was laying the foundation on which I would later develop a philosophy for raising children.

Webster defines *discipline* this way:
1. To instruct or educate; to inform the mind; to prepare by instructing in correct principles and habits; as, to discipline youth for a profession, or for future usefulness.
2. To instruct and govern; to teach rules and practice, and accustomed to order and subordination; as, to discipline troops or an army.

Webster defines *punishment* as:
1. Any pain, suffering, or loss inflicted on a person because of a crime or offense.

There is a big difference between the two concepts, but I am afraid a lot of parents get them confused. I like to think of it this way. Punishment, when not used as discipline, is a useless burden. Notice the key words from Webster's definition of discipline: prepare for usefulness. That is exactly what our efforts as parents should be centered on. Going back to Dr. Edwards' philosophy, education was preparing us for usefulness and school was only a small part of that education. Likewise, punishment is only a small part of discipline when it comes to preparing our children for usefulness.

For this reason, every decision we make in regard to discipline, punishment, behavior management, correction, or whatever word we want to use, should all revolve around preparing our children for future usefulness. Every time we have to administer a consequence we should first ask ourselves if that consequence is going to help prepare those children for a better future.

If we adhere to this definition then everything we do in terms of behavior should be done as *discipline*. In the remainder of this chapter, therefore, I will only use the word discipline to refer to anything concerning behavior, punishment or consequences applied.

If our efforts to discipline our children are all designed to prepare them for future usefulness, then we must be *intentional* each time we discipline. Take the example of tobacco use. We all know smoking cigarettes is a nasty, costly, and useless habit, but is that the reason we discipline our children when we catch them smoking? We discipline them because we do not want them to stink, be poor, or have to have an oxygen tank in order to breathe. These things are clearly not a part of a useful future. Therefore, when we discipline concerning tobacco, we have to ask the question, "How will my chosen method of discipline (possibly punishment) help prevent them from being stinky, poor, and in bad health?" Believe it or not, this question changes your perspective and can help you address the issue in ways that are helpful rather than solely punitive. At Eagle Rock, we used several forms of discipline if a boy was caught smoking cigarettes. To help him counteract the damage to his health, we might have him run wind sprints until we felt all the smoke was burned out of his lungs. To help him understand what the smell does, we might have him hand wash his clothes, reasoning that the other family members don't want their clothes to be washed in the same washer with all the nasty smoke. To help him understand the health risk we might have him read a pamphlet that describes them. (we made sure it had plenty of nasty pictures of people who were dying of tobacco-related diseases). To help him understand the economic impact we would have him donate money to the American Cancer Society to help fund their research in finding a cure for cancer - a cure he would possibly need someday. The whole idea is instead of punishing a boy for smoking we were disciplining him – always thinking of his future usefulness. Every form of punishment was designed to teach him something that would be useful to his future. With this in mind, there was no need to become angry or oppositional. We were just teaching him things he needed to know.

Parents in general have a tendency to use punishment instead of providing discipline. This is done because we get disappointed, frustrated, and even angry with our children. When punishment becomes solely a way for us to deal with our personal issues, we miss the point. Punishment outside of being a piece of the discipline equation is little more than a way for a parent to deal with his/her personal frustrations.

VPs often experience stress because they feel they have to capture every little misbehavior their child commits. That is not necessary. In fact, there are times when it is best to turn your head the other way and ignore misbehavior. Sometimes we can go into discipline overload. Instead of trying to deal with every little issue, we need to take issues one at a time and consider our ultimate goal, that of preparing our children for productive adulthood.

One time we had a couple of boys do something that I thought was rather creative. Someone donated a large can of powdered Kool-Aid mix. These boys discovered they could put small portions of the mix into ziplock bags, take them to school and sell them to fellow students. They had a pretty good business going until they got caught. I had not given them permission and it was against school rules, so something had to be done. The principal called to tell me about their little business and asked me to deal with it. I had to stop and think about the matter. How could I discipline the boys for doing something that was creative, entrepreneurial, and showed a good work ethic? If everything I do is supposed to prepare them for future usefulness then I'm not about to discourage them from developing a skill that might help them become good businessmen. I called the principal back and asked him to deal with the matter at school. The school had a policy against selling food and there was a consequence for breaking school policy. I explained to the boys that while I admired their initiative, they had broken a school rule and that part of their plan was going to cost them. Instead of being punitive, we used the opportunity to teach that although initiative is a good thing, in society we have to go by the rules.

One of the mistakes VPs make is failing to realize the value of logical and natural consequences. Actually, I believe these are God-given tools for effective discipline. Natural consequences are those things that occur naturally to teach us how to get through life. We had a boy who refused to wear shoes. It did not matter how often we reminded him, he was just too lazy to find them and put them on. One day he cut his foot on a piece of glass and had to have stitches. That was a natural consequence and we did not have to say a word. He had learned his lesson. To add to the lesson we had him pay part of the doctor's bill. That was a logical consequence. Logical consequences are similar to natural consequences but they require a little assistance from the parent. The boy learned not only that he should be wearing shoes, but it was not fun to pay the doctor's bills that came logically as a result of his disobedience. As VPs we all need to earn our Master's Degree in the administration of natural and logical consequences. I am not saying we need to let our five-year-olds touch hot stoves or let our teenagers ride bicycles on the interstate, but I am saying that God has put a plan into nature itself, and if we pay close attention and stay out of the way, many of life's valuable lessons will occur with little or no intervention from us. Logical and natural consequences have a wonderful way of preparing our kids for future usefulness if we will let them.

Jesus said some rather interesting things in Matthew 5, known as the Sermon on the Mount. In verse 17, Jesus says, *"Do not think that I came to destroy the Law or the Prophets. I did not come to destroy but to fulfill."* He goes on to say in verse 20, *"For I say to you, that unless your righteousness exceeds the righteousness of the scribes and Pharisees, you will by no means enter the kingdom of heaven."* Later, in verse 22, He says, *"But I say to you that whoever is angry with his brother without a cause shall be in danger of the judgment."* Finally, in verse 28, He says, *"But I say to you that whoever looks at a woman to lust for her has already committed adultery with her in his heart."*

Jesus spoke these words to the Jewish people who had been given the law we find in our Old Testament but had also developed a lot of rules to keep them in compliance with that law. The Pharisees focus a lot of energy on following these rules, but Jesus points out that they are not really accomplishing anything by doing so. Furthermore, he teaches that what comes from the heart is really a lot more important than following all the rules. Jesus is basically saying that the laws are not there to rule the people; they are to be a guide to them. People rule themselves from within – from the heart.

In terms of discipline for our children, our objective should be to raise kids who are controlled by internal controls rather than external controls. In terms of spiritual maturity, the same principle applies. God wants our hearts to be right first. This is an extremely important concept to grasp, one that will revolutionize our thinking about discipline. Every action we take should be toward teaching our kids to do things right because it is the right thing to do rather than as a result of external pressure (or punishment).

Therefore, discipline is really more about *teaching* than it is anything else. Unfortunately, we get so caught up in our frustrations that we forget this important fact. So how do we keep the focus on teaching? I have already suggested that we use logical and natural consequences, but there are also some other important strategies we can employ to make discipline more about teaching and less about forcing obedience to external rules.

TEN THINGS TO REMEMBER ABOUT DISCIPLINE.

1. Don't try to control the child. Control his environment. Children have to learn that poor behavior has an effect on them. When they begin to realize this, they become motivated to change so their environment will become more suitable for them. For example, if your child destroys his clothing, do not replace it. Eventually, he will realize his behavior is creating natural challenges. No kid wants to wear the same shirt to school every day. He will internally learn the value of taking care of his clothes.

2. Don't think that consequences are always required to teach a lesson. Many times a simple talk will do the trick. I recall numerous incidents when all I had to do was have a heart-to-heart talk with a child. There was no need to punish or administer a consequence. The talk alone was enough to accomplish

the goal; prepare him for future usefulness.

3. Let him learn naturally from his mistakes. If he refuses to take a shower every day, let him stink. Eventually, the kids at school will say something and he will suffer their disapproval. All you have to do is notify the school of your tactic.

4. Don't nag. Nagging is not a good teaching method. When we nag we send the message that there will always be a warning shot or a second chance. Instead of nagging, take action.

5. Try to show kids the benefits of good behavior – particularly good social skills. When they see that others respond to them more positively when they carry themselves in the proper way, they will also recognize the personal benefit. The result is some internal motivation. When a boy figures out that those who know how to give a firm handshake and look someone in the eyes get paid more money than those who stare at the ground and mumble to their boss, he will then be internally motivated to look people in the eyes and give firm handshakes.

6. Remember - there is a time and a place for a good chewing out but it should be rare. I became very skilled at this and I could turn it on and off as easily as switching a lightbulb. I could become very animated and intimidating, but I only used this tactic on rare occasions – maybe once per year. I once chewed out a little boy because he complained about his Christmas gift. I reminded him that many children around the world are happy just to have a full meal to eat on Christmas. I believe I made a point that this boy will never forget. I also reserved chewing out for situations in which larger or older children were beginning to be aggressive toward weaker children. Finally, I used it when I saw entitlement attitudes developing.

7. Don't lose your composure. When children sense they have gotten the best of you, it empowers them. They feel like they are in control. Instead, maintain your cool and they will begin to realize instead of hurting you with their misbehavior, they are only hurting themselves.

8. When administering consequences as part of discipline, always try to connect the consequence to the misdeed. Help them

make a connection so they realize the purpose of the consequence.

9. Allow them to suffer the consequences of their mistakes. If a child misbehaves at school it is best to let the school handle the situation without you. When the school asks you to get involved, it undermines their authority. Unfortunately, schools are often reluctant and will likely call on you. That is understandable and correct, but try to give the school as much freedom and authority as you can.

10. Remember that talking with some teenagers is a waste of time. Know when to shut up and let them learn the hard way.

CHAPTER 20

- *POINTS AND LEVELS* -

If you read the book of Proverbs you might easily get the idea that in Solomon's time the only method of correcting children was to spank them. He refers on several occasions to the *rod*. I would like to briefly visit this matter. We won't spend too much time here because foster parents and congregate caregivers are no longer allowed to use corporal punishment. If you are an adoptive parent without a full history of your child's prior background you may not want to use it either. Nevertheless, we can learn a few things from Solomon's teaching.

Solomon obviously wrote before the industrial revolution, so there were a lot more farmers and herdsmen in his time. The general public at that time would have understood that Solomon's reference to a rod was that which a shepherd used to herd his sheep. Modern-day Christians debate over the exact use of the rod. Some say it was used to count sheep. Others say it was used to tap them on the head and steer them in the right direction. Still, others claim it was to beat the sheep to get them to stay within the herd. It has even been said that the rod was used to break the leg of a sheep that tended to stray to keep it close to the shepherd. Do you want to know what I say? I say we really don't know what a shepherd five thousand years ago did with his rod! It doesn't matter anyway.

I happen to own a sheep and I can tell you she is the dumbest animal on the face of the earth. Sheep are so dumb that they sometimes have to be reminded to drink water. My sheep cost me a lot of money when she saw her reflection in the door of my friend's Porsche. She thought it was another sheep and she headbutted him. That is a true story, and guess what? I did not use my rod to tap her on the side of the head to redirect her. She needed a real good whack on the backside – if you know what I mean. Therefore, I lean toward believing that the shepherd's rod was probably used to give the sheep more than a tap on the side of the head. I probably saved my sheep's life. If I had let her continue to head-butt cars, my friends would have drawn weapons and we would have eaten leg of lamb for dinner. I believe the shepherds of ancient times knew that sometimes their sheep needed a good whack on the behind in order to save their lives.

Somehow, I became the last person in our state to use corporal punishment with foster children. In the early 2000s, my licensing agent kindly told me it was being outlawed and I would be the last to use it. I can tell you from experience that a good paddling has its place and can be highly effective. I documented an average of seven paddlings per year for the six or seven years I used corporal punishment. I used a very thin paddle that I found in a Christian bookstore. You can guess what Bible verse was printed on the paddle. Ironically, prior to the removal of corporal punishment at our ranch very few of our boys required psychotropic medication. After paddling was taken away it seemed everybody mysteriously needed Ritalin. In addition to that, we had to develop creative alternative methods of correction which the boys hated. On numerous occasions, a boy would say "Mr. Scott, can you please just paddle me and get this over?" I could not.

For those of you who serve in congregate care settings, you are probably very familiar with some sort of *points and levels* system of behavior management. They usually consist of a set of house rules and behavior expectations that are tightly connected to a point or level system. The points and levels are then connected to a privilege system. For example, if little Johnny makes his bed every day and says "Yes, sir" to adults he might get a chance to advance from level 1 to level 2. His houseparents, along with other staff have a meeting once a week to count how many times he makes his bed. Then they decide whether or not he can move to level two. If he makes level two he gets to play outside for an extra hour every day. This is an oversimplified explanation, but I assume most of you are familiar with a similar system. These points and levels systems are a consistent way to manage behavior. I would like to point out some pros and cons to this sort of system.

PROS OF A POINTS AND LEVELS SYSTEM

1. They help maintain consistency. If you are in a congregate care setting there is a good chance you are working alongside other adults who are all trying to help the children. Spouses, relief parents, counselors, and program staff are all part of the team. You may also be in a place where there are several houses or families working as part of the organization. When you are working with multiple children and multiple adults there is a need for consistency. For this reason, many group care homes develop points and level systems. Additionally, some foster parents have also resorted to these sorts of systems to help them manage behavior. There are thousands of systems out there and they are fairly easy to find or develop. Therefore, they are quite popular.

2. They are easy to teach. We all know that unfortunately there is a shortage of people with the calling to care for other people's children. During all of my years of operating a boys ranch, this was my single most difficult challenge. Unfortunately, there is also a high turnover rate. When you have a points and levels system of behavior management it is much easier to train your staff. It takes years to train people to do parenting the right way and it really only comes through experience. However, with a points and levels system, you can hand them a manual and within a few weeks, they can master the system.

3. It decreases adult disagreement. In an organization where there

are several people involved in helping children, there will be inevitable disagreement. However, if you have an objectively understandable system of behavior management people are less likely to disagree because they all know from the beginning the decision has already been made. As long as others are working on the system, they don't have much room to complain (although they will still disagree from time to time).

4. Points and Levels systems tend to keep extreme parenting styles in check. If there is one thing on which people disagree, it is the subject of how you should raise a child. There is a good reason for this that we will get to later. However, consistent behavior management systems keep people from being too liberal or too conservative. They keep people in the middle.

5. Points and levels systems can decrease the chances of children sensing injustice. In another chapter, we discussed the importance of fairness and justice in the lives of children who have been hurt. Non-subjective behavior management systems can reduce this problem – although it will not make it go away.

6. These systems help children learn that behaviors have consequences. Although points and levels systems are rarely good at connecting specific behaviors to specific consequences, they do teach the general concept of good behavior resulting in positive benefits.

7. The systems can be a good primer for children who will someday work in big corporations where points and levels are often used as incentives for productivity. For example, a certain big-box retail store has a policy calling for job termination after earning a certain number of points. You earn two points each time you are tardy, four points for not finishing your assignment, two points for dress code violations, and so on.

CONS OF A POINTS AND LEVELS SYSTEM

1. Points and levels systems are not relationship based. In fact, they tend to sterilize the relationship between adults and children. Adults become comfortable with managing behavior in-

stead of teaching discipline. Relationship building is hard work. It takes sacrifice and commitment. When a points and levels system is used, the adult tends to resort to the system's power instead of the power of relationship. We all know that the single most important thing we can give a child is a loving relationship with a caring adult.

2. Points and levels systems are a form of behavior management. That is not necessarily the same thing as discipline. When we discipline children, we are teaching them to gain control of themselves. That is our ultimate goal – that they would develop a sense of internal control. Points and levels call for external controls. They are a *management* tool instead of a *discipline* tool.

3. When points and levels systems are used they very often take the place of logical and natural consequences. The absolute best teachers are those that nature and logic have given us. At Eagle Rock, we always preferred children learned via natural and logical consequences as long as they were not in danger. For example, if we told a boy to wear shoes but he refused, the best teacher would be for him to cut his foot. That is a natural consequence that teaches a quicker lesson than the one learned from having his level dropped for disobeying. If a boy stole from a store, the logical consequence would be no longer being allowed to go to stores. Any VP who learns the value and use of natural and logical consequences will find himself much more relaxed and much more effective in teaching his children the things they need to know to be successful.

4. The key issue with discipline is humility. Proverbs teaches that humility is the beginning of wisdom. Our objective should always be to help our children become wise so that they can make good decisions for themselves. We are not always going to be around to keep them out of trouble. If humility is at the core of wisdom, then helping our children humble themselves is one of the most important components of discipline. Points and levels systems do not always incorporate the component of humility development. They focus on behaviors and consequences, but

not the internal change of heart.

5. Points and levels systems lack effectiveness in helping children connect behaviors to consequences. In most of these systems, the child's overall behavior determines his overall level of privilege. Therefore, he is not pushed to zero in on his exact deficiencies. For example, if a child loses his level for making bad grades and talking back to the teacher, he does not really care which one cost him his privileges. Only that they are lost. Fair enough. However, would it not be better if he could make a connection? For example, he might have extra study hall hours as a result of the bad grades and separately write an essay about respecting adults as a consequence of talking back. He can then handle the issues one at a time. This does two things. First, it keeps him from becoming overwhelmed. He can compartmentalize and tackle one issue at a time. Secondly, he can more clearly focus on the corresponding issue behind each behavior

6. Point and level systems are usually not individualized. They are usually *one size fits all*. However, children are individuals with specific sets of circumstances. They have different backgrounds and different lenses from which they see the world based on their own personal experiences. I find it ironic that we often call our treatment plans Individualized Service Plans while at the same time we expect a one size fits all system of behavior management to be effective.

7. These systems very often do not allow enough flexibility to accommodate acute life stressors. For example, if a child has had a visit with his birth family and it does not go well he is likely to be very frustrated and much more likely to act out inappropriately for a short period of time. In a point-and-level system, that child is probably going to suffer a long-term consequence for short-term behavior. Systems should be in place to look the other way occasionally, but it has been my experience that houseparents are hesitant to do so for fear of compromising the effectiveness of their behavior management system. In other words, the points and levels systems are, by nature, not personalized.

8. Perhaps the biggest problem I see with point and level systems is their inability to deal with the issue of immediate reinforcement. Most of the systems are set up so that levels are gained and dropped once per week, maybe even once per month. Behavioral research is clear that the best way to correct or reinforce a behavior is via immediate reinforcement. As a crude example, laboratory rats who are rewarded with food immediately after figuring out a maze are more likely to remember the correct path, while rats who are rewarded with food several hours later often forget. Negative reinforcers such as dropping levels immediately for poor behavior are probably more effective, but if there is no way to regain that level quickly it creates other demotivators.

9. Closely connected with #8 is the fact that positive reinforcers are forced to wait. For example, if little Johnny knows he cannot advance his level for ten more days he is going to feel frustrated, overwhelmed, and more quickly give up. To him, that may seem like an eternity. I have even seen situations in which children had little chance of improving their status for a month or more. This frustrates children at varying degrees. For many, the deferred hope will lead to further misbehavior.

Proverbs 22:6
Train children how to live right and when they are old they will not change. (NCV)

Proverbs 29:17
Correct your children, and you will be proud; they will give you satisfaction. (NCV)

If our behavior management systems are just managing behavior and not providing training and correction they are falling short. Correction does not necessarily give the result of getting the desired outcome. It has more to do with the process by which that outcome is obtained. The learning *experience* is as important as the *outcome*. Outcome can be temporary, but when we train children and teach them correct thinking the outcomes last a lifetime.

At Eagle Rock, we managed to get by without ever using a points or levels system. I may have tried it in my early career but soon realized its shortcomings. We eventually developed a system that worked very well, was not complicated, and got long-term results. The following tips are for anyone who wants to improve or do away with a points and levels system.

TEN PRACTICAL THINGS TO DO WITH A POINTS AND LEVELS SYSTEM.

1. Relationship building must be your number one priority. Even if you have to use a points and levels system, place your main emphasis on relationship building. I have included an entire chapter on this topic. I have talked to lots of kids who completed 90-day tours in juvenile corrections programs which were punitive in nature. They will all tell you that the most important thing that happened to them in those programs was the relationships they built with the adults who worked with them. Regardless of the setting, relationships with caring adults are the most crucial thing you can provide. Unfortunately, this is the most difficult thing for adults to do. If your points and levels system is letting adults get by without building relationships, you have a problem.

2. Use logical and natural consequences before resorting to the system. Your goal should not be to get a child through your program. Your goal should be to teach them and help them develop internally-driven motivation to do the right things in life. If a logical or natural consequence can accomplish this goal, let it happen.

3. All behaviors do not have to have a consequence. We often

make the mistake of thinking they must. This is not true. The only purpose of a consequence is teaching for usefulness. If that teaching can be taught via simpler means, (ie . a simple discussion of the matter) then let that be the course of action. Don't try to fit every little detail of a child's life into a system. Deal with some things via common sense.

4. Make sure consequences are immediate. Children and teenagers have a hard time connecting the dots when a long period of time lapses between behavior and consequence. At Eagle Rock, we had a system where a child immediately lost all privileges if a forbidden behavior occurred. There was no waiting period.

5. Provide an opportunity to immediately begin action to make amends for misbehavior. As I noted, Eagle Rock's system immediately removes all privileges when forbidden behaviors take place. By the same token, we provide a way for the child to immediately begin working his way back up.

6. Always figure out a way to incorporate the learning of humility. Any system that allows a child to progress without demonstrating some humility is missing the point. Humility can come in very small ways. Don't try to force the child/teen to be totally humble. They have to start somewhere; even a hint of humility is progress.

7. Consider the 72-hour rule. Corrective action should be completed within 72 hours in a worst-case scenario. Most should be much, much quicker. In other words, if the child shows humility and pays the price for his misbehavior, he should be able to move on in no more than 72 hours. Of course, criminal activity would be excluded because it should carry a logical consequence - involvement in the juvenile justice system if possible. Additionally, you have to use some common sense when issuing consequences. For example, if little Johnny gets to visit his birth parents on weekends but uses this opportunity to smoke pot, those visits probably need to be moved to your facility for several months instead of his birth family's home.

8. Allow room for adult caregivers to use some discretion. There is no way that a points and levels system can anticipate every possible situation or circumstance. It is possible to maintain a system while making allocation for flexibility.

9. Avoid the use of grounding. The last thing we want our kids to do is to learn to enjoy sitting in their bedroom for days at a time. We had a rule at Eagle Rock that during the time your privileges were suspended you were not allowed to go to your bedroom. In fact, during good weather, the boys were not even allowed inside the house (our houses are all in rural areas with lots of acres surrounding them). I cannot say that all grounding is a bad idea, but I can say that we never used it even though some kids would have loved it if we had.

10. Avoid *death penalties*. Kids have to feel like they have a path to get out of their situation and it cannot be so far in the future they feel like they will never get there. I would recommend if levels are used, they should be reset every three days. I realize this may not be practical for adults, but it will probably pay off in terms of motivating children.

If you must use a points and levels system, below is a checklist of characteristics it should have:
- Focuses on relationships
- Is not complicated to understand
- Is not hard to teach
- Emphasizes the development of humility and wisdom
- Reduces frustration
- Allows room for individualization
- Focuses on long-term development instead of short-term management
- Allows room for modification without compromising the system
- Is easily transferable into adoption or returned to birth families.

FOUNDATION 5

- GENERATIONAL CURSES -
AND BLESSINGS

A Biblical Perspective
Genetic Generational Curses
Social Generational Curses and Blessings
Breaking Generational Curses
Demonic Possession and Oppression

CHAPTER 21

- GENERATIONAL CURSES + BLESSINGS - A BIBLICAL PERSPECTIVE

I imagine anyone who has ever adopted, fostered, or served as a houseparent has, at some point, asked the question, "Are generational curses real?"

Michael was a very special child to my family. He came to live with us when he was nine years old. For the next ten years, we shared him with his two aunts who were both solid, Christian ladies with stable homes. Michael had plenty of proper training, encouragement, and structure for ten years, but soon after high school graduation he found trouble and ended up going to prison. While in prison he met his biological father for the first time. The man had committed a murder shortly before Michael's birth and had been in prison since before Michael was born. The two had never met. Michael did not even know where his father was until someone approached him in prison and asked, "Do you want to meet your 'real' dad? He's in block C." Michael laughed when he told me about meeting his birth father for the first time. He said it was like meeting himself.

How can children who have never met their birth parents turn out to be just like them? It is a mystery that puzzles us all. In this chapter, I will attempt to demystify the matter of generational curses and blessings from a Biblical perspective.

In both Exodus 20 and Deuteronomy 5, we find the story of God giving the Ten Commandments to Moses. The second commandment that God gave to His people is this:

"You must not worship or serve any idol, because I, the Lord your God, am a jealous God. If you hate me, I will punish your children, and even your grandchildren and great-grandchildren."
Exodus 20:5 NCV

Later, in Exodus 34, we find these words:
The Lord forgives people for evil, for sin, and for turning against him, but he does not forget to punish guilty people. He will punish not only the guilty people, but also their children, their grandchildren, their great-grandchildren, and their great-great-grandchildren.
Exodus 34:7 (NCV)

Again, Moses repeats this in Numbers 14.
The Lord doesn't become angry quickly, but he has great love. He forgives sin and law breaking. But the Lord never forgets to punish guilty people. When parents sin, he will also punish their children, their grandchildren, their great-grandchildren, and their great-great-grandchildren.
Numbers 14:18 (NCV)

I have to confess that many times during my career working with troubled boys I felt as if some boys had been cursed by the sins of their parents, grandparents, and great-grandparents. There was a good reason to feel this way. Those boys seemed not to be able to help themselves overcome negative traits and behaviors. You probably know what I mean.

The scripture seems clear. Just read it. It clearly says God will punish the children for the sins of their fathers.

I have often wondered how this could be true. Isn't God a loving and forgiving God? Are we not all supposed to be held personally accountable for our own actions? How could a loving God punish innocent children for things their parents did? We must admit it creates a theological dilemma.

Even though it seems contrary to the nature of God, I came to accept the possibility that God did mean exactly what He said. In fact, we see it in the Israelites to whom these passages are addressed. They had a long history of rebelling against God and their children, grandchildren, and great-grandchildren suffered the consequences of their rebellion.

In my earthly life I know I will never fully understand the nature of God. He may not fit my neatly wrapped image of who I think He should be. Maybe He's not *Dr. Feelgood* after all. Maybe He is exactly as Moses described in these passages.

Notwithstanding my thoughts, however, after careful study of the Bible, I realized I had been wrong in my belief concerning generational curses.

The prophet Ezekiel is believed to have written in the 6th century BCE. As Christians, we believe he was a messenger of God and his prophecies point to the coming of Christ and a new covenant. Ezekiel 18:3-4 reads:

As surely as I live, says the Lord God, this is true: You will not use this saying in Israel anymore. Every living thing belongs to me. The life of the parent is mine, and the life of the child is mine. The person who sins is the one who will die. (NCV)

The proverb he references is stated in verse 2,
The parents have eaten sour grapes, and that caused the children to grind their teeth from the sour taste. (NCV)

Basically, this old proverb means children suffer the consequences of their parent's actions. It is a proverb that seems to have been taken from the teaching we find in the second commandment. Notice that verse three states *you will no longer*. This tells us things will change under the new covenant.

The prophecy is repeated in Jeremiah 31:29-31 and it is a little easier to understand here.

"At that time people will no longer say: 'The parents have eaten sour grapes, and that caused the children to grind their teeth from the sour taste.' Instead, each person will die for his own sin; the person who eats sour grapes will grind his own teeth. "Look, the time is coming," says the Lord, "when I will make a new agreement with the people of Israel and the people of Judah. (NCV)

So you have to be asking, "Did God change his mind?" I realize that question offends some people but the answer is yes. He established a new covenant with his people. For those who think God cannot change his mind, please read the story of Abraham when he negotiates the deal for God not to destroy Sodom. He changed his mind there, too (Genesis 18:16-33).

The most direct New Testament passage regarding generational curses seems to come from the John 9. Jesus and the disciples were walking along a road when they came across a man who had been blind from birth. The disciples asked him in verse 2, *"Teacher, whose sins caused this man to be born blind - his own sin or his parent's sins?"* (NCV) The question reveals a clue to understanding the mindset of the people of that day. Apparently, at that time people felt that deformities were the result of the parents doing something wrong – parental sin. Jesus dispels the idea in one simple phrase in verse 3, *"It is not this man's sins or his parent's sins that made him blind."* It must have been a strange concept for the disciples to grasp because, at this point, they did not understand the new covenant God had sent.

My conclusion is that God no longer punishes children for the sins of the parents to the third and fourth generation. Maybe he did so at one time, but this practice was discontinued. This does not mean children cannot suffer for the sins of their parents. There really are generational curses but not in the sense that we see described in Exodus and Deuteronomy.

GENERATIONAL BLESSINGS

I will never forget one particular night I spent at my grandparents' house. I slept on the couch. At the end of the couch, there was a bookshelf on which sat individual pictures of each member of our family-my parents, aunts, uncles, and cousins. During the night I awoke to find my grandmother standing at the end of the couch with her back to me. She thought I was asleep but I watched for several minutes as she quietly placed her hand on each picture and whispered a prayer and a blessing for every member of her family. It was a moving moment for me that made a lasting impression.

My father-in-law is eighty-three years old at the time of this writing. Every morning he sends a blessing via text to each of his three children. Don't bother asking my wife if she believes in the idea of blessing your children. She has no doubt it is a powerful tool. She has continued the practice with my children. Does it work? You be the judge; my wife and her siblings are committed to the Lord, live good lives, and are deeply involved in ministry. My grandmother's only son served in full-time ministry for fifty-five years and impacted thousands of lives. Both of her grandsons married committed Christian women and founded strong ministries that have impacted thousands of children. Along with my wife, I am convinced that I am also a recipient of generational blessings passed down from my grandparents.

One of my favorite passages of scripture is found in Mark 10:16. Jesus was teaching the crowd when people started bringing little children to him and asking him to place his hands on them. This agitated the disciples so they rebuked the people. The NCV says Jesus *got upset* but the NIV says he *became indignant*. I think that means it ruffled his feathers a little. Anyway, Jesus instructed them to let the children come to him, and then he did a beautiful thing. Verse 16 says, "He took the children in his arms, put his hands on them and blessed them" (NCV). The English word *blessed* comes from the Greek word *eulogeo*. It literally means *to speak well of*, but sometimes English words do not fully describe the meaning of the Greek. Looking at other places where eulogeo is used we get the idea that to bless someone really means *to give them something*. When Jesus blesses the children he is bestowing something upon them that goes beyond mere words.

We all know that the words we speak directly to our children can have a dramatic impact. However, the words we speak over them can do the same thing. Notice in the Mark passage Jesus did not feed the children or heal their diseases. He did not counsel them or give them any medicine. He simply spoke blessings over them. We may not be able to heal or counsel, but I believe we all have the power to speak blessings over our children. I have seen it work in my own family. Because the children in our care, unfortunately, do not always have a grandmother, a mom, or a dad to bless them, that becomes our job.

TEN PRACTICAL THINGS ABOUT BLESSINGS AND CURSES.

1. Put a picture of your child in a special place. Make a routine of going to that picture, placing your hand on it, and blessing that child. There is nothing magical or mystical about the practice and it won't cost you anything to try.
2. Occasionally give your child a blessing in the form of a card or letter. Surprises found in lunch boxes or backpacks can be very meaningful to children.
3. Every year, on the first day of school, pray with your children and speak blessings over their new school year.
4. Use technology to bless your children. A daily text blessing can be a source of encouragement. (Just don't send it too early. Nobody likes to be awakened by an early morning text!)
5. You do not have to over-spiritualize the concept of blessing your children. Some people have developed elaborate techniques. Just know that Jesus blessed the children and we can follow his example.
6. Understand that generational curses still occur, but they are not handed down by God as a result of the iniquities of a

child's ancestors.

7. Remember - you may be the only person in a child's life who is blessing him or her, so persevere!

8. Don't be discouraged if your child's behavior does not change as a result of your blessing. When we bless a child we are not doing it as part of our attempt to change behavior. Blessings can have that result, but that should not be our sole motivation.

9. When appropriate, help your children understand they are not going to be held responsible for the sins of their parents. Show them what the Bible says in Ezekiel, Jeremiah, John, and Mark.

10. The whole concept of blessing and curses can seem a bit mysterious and worthy of our skepticism. Remember we are not practicing witchcraft nor do we have to fully understand how blessings and curses work. Do like Granny did and bless your children anyway. The results may surprise you.

CHAPTER 22

- *GENETIC GENERATIONAL CURSES* -

Have you ever read something in the Bible and thought to your-self, "Well, that is odd..." or "What is that supposed to mean?" or "Why is this in the Bible?" There is an interesting story in Genesis 30 that I find to be peculiar in this way. The story is about a guy named Jacob, Abraham's grandson who was married to two sisters, Rachel and Leah. You may remember the story. Jacob was in love with Rachel, so he cut a deal with her father, Laban; he would work seven years for Laban in exchange for Rachel. But Laban tricked Jacob and gave him Rachel's sister Leah instead. Jacob had to work an additional seven years for Rachel, but he eventually earned them both. In the process, Laban was dishonest and often changed the rules. However, God blessed Jacob in spite of his dishonest father-in-law. For example, Laban told Jacob he could have all the spot-ted and speckled sheep. The sheep would be his pay and, because Jacob's were all marked, they could easily be distinguished from Laban's sheep. After they made the deal God caused all the new-born sheep to be spotted and speckled. Because God was blessing him Jacob became very rich. Eventually, Laban and Jacob got into a big disagreement and decided to part ways. They had agreed Jacob could have all the speckled or spotted sheep, every dark-colored lamb, and all the speckled or spotted goats. Laban would keep all the other animals for himself.

However, Laban had a trick up his sleeve. He had his sons remove all the speckled, spotted, or dark-colored animals while Jacob was at work. Basically, he stole what was supposed to have been Jacob's flock.

The whole story is a big mess up to this point, but in verse 37 of chapter 30, a fascinating thing happens. Jacob took freshly cut branches from poplar, almond, and plane trees and, by peeling the bark to expose the white inner wood, made the branches appear striped. Then he put the peeled branches in the watering troughs so the animals saw them when they came to get water.

Here is the crazy thing: all the animals that mated in front of the trough where the white branches were placed had babies that were speckled or spotted. Furthermore, Jacob positioned the strongest of the females close to the trough to be sure they mated in front of these mysterious branches. This ensured the stronger babies would be spotted and speckled. These would belong to him. Eventually, Jacob owned all the strong animals and Laban owned all the weak ones. This is interesting, isn't it?

As I read this I thought to myself, "Did this really happen or is this just Hebrew folklore?" Regardless of what you think of the story, it says one thing for sure: the ancient Hebrew people must have believed you could influence genetics by controlling the environment at the time of conception. Therefore, if these sheep saw the white branches during the time they were mating, the result would be offspring with spots.

I am not suggesting that only spotted lambs will be born to sheep who mate in front of white branches in today's world. I am suggesting, however, that the ancient Hebrew people knew something that it has taken modern scientists 5,000 years to discover: genetic makeup can be altered by environmental influences at the time of conception.

Oh, the secrets the Bible may hold below the surface!

Consider these excerpts from an article by Lifehacker writer Chris Jager, first published August 15, 2014, titled "How Your Diet Affects Your Offspring's Health (Even Before Conception)."

Most parents realize their dieting habits can have an adverse effect on the development of their baby. However, it turns out that environmental factors prior to conception have more influence on a child's future than previously thought. Your lifestyle choices can greatly influence your offspring's genes and impact their long-term health — before they even exist. A new research paper in the international journal, science has cast fresh light on how parental influences can affect the health of potential offspring before they are conceived. It has only been over the past decade that the science community has begun seriously discussing how parental health affects offspring at the moment of conception. This new report follows five years of international research. "We can now say with great certainty that the [unborn] child doesn't quite start from scratch – they already carry over a legacy of factors from their parents' experiences that can shape development in the fetus and after birth. Depending on the situation, we can give our children a burden before they've even started life.

It seems crazy to think that our grandparent's health could have had an impact on us from a medical point of view, but this kind of thinking is widely accepted in the scientific community. In an even stranger twist, researchers are now discovering that our Grandparents' experiences can have an effect psychologically as well.

Consider this excerpt from a July 1, 2019 article by the International Center for Multigenerational Legacies of Trauma: "Major Neurological Study Reveals Long-Term Mental Health Impact of Holocaust on Survivors and Their Descendants."

A new study by Europe's leading professional association for neurologists has found that survivors of the Holocaust suffered long-term damage to their brain structures as a result of their trauma, with mental health problems being passed down to their children and grandchildren.

Imagine that – the things our grandparents experienced can

have an effect on our mental health. However, this concept gets even more interesting.

In 2013 at Emory University researcher Gary Brian Dias, Ph.D. discovered something that got the attention of people worldwide. Dias exposed a group of female laboratory mice to a distinctive odor, issuing a small electric shock each time the rats got near the odor. Eventually, the rats began to associate the shock with the odor. They were essentially traumatized and began to associate their trauma with a distinctive smell. This was not a surprise – we all remember from Psych 101 the experiment Pavlov did with his dogs when he associated a ringing bell with food and eventually had the dogs salivating when they heard the bell. However, the Dias experiment went a step further. Shortly after establishing the aversion in the rats, he allowed them to become pregnant. Guess what happened! The offspring, who had never received the electric shock (the trauma) had the same aversion to the same odor. Dias found that even the second-generation offspring experienced the same aversion as their grandparents. This study fascinates me personally because it opens the door for us to consider an outrageous possibility – that trauma can be passed along genetically. We can be traumatized by something we never personally experienced or even knew about.

To go a step further, it opens the door for the possibility that we may have memories in our minds of things that happened to our grandparents years before we were born. I want to be careful to point out that this matter is highly debatable in the scientific community, but the idea of transgenerational memory transmission is not as far-fetched as you might think.

There is a relatively new field of science called epigenetics. I am not articulate enough to scientifically explain it, but in layman's terms, it is the study of how things get passed down from generation to generation via genetics without changing one's DNA. It opens the door for us to consider the possibility that all sorts of behavioral (non-biological) traits are genetically transmitted from one generation to the next.

Before you assume I am another crazy conspiracy theorist I

would ask that you read the following information about memory transmission. If you think all of your memories are always a result of something you directly experienced, you are in for a surprise.

For many years I have heard the story of a young girl who was brutally attacked by an unknown assailant. She eventually died from her injuries but her heart was donated for transplant. The transplant recipient, another young girl with no knowledge of her donor, received the heart. Shortly afterward she began to have frequent nightmares in which she was attacked by an unknown man. She reported these nightmares to her parents and described the attacker to them. Through this description, police identified the attacker who had killed the donor. The story seems to indicate that the memory of the experience was passed along via the tissue of the heart (through the cells). Because I questioned the validity of this story, I began to look around to find verification. In my search, I discovered a research paper titled "Changes in Heart Transplant Recipients That Parallel the Personalities of Their Donors" by Paul Pearsall, Ph.D. University of Hawaii; Gary E. R. Schwartz Ph.D., Linda G. S. Russek, Ph.D. The University of Arizona. The paper documents interviews conducted with people who received heart transplants and their families. Independently, interviews were also conducted with the families of the donors. Some interesting things were discovered:

1. One recipient reported after his transplant he developed a strong liking for classical music. He did not know that his donor was a classical musician and in fact, had died with an instrument in his hand.
2. Another recipient reported she had never eaten junk food or even chicken nuggets but after her transplant, she had a strong desire for chicken nuggets. The donor family revealed that the donor loved chicken nuggets and, ironically, when he was killed had an order of McDonald's chicken nuggets in his pocket.
3. A lady receiving a man's heart reported she was always mild-tempered and passive, but when she came out of the

transplant surgery in which she received the heart she was angry and even screamed at doctors. She further reported she did not know why she became so enraged. When her donor's family was interviewed, it was discovered that the donor had died as a result of injuries received in a bar fight.

4. The family of one young female recipient reported prior to her transplant she always had lesbian tendencies and was, in fact, very open about the matter. Following her transplant from another woman she lost her lesbian attraction and decided to marry a man.

5. A male recipient who received a heart from a female donor stated that following his transplant he became much more sensitive to his wife's sexual needs. His wife reported he seemed to know exactly what she wanted.

6. Numerous transplant recipients have reported following their transplants they developed appetites for things they never wanted prior to their transplant – including alcohol.

7. A little boy who received a heart from a drowning victim is said to be terrified of water despite having never known that his donor had drowned.

Actually, this is only a sampling of the many stories available. Previously, we might dismiss such tales as exaggerations or outright lies. However, via the internet and with transplants becoming so common, it is hard to deny the possibilities. Where there is enough smoke, there is probably some fire.

Up to this point, I have been trying to establish the possibility that genetic blessings and curses can be passed along to us from our ancestors. These curses and blessings may not only be in terms of our biological makeup but of our mental health and personality as well. There is even the possibility that we inherit memories of things we never personally experienced. The peculiar Biblical story we looked at may even suggest ancient people thought about these things and may have even been far ahead of us in their understanding of genetics. I have to ask one simple question: "What good does it do for us to understand these things if there is nothing we can do about it? Genetically, we get what we get and then we learn to live with it." I have three answers to this question:

First, we are living in an unprecedented time in the history of the world. Scientific and medical advancements are occurring faster than ever before. Information sharing is more global than it has ever been. I believe in the 21st century we are on track to unlock mysteries that have perplexed people for thousands of years. Namely, I believe we will make great advances in settling the age-old question of nature versus nurture. The possibilities of what we will discover are almost limitless. Will we someday discover that a woman's exposure to a particular chemical resulted in her grandchild having ADD? Don't laugh, one study already points to this. Will we be able to identify an obesity gene and figure out how to turn it off and on? Don't laugh, it's currently being studied. Will we discover that the phobias our children experience could be attributed to the trauma our grandparents experienced? Don't laugh, there is already evidence. Will we be able to trace the origins of panic attacks that seem to have no rational basis? Who knows? Will we discover that the voices some schizophrenics hear in their head are actually the voices of people their ancestors encountered 100 years ago? Ok, maybe I'm taking that one a little too far!

I realize it all seems like science fiction and conspiracy, but as a guy who spent thirty-two years working with hurting children, I say we should exhaust all possibilities when it comes to helping our children overcome psychological pain and suffering. Just as we do research to help prevent and battle cancer, we certainly should be doing research to prevent and battle mental health issues in children. Just as cancer has a genetic link, we know that mental behavioral health has one too.

Secondly, a better understanding of genetic generational curses may very well help us develop better therapies for the treatment of behavioral and mental health challenges in hurting children. Could it be that talk therapy is not the most effective method of treatment? For decades, our main strategy for dealing with behavioral health has been talk therapy. We like to call it *counseling*. I am professionally trained and have years of experience, but I can tell you that it does not always work. Any good counselor with an ounce of honesty will tell you that many times we simply do not have all the answers. Our craft falls short.

It is exciting to know that treatments such as Eye Movement Desensitization and Reprocessing (EMDR) are finding success in the treatment of victims of childhood trauma. Doctors are also finding success with Transcranial Magnetic Stimulation (TMS) which is a noninvasive procedure that uses magnetic fields to stimulate nerve cells in the brain to improve symptoms of depression. Wouldn't it be great if such treatments could supplant the use of invasive psychotropic medications?

Finally, and most importantly, I am reminded that literally thousands of VPs both now and in the future will deal with guilt, confusion, and a sense of failure because the children they care so deeply for have not responded to the love and sacrifice the VP has been given. I know, from my personal experience, that I gave all I had to give but in many cases, there were no positive results for my efforts. I prayed, gave of my time, had empathy, used all the latest psychology and medicine, and yet things still did not turn out the way I envisioned. It can be very, very frustrating.

We are taught to believe that a new environment combined with good psychology and a dose of faith will fix whatever problem exists in our child's mind. However, sometimes nothing works.

Could it be that humans are not really born as blank slates? Could it be that genetics plays a much larger role than our current mindsets are prepared to accept? If so, some of us might take a big sigh of relief in realizing we really do wrestle with powers that are beyond our control. There may be some things that are not within our power to correct. Just as a doctor is not always successful in efforts to cure cancer, VPs will not always be successful in redirecting the lives of our kids. Maybe we need to take a deep breath and say, "I will do all I can do, but if it does not work, it is not a reflection on me, my efforts, or my skill."

TEN PRACTICAL THINGS TO KNOW AND DO ABOUT GENETIC GENERATIONAL CURSES.

1. Learn all you can about your child's past; not just his five-page social history but also about his ancestors, their experiences, and their traits. It could be enlightening.
2. Share information with others. Don't break confidentiality, but share your thoughts and observations with other VPs. When we share, we develop ideas. Those ideas can become theories, and those theories can lead to solutions.
3. Consider alternate therapies and treatment protocols. Talk therapy may not be all your child needs.
4. Identify your own generational genetic blessings or curses. Understanding them may help you become more thankful as well as help you identify areas in your life that still need some work.
5. Try to identify your child's generational blessings or curses. This will not only help you find ways to help him, but it may also aid in your development of empathy and understanding.
6. Remember that most of the kids VPs care for are the victims of genetic and social generational curses. They will require more patience than children who are the recipients of generational blessings.
7. When working with our children's parents, it is beneficial to realize that they, too, were probably the recipient of generational curses. Sometimes we forget that. They may need an extra shot of mercy from time to time.
8. Do not let genetic generational curses be an excuse. Regardless of the hand of cards we are dealt, we are all still responsible for our own choices and actions.
9. Always err on the side of mercy.
10. Don't beat yourself up when kids turn out differently than you hoped they would. Sometimes it just happens that way and has nothing to do with the efforts you made. Trust me: been there – done that.

CHAPTER 23

- SOCIAL GENERATIONAL CURSES + BLESSINGS -

We tend to think of curses and blessings as being mysterious, paranormal, or without logical explanation. However, curses, whether they be explainable by the laws of nature or not, are still curses and they can hurt our children just as much as the curses that seem to be passed along mysteriously.

My family's oral history tells me my great grandfather fought in World War I and that he was a carpenter and a farmer. In fact, he was the casket maker for the community. His daughter, my grandmother, lived to be ninety-nine so I received a lot of first-hand oral history. Two of her stories have always been of particular interest to me and I sometimes contemplate the possibility that these stories have impacted me and my attitudes toward life. Granny says that during the Civil War the Union troops came through and burned the family farm, destroying all the crops and buildings. However, prior to their arrival, one of Granny's aunts collected all the seeds needed to plant the next year's garden. The seeds were hidden in a tree trunk in the forest. Tuck that tidbit of information away for a moment.

The second story occurred many years later when the great depression occurred. Granny said that her father was not at all happy about Roosevelt's "New Deal." Students of history will recall that the

"New Deal" amounted to a government bailout and some people blame it for starting the modern *welfare state*. My great-grandfather wanted no part of a government bailout and stated emphatically that it was his role to take care of his family – not the government. My Dad says he remembers his grandfather complaining that men were being paid to "lean on their shovels." Tuck that information away for a moment.

Finally, Granny said that throughout the depression she never went hungry because her "PaPa" always had a garden and some hogs, chickens, and a milk cow. She said that after he fed his thirteen children there was usually enough to share with the community so they bartered and gifted what was left. Tuck that information away for a moment.

I never personally spoke to my great-grandfather about these matters. I was only three years old when he died. I never heard these stories about my great-grandfather until I was about forty years old. My grandmother nor my Dad ever said anything to me about preparing for emergencies, being self-sufficient, or disliking the welfare state. (they felt the same way but it was never talked about). How is it, then, that fifty years after my great-grandfather died, his great-grandson shares the exact same values? It is an interesting question. My theory is that those core values became part of our social DNA. It could have been passed down by conversations we had or it could have been passed down by the examples we set for one another. It could also be genetically transmitted (I discussed that in a previous chapter). Whatever the case, generational curses and blessings that take the form of family values seem to be passed from one generation to the next.

I share this information for a reason; our family histories can be a blessing or a curse to us. Those histories can form our identity and shape our values in ways that we probably never realize. Think for a moment about that child you are caring for. What kind of generational curse or blessing might they be the recipient of? How was that curse or blessing transmitted? How has it affected them?

Granny and Granddaddy got married at an early age and soon he was shipped off to war, leaving Granny with two small children.

They certainly faced trials and difficulties. They lost a child. Grandaddy had a nervous breakdown as a result of several traumatic events but none of us ever knew it until after his death. They faced all the challenges of a normal family but they held strong. Both of them taught Sunday School and at the age of eighty, Granny finally quit teaching the junior high boys class. She said they needed somebody who could understand them better. In their seventy years of marriage, they never borrowed one cent and never had a credit card. They lived a quiet, humble life and they were happy. I was blessed to be able to spend a lot of time with them.

I was also fortunate to spend a lot of time with my mother's parents. They were two of the most loving people I have ever known and I knew they always had my back and would be there for me through thick and thin. They flooded my life with wonderful memories and lessons. Paw Paw had been an orphan and he had a very tender spot in his heart for hurting children. He broke his generational curse to become a great father and an awesome grandfather. My Grandmother's father had been an alcoholic but she, too, broke the generational curse and was the most awesome Granny any kid could ask for.

So you may be asking how all of this history affected me. I'm glad you asked. From Dad's side of the family, I learned the importance of living a simple life, serving others, and trusting God to bring you through difficult times. I learned that there is honor in all work and that to make it in life you need to plan ahead and not wait on someone else to feed you. From Mom's side, I learned how to truly love people unconditionally and I learned that no matter how bad life may have treated you, you can still be an overcomer. You can still break the cycles of dysfunction.

I hope you are able to see through my personal story how social generational blessings work. As you read this book you will probably see trends in my thoughts that can be attributed to my grandparents.

Unfortunately, not everyone is as fortunate.

I was a nineteen-year-old college freshman when my world got turned upside down. I played sports all my life and had planned to play football at my small university. During team physicals, the doctors discovered I had a heart problem and I gave up football. For days I sought God's guidance regarding what I should do now that football was gone. I soon found myself sitting in a juvenile detention center with fifty of the finest delinquents ever known to man. I was a volunteer mentor. On day one, a fifteen-year-old boy named Bruce wanted to talk with me. I was curious to know what his family history was, so I asked. He said his dad owned an *import/export* business and his mom was *self-employed*. I thought that sounded pretty good but I could not figure out how this nice young man from this nice family ended up in so much trouble. Bruce and I developed a strong bond. I went to see him twice per week for two hours and we played games and talked about a lot of things. Several months passed and I was always perplexed by the fact that Bruce came from such an outstanding family but had gotten into so much trouble. Knowing I had gained his trust after several months, I asked him again about his parents. He paused, dropped his head, and said, "I didn't lie to you. My Dad really is in the import/export business. He sells drugs. My mom really is self-employed, she is a prostitute". He went on to tell me that his role in the family business was to collect the money when customers came to pick up drugs or visit his mother. For a moment in time, my world stood still. My heart sank. I was speechless. A few minutes later I excused myself and told Bruce I would see him in a few days. I vividly remember that as I walked out of the building, I looked up between the branches of some trees. I could see the clouds and it was as if God spoke to me as clearly as I have ever heard him. He told me that if I had been born into the family that Bruce was born into, I would probably be locked up in prison instead of heading back to my comfortable college campus. That day changed my life and eight years later I founded the boys' ranch. I did not know it at the time but I now realize something. During all those years at the ranch, I was just trying to do one thing – break the social generational curses of young men who had not been as fortunate as I had been.

I am happy to report that for a lot of boys who came to our ranch, the social generational curse was broken. We saw kids who had never known their fathers, grow up to be great daddies to their little babies. We saw young men who never had a man model what it means to be a good husband and grow up to be great husbands. We saw young men from families in which nobody held a job grow up to be great employees. By the same token, we saw numerous young men fall into the same patterns of dysfunction that generations of their families had exhibited. The social curses held on. They never rewrote their family history. As the kids now say, "They failed to flip the script."

So how do we help our kids *flip the script*? How do we help them interrupt those generational patterns?

TEN STEPS TO HELP KIDS BREAK SOCIAL GENERATIONAL CURSES

I would like for you to imagine being in a small boat in the middle of a large river. The boat has sprung a leak and is slowly taking on water. If something is not done you are going to sink. This is the analogy we will use to understand the process of helping our children break the social generational curses they face.

1. FIND THE LEAK

The first thing you have to do is find the leak. You may find more than one. Grab whatever you can find to temporarily plug the hole(s). It may be an old rag or it may be a piece of chewing gum. It does you no good to start dipping water out of the boat if it is going to continue to fill back up.

Too many times when we take children into our care we feel like we have to immediately move forward. We have to immediately start making "progress". We often develop a "treatment plan" in which we outline all the goals and steps we need to take to get the kid to the place where we know they can be. This is not always a good thing. Our tendency is to start dipping water out of the boat but it keeps filling back up. From an emotional standpoint, sometimes the children just need a temporary fix to keep from sinking. Sometimes the best thing we can do is put our finger over the leak in the bottom of the boat and hold on. We may not be making progress but we are not sinking. We should never forget that it is better to stay afloat than to sink while dipping out of the water.

2. START DIPPING THE WATER OUT

Once you are confident you're not taking on more water, you can start to dip water out of the boat. Slowly, as the water is thrown out, the boat will start to rise and you might begin to come out of the panic stage. Just remember that there is a possibility that your chewing gum patch may break loose and you will start taking on water again. It's a strong possibility so keep watch on it.

As it relates to children this is the stage at which they are just beginning to even be able to think about making progress. Those holes need to be patched just to keep them from sinking but that does not mean they are ready to be well. They may not even have the strength to be well but you can still slowly begin to dip out the negative things that are causing them to sink.

3. PADDLE TO SHORE

You may have the holes temporarily plugged and you may have dipped some water out but you are a long way from being on solid ground. As the saying goes, "you are not out of the water yet". Your focus at this stage is to get the boat to shore so you can rest and think through the situation more clearly. Dry ground will provide you with some stability.

With our children, this is the step where you can spend days, months, and years before you move on to the next step. Children are not going to be able to address their curses until they are on stable ground and feel secure and confident. In foster care, we tend to move kids around from home to home and then we wonder why they do not make any progress. It is because they can't make progress when there is no stability. You cannot properly patch a hole in a boat if you are still dipping out water and trying to stay afloat. With children, this can take years but it is an essential step in the process.

4. IDENTIFY THE PROBLEM.

Now that you are on shore and things are drying out, you can start taking a real close look at the root of the problem. You can figure out exactly where the leak is.

With our children, this is really the first step in breaking curses. This is the point you reach after many days, months, and years of fighting to bring some stability. It is also a step that can only take place when the child is ready for it to take place. They may still be standing on the shore trying to catch their breath after fighting to keep from sinking. Frankly, sometimes they do not seem to ever recover from that. However, for those who do, they will eventually come to a place where you can help them say, "OK. Here's the problem. How am I going to deal with it?"

5. MAKE A DECISION

Decide whether or not you want to experience that problem again. You have to go out in the boat again but you don't have to sink again. However, some people are just reckless enough and careless enough to push that boat right back in the water with a chewing gum patch and in due time they will sink again.

With social generational curses, there is only one person who can break the curse. That is the child himself/herself. As the VP you cannot do it for them. You cannot make the decision for them. You cannot do all of the hard work. They have to make up their mind for themselves. Unfortunately, a lot of the kids will choose to keep their bubble gum patches and they will push their boat right back out and they will sink just like their parents did. The cycle will go on generation after generation.

Your role as a VP or sometimes as the therapist is to help the child see what the problem is and help them see where it will lead them. At this stage, you are not really looking to solve problems.

You are just trying to help your child determine whether or not they want to continue. You are just looking to identify it and recognize its consequences. The child has to decide whether or not they like their family situation. Frankly, some kids just seem to enjoy passing along the curses. It is the path of least resistance. Leaving what is familiar to them is scary. For them, it is not a matter of how dysfunctional their family life, values, and culture may be. It is a matter of having the courage to turn their back on all they have ever known. There is not much you can do with those kids. Hopefully, though, your child will decide they want to flip the switch on their family curses.

6. CUT OUT THE ROTTEN PARTS

Now that your boat is dried out and you've identified all the leaks and you've decided that you would rather fix them than leave the temporary patches in, you can start making a plan to do the repairs properly. You will probably see that in order to repair the leaks you need to cut out and replace spots that are much bigger than the leak itself. You have to cut out all the rotten parts around the leak.

This is the point at which actual teaching begins. You start to teach the child what causes generational family curses. This is not the place for mystical and confusing concepts to be taught. This is the time to be very practical. For example, if poverty is the generational curse your child wants to break, you can ask him to identify the things that have caused poverty in his family. Write them down. They will be things like, "My parents are lazy and won't work," "My family members get fired from jobs a lot," "My family members rent their furniture," "My family members buy things they don't need," "My family does not take care of material things..." You get the idea. This is not the place to present a plan. I'm just trying to give an example. Approach these things from a very practical point of view. Teach better ways of doing things.

7. DEVELOP YOUR REPAIR PLAN

Develop your plan to fix your boat. This step does not require a lot of explanation. With your children, you do the same thing. You help them figure out exactly what they can do to break their generational curse. It even helps to write it down. For example, "I am determined to be a hard worker," "I will not buy something unless I can pay cash for it," "I will drive old clunker cars until I can afford something better," and "I will take good care of the material things I acquire." You get the idea. It is all about teaching again.

8. COUNT THE COSTS.

Count the costs of making your repairs. If you are going to fix your boat you have to know it is going to cost you something. Make sure you have a clear understanding of that cost.

With children, they have to know that breaking generational curses is hard work. Nothing good is going to come easy. You need to prepare them for the fact that they are going to have to make some sacrifices and those changes are not always going to make them popular amongst their birth families. They may lose some friends and they may even lose some family members. I have been amazed that some birth parents resent their children who have broken the curse and gone on to become much better people. It is almost as if misery loves company and some parents just don't want their children to move up in the world. We had one boy rise so far above his family's curses that they disowned him. Success was not allowed in his family so part of the price he paid was ostracisation from his family. Some kids are not willing to pay that price. They will have to decide. While they are deciding it is helpful for you to reassure them that they will always have you as a family and will have your unwavering support.

9. ROLL UP YOUR SLEEVES

Roll up your sleeves and fix your boat. It won't be easy but you can do it. Your children will need a lot of strength to break those curses. You will need to cheer them on. Your encouragement of your children will empower them to do things they never thought they were capable of doing.

10. VISUALIZE YOUR FUTURE

Visualize what it's going to be like when you float back out into the river in your newly repaired boat. This will drive you to carry through.

With the boys at the ranch, I regularly gave subtle hints to them to describe what their life might be like. They seldom realized I was doing it because I sneaked it into everyday life. For example, we might drive by a nice house and a boy might comment about how nice the house is. I might say, "One day that might be your house." We might see a family walking hand in hand in a park and I might say, "That's the way you're going to be one day with your family." We might notice a son and his dad tossing a football and I might subtly say, "That's probably how you're going to be with your son." I was tossing subtle visions to the boys but you don't always have to be so subtle. Sometimes it is ok to be deliberate and open. Cast a vision for what their life can be like. Expose them to people who have broken their own generational curses and show them that they can do the same. Give a vision of what life can be like.

I have good plans for you, not plans to hurt you,
I will give you hope and a good future.
Jeremiah 29:11 (NCV)

CHAPTER 24

- *BREAKING GENERATIONAL CURSES* -

If you have read this book in chronological order you know my position on generational curses from a Biblical perspective. You also have an understanding of how generational curses can occur genetically and socially. However, none of that matters if you do not know how to break those generational curses. It is one thing to understand how the game is played, but it is an entirely different thing to play the game. In this chapter, I want to take you off the sidelines and put you into the game of battling and breaking generational curses.

Allow me to begin with an apology to those who desire quick and easy fixes or mysterious techniques. Breaking generational curses is not a matter of knowing the right incantation or saying a prayer in a specific way. It is not always a matter of laying on of hands or a special anointing by clergy. For the most part, breaking generational curses is a matter of hard, dirty, persistent grinding. Sorry to disappoint you.

I am a counselor by profession and believe in the power of good mental health workers. I believe we should develop our skills to our fullest potential. However, in my thirty-two years of working with troubled kids, I can tell you there are some things professionals simply do not know how to handle. Anyone with an ounce of honesty and experience will admit the same. It is in those cases that we have to accept the fact only God can fix some situations. It is these situations that are the focus of this section.

In the ninth chapter of John, there is an interesting story of Jesus healing a man who had been blind since birth. The Pharisees were complaining about the healing on the Sabbath, so they launched a full-fledged investigation. This investigation occurs over several verses and the man, his parents, and several others are all questioned. Finally, in verse 25 the guy who had been healed says, "Hey Mr. Pharisee, look, I don't really know what else to tell you. I'm not sure who the guy was, how he did it, or where he went. All I know is that I was blind and now I see. That's all I know" (my paraphrase). In many situations, mental health professionals have theories and treatments which often work. At other times, we just have to say, "Hey Mr. Mental Health World. I really don't know what to tell you. I'm not sure what the problem was or how it got fixed. All I can tell you is that something changed in this kid's heart."

While God is the first player in breaking generational curses, the second player is the person with the curse. It is evident that the blind man had a role in his healing. In verse 7, God gave him a task and he obediently did it. Healing does not usually occur unless the person in need of healing takes action of some sort. In the case of breaking generational curses, the cursed person must first understand he needs healing and then secondly, must take some action to become whole.

You, as a VP, can drive yourself crazy wanting a child to do something to better his or her life. Sometimes you can clearly see the trouble ahead and intently desire to steer them a different way, but the fact of the matter is until they make a choice to follow the right path, there is not much you can do. In order for those generational curses to be broken, our children have to want them to be broken. I can point to dozens of young men who apparently did not care. Fortunately, there were a few who did want to change the course of their family history, and I was blessed to be a part of that process.

So, you may be wondering about your role as a VP in breaking generational curses. It is a huge one. Below, I outline five things you must do:

1. PRAY.

Christians frequently list prayer as the tool of choice when it comes to handling difficult situations. Unfortunately, this is often just our default answer. We have all heard the story of the parents who asked their little boy what he learned in church. The boy had not been paying attention, so he turned to his default answer: "God and Jesus and the Bible." For prayer to be effective, it has to become more than your default answer. It needs to be real. We need to remember the following things about prayer:

Prayer is our way of petitioning God. I am fascinated with the petition Abraham presented to God when God had decided to destroy Sodom and Gomorrah. He really went to bat for the city. He bargained with God and, even though God did not completely change His mind, he did spare Abraham's nephew. He originally planned to do away with everyone. There is nothing wrong with us going to bat for our children. Prayer is our tool and, although we should never see prayer as a way to twist God's arm, there is certainly nothing wrong with being an advocate for our children.

Prayer is not all about making requests and negotiating with God. In my life experience prayer has often been much more about me learning from God. It is through prayer that I get direction. Late one night, while sitting under a tree on the campus of Samford University, I began to pray for direction in my life. I can tell you the specific moment and circumstance during that time of prayer when God told me what he wanted me to do with my life. I was not making petitions, twisting His arm, or asking for anything. I just needed to hear from him, and it was through prayer that that happened. When we pray for our children, we need to remember that making petitions and acting as an advocate are only part of the process. Listening for direction is equally important.

As a VP, one of the most important things you will need to learn is that the problems your children have are not yours. If you try to own those problems and assume responsibility for fixing all of them, you are going to drive yourself crazy. It always hurt me to see my boys make mistakes and fail, but I finally had to realize it was not my responsibility to make them successful. It was my responsibility to make sure they had the environment, the structure, the encouragement, and the instruction needed for them to overcome obstacles and live happy and productive lives. Beyond that, somebody else (either God or the boy) was going to have to take the responsibility. Very often it was through my prayer that I was able to give them over to God and find relief from a lot of pressure.

2. EMPOWER.

In sports, we have a phenomenon called the *home-field advantage*. It is what happens when we play on our home fields or courts. Sometimes, inferior teams win games just because they have home-field advantage. There is something empowering about having people cheering for and supporting you when you are in the game. It gives you extra strength and courage. I remember in high school when we would have powerlifting competitions in our weight room and would all gather around when a guy was trying to break a record. We would yell encouragement, chest bump each other, and do Tarzan imitations. We did all sorts of crazy things to get one another fired up for the big lift. Then, in the midst of the lift, if it looked like the guy was not going to make it, we would shout words of encouragement. "You can do it! Push, Push. You're almost there. Don't give up man, don't give up!" When a guy broke a record, everybody went crazy. We slapped each other, growled like rabid dogs, barked at one another, flexed our muscles, and pounded our chests. We were empowering each other. As a 160-pounder, I broke the school record for my classification by squatting 455 pounds. As I struggled to finish the lift, my teammates began to scream all sorts of encouraging words. I wanted so badly to quit. I was in terrible pain and thought there was no way I was going to stand up with all that weight on my back. I pushed and pushed and somehow became stronger than I really was. There was no way I was going to let my friends down. I could not face them if I failed. I finally finished the lift and there was a collective "WooHoo" in the weight room.

My friends had empowered me to do more than I should have been able to do. (Thanks, guys. I still have a hemorrhoid from that day!) Our children face a difficult task in breaking generational curses. Sometimes they need to become stronger than they really are. We have the resources to empower them by our encouragement - let them know they have the home court advantage.

3. ACCLAIM.

Webster defines acclamation as *a loud, eager expression of approval, praise, or assent.* That may sound a lot like empowerment but there is a big difference when it comes to our children. There is power in the words we use. As the director of a ranch, it always bothered me that my boys were often referred to as *ranch boys.* Something about that just never settled with me. From the perspective of social curses, it is rather easy to understand how that might affect a boy. If he hears himself described in those terms he eventually begins to develop that identity. The same thing applies to other sorts of descriptive words. So what happens when we use terms like *"foster child"* or *"adopted"* with our kids? Sometimes they take those words as their identity. When such identities become ingrained in our children over long periods of time it becomes part of their *story.* In terms of social curses, stories are where they begin. A person's family story can become his or her curse. In terms of genetic curses, let me ask you to think outside the box for a moment. What if every time a boy hears himself referred to as a foster child a little mechanism in his DNA gets turned off or on? That mechanism says this genotype is not capable of properly raising children. If we believe memories can be passed down genetically then what is the little voice in the next generation's head going to be hearing? "We are not good family people. We are not good family people." Thus we have a genetic family curse. Of course, I am not presenting this conspiracy as a theory, but I can tell you that after thirty-two years of working with children I have to wonder if it is a possibility. Generation after generation, in some families the cycles are repeated. The confusing thing is many times the children repeating the family dysfunction have been removed from it for most of their lives. If you are a VP long enough you will start to consider believing things you might have once thought ridiculous. When I operated the ranch we treated every boy as if he were automatically going to college. We knew the overwhelming majority of them would not go, and some were far from capable, but we still spoke those words over them. It had nothing to do with self-fulfilling prophecy. It had everything to do with speaking blessings rather than curses over our children. The words we use and the expectations we have for our children are of extreme importance in the difficult process of breaking generational curses. Kids need to hear who they are from adults in positive terms in order to build a healthy self-image.

4. *CORRECT.*

Generational curses can come in the form of incorrect thinking. I believe there are three generational curses clearly evident in modern American society. They are the curses of victim mentality, laziness, and poverty. It is fairly easy to identify these as social generational curses. They are family values that are taught and passed down through the family bloodline and the family story. We often say *the apple doesn't fall far from the tree* or *blood is thicker than water*. These are common idioms for the idea that social generational curses are passed down via environment and family culture. Interestingly, you should be aware that some theories exist to support this idea. It is almost as if our ancestors had the power to say, "This family is lazy" or "This family is a victim." Then, that memory gets passed along to the third and fourth generations via genetic code. It is almost as if you can flip the lazy switch on or off and it will remain in that position for subsequent generations. (Again, if you think that is foolish nonsense, just talk to a few people who have raised dozens of foster kids. They might tell you it makes sense. Ask the adoptive parent who raised a child from birth to explain how their child has the same work ethic as their birth parent whom they never met. They will tell you this conspiracy theory may have some merit.) Regardless of how we feel about the transmission of curses, it is still our responsibility to teach our children that their thinking, no matter how natural it may seem to them, is flawed. They will likely have a hard time understanding because they are probably wired differently, but it is through our educating process that we can help rewire their brains. Hopefully, this rewiring will be passed down to future generations. This is what we call breaking the cycle or breaking the generational curse.

The Greek philosopher, Plato, wrote a fascinating piece called "The Allegory of the Cave." This is my paraphrase. Assume we are born in a cave and are never allowed to go outside or to even look outside. We spend our lives sitting at the door facing the inside of the cave. As people walk by outside, the sun casts a shadow on the inside wall. These shadows occur several times every day and are the only thing we see. Plato says that the shadows become reality to us. Our perception is skewed because of our limited experience. Our reality is based on the only thing we have seen – the shadows. That is often how it is with the children we are trying to help. They may have seen only one way of doing things and to them, it is the only way it can be done. This becomes their reality. As VPs, we know better and it is our responsibility to figuratively pick them up at the door of the cave and turn them around. We have to show them the deception of generational curses they are living under is not the only thing available to them. When we do this, we flip the switch. There can be an *aha* moment when they see that everything they had ever known was wrong.

5. SET AN EXAMPLE.

The best way to flip the switch is to set a better example. I will never forget sitting in a car one night with one of my boys. This boy had never had a family and he was twelve years old. As we sat there, a husband and wife walked past our car. They were holding hands with a little girl I presumed to be their daughter. The three of them walked along joyfully holding hands, laughing, and enjoying their time together. My boy became very silent as he intensely watched them cross in front of us and then walk up the street. He then sat up in his seat, stretched his neck, and watched the little family walk as far as his eye could see. I was curious as to what had caught his attention, so I asked him. I will never forget his reply. "I have never

221

seen a family like that. Mr. Scott, do you think I can have a family like that one day?'"

In the That's My Dad Podcast, I interviewed several men who had grown up either without fathers or with abusive fathers. Each of the men I interviewed had become outstanding fathers to their own children – they had broken the generational curse. I wanted to know why and how they did it. I was surprised the answer was so simple. Every man I interviewed told me the same two things. First, they remembered making a conscious choice to be a good father. Time after time the men would tell me the exact place and time of that decision. One described being fourteen years old and standing in a bathroom when he made the decision. He could even describe the size of the bathroom and the colors. Another told me exactly where he was and even who was present when he made that decision. None of the men knew it at the time, but they were breaking generational curses.

The second thing each man told me was even more striking. Every man I interviewed who had broken a generational curse recalled at least one adult in his life who reached out to him, gave him encouragement, set an example for him, or spoke positive things about him. Each person I interviewd named the person and could tell me intricate details about that person's life and, specifically, what that person had done for him. They could even quote things the person had said to them over 30 years prior. You may be that person in the life of a child in your care!

TEN PRACTICAL THINGS ABOUT BREAKING GENERATIONAL CURSES.

1. There are no secret formulas, magical spells, or special prayers to recite. It is dirty, frustrating, and hard work.
2. Remember - you are fighting against forces that you probably cannot see.
3. Remember that the only way a curse can be broken is if the cursed is willing to participate.
4. Know your limitations. There are some things you can do and there are some things that only God can do.
5. Children who deal with generational curses are dealing with things that you might not understand because you have never been in their shoes. Be sympathetic but not enabling.
6. Prayer is your opportunity to commit an issue to God and relieve yourself of the responsibility.
7. Never underestimate the power of genetics. It is easy to assume that children are the products of their environment and simply need to re-learn what they have been taught. However, there is good reason to believe children struggle with issues caused by unseen genetic forces we cannot fully understand.
8. Be sensitive in your choice of words. Words can be very powerful and can affect children consciously as well as subconsciously.
9. Never forget that everything you do and say with or to a child has the potential to affect many generations to come.
10. Don't beat yourself up when children fail to break generational curses. It happens.

Our fight is not against people on earth but against the rulers and authorities and power of this world's darkness, against the spiritual powers of evil in the heavenly world.
Ephesians 6:12 (NCV)

C H A P T E R **25**

- DEMONIC POSSESSION + OPPRESSION -

I must admit from the beginning that I don't have much experience helping kids who are demon-possessed. I have raised some boys whom I thought might be the devil himself, but not any that I thought were "possessed." I have had a couple who I felt were under spiritual oppression. We will discuss that concept and how we handle it, but for starters, I believe we need to try to figure out how we know the difference between demonic possession and mental illness.

The Bible gives us several examples of possession and oppression. Let us take a look at some of them.

In I Samuel 16:14 we read, *"But the Lord's Spirit had left Saul, and an evil spirit from the Lord troubled him"* (NCV). At first glance, this is a rather strange occurrence. It is hard for Christians of the 21st century to imagine that God would evoke an evil spirit to haunt someone. The scripture proceeds to tell how the evil spirit tormented Saul until his attendants finally went out and found someone to play the lyre to comfort him (the first documented case of music therapy). Verse 23 says that whenever the spirit came from God the lyre player played. This would relieve Saul and the evil spirit would leave him. The story requires some background understanding. Saul had at one time gained great favor with God and was appointed King of Israel. However, he had become arrogant and prideful. This led to him doing things his own way instead of following God's orders. God was not happy with him and in Chapter 15 verse 10 we read these words, *"Then the Lord spoke his word to Samuel: I am sorry I made Saul king because he has stopped following me and has not obeyed my commands"* (NCV). Saul was dethroned and humiliated. For the moment let us tuck away one little fact to which we will return later; God turned Saul over to an evil spirit because Saul became proud and decided he didn't need to do things God's way. We will come back to this.

In Matthew 12:22 we find people bringing a blind and mute man to Jesus. The Bible says the man was *demon-possessed*. Jesus heals him so that he could both talk and see.

In Matthew 9:32 and Luke 11:14, we find Jesus healing a man who had been mute. Again, the Bible refers to the man as being *demon-possessed.*

Luke 8:2 says Jesus traveled around with his 12 disciples but also some women who had been cured of evil spirits and diseases. One of them, Mary Magdalene, is said to have had seven demons come out of her.

Matthew 4:24 says that as news of Jesus spread over Syria he healed people from diseases, severe pain, seizures, paralysis, and demon possession. The same thing is said in 8:16 and 15:22.

Mark 1:32 gives the same accounts we find in Matthew but adds a piece of additional information. It says Jesus would not allow the demons to speak because they knew who he was. Mark 3:11 adds that whenever the impure spirits saw Jesus they fell down and shouted, "You are the Son of God!"(NCV).

Mark 7 provides us with an interesting story where Jesus casts out a demon from a girl who was not present at the scene. Her mother had begged him to drive the demon out. We are not told how the demon manifested itself.

Luke 4:33-35 says, *"In the synagogue, a man who had within him an evil spirit shouted in a loud voice, "Jesus of Nazareth! What do you want with us? Did you come to destroy us? I know who you are -- God's Holy One!" Jesus commanded the evil spirit, "Be quiet!*

Come out of the man!" The evil spirit threw the man down to the ground before all the people and then left the man without hurting him" (NCV).

Mark 9:17 tells the story of a man whose son was robbed of speech and whenever this spirit seized him it threw him to the ground. He foamed at the mouth, gritted his teeth, and became rigid. When Jesus commanded the spirit to come out it shrieked and convulsed violently and came out. Then the boy looked like he had died but Jesus took him by the hand and lifted him to his feet. The disciples who had tried to cast the demon out but were unsuccessful asked Jesus why they could not drive it out. Jesus simply replied, *"That kind of spirit can only be forced out by prayer"* (NCV).

Mark 5 gives what I consider to be the most interesting account of exorcism. A man was living among the tombs and nobody could bind him. Several times people had bound him with chains on his hands and feet but he always broke loose. He had supernatural strength. He spent his days and nights cutting himself with stones and would cry out loud. When he saw Jesus he ran and fell to his knees in front of him and said, *"What do you want with me, Jesus, Son of the Most High God? I command you in God's name not to torture me!"* Jesus replied by telling the unclean spirit to come out of the man and then asked the man what his name was. The man replied, *"My name is Legion, because we are many spirits"* (NCV). He then begged Jesus not to send them out of the area. About that time a large herd of pigs was grazing on a nearby hillside and the demons begged Jesus to send them to the pigs. Jesus gave his approval and the impure spirits came out of the man and went into the pigs. 2,000 pigs rushed down the steep bank and into the lake where they drowned. It must have scared the pig herders to death so they ran to town to tell everybody what happened. When people came out to see what happened they found the formerly possessed man sitting there in his right mind. It apparently freaked them out so they asked Jesus to leave the area.

In Acts 16 we hear the story of a fortune teller who pestered Paul for several days. He seems to have had enough of her nonsense so he turned around and said, *"By the power of Jesus Christ I command you to come out of her!"* (NCV). The spirit left her.

I am a rational person and not afraid to challenge some traditional views. Therefore, I will say what I believe a lot of people are thinking. Some of the conditions referred to as *demons* or *evil spirits* in the Bible sound an awful lot like modern medical and mental health conditions. We might attribute these *possessions* to things like epilepsy, deafness, paralysis, and muteness. I would remind you that the gospels and Acts were written in the first century – long before the field of psychology and psychiatry were developed as we know them today. The writers were not so much trying to show the cause of the condition as they were trying to show that Jesus was healing people. There seems to have been an idea at that time that if you could not understand something it must come from an evil spirit. There also seems to have been an idea that illness was the result of sin. Therefore, it must have a spiritual cause. Today, we have a better understanding of what causes things like epilepsy, paralysis, and mental illness. Back then they may not have. They basically threw all the mysteries into the basket of unclean spirits, demons, or evil. This should not make us uncomfortable or lose confidence in the scripture. I have no problem, for example, saying that the boy in Mark 9:7 was epileptic. I have witnessed an epileptic seizure and I would describe it exactly as the Bible describes what happened to this boy. The fact that the boy often fell to the ground is easy to understand and if I had been the boy's father at that time in history I would have assumed the evil spirit was trying to kill him too. It does not negate the fact that Jesus healed the people. That was the message the writers were trying to convey. There is no evidence they wanted to make any of these incidents mysterious.

For the sake of this study, we are going to assume it is possible that a few of the cases of exorcism described in the New Testament should be classified purely as miraculous healings. However, that does not explain all of them.

If we take into account the things the Bible says about demon possession and add to it our contemporary experience I think there are some key signals that tell us when something is demonic versus medical or mental.

1. Supernatural physical strength should be our first clue. The man living among the tombs reportedly broke himself free of iron chains and nobody could contain him. To my knowledge, there are no mental or physical health conditions that cause a person to have supernatural strength. Some might argue certain drugs make you strong but in reality, they are only serving to release your full strength. I have not heard any stories of meth addicts breaking out of iron chains. One of the most common things people who have witnessed exorcisms report is supernatural strength in the victim. They will toss objects and people around like ragdolls.

2. The ability to manipulate material objects via mental control. This would include the ability to levitate. It might also include the ability to inflict harm on others via mental will – in other words, they can hurt you without ever touching you. No mental or physical diagnosis can explain that ability. Of course, we have to be careful here because some illusionists are very proficient in making it appear they have this ability.

3. Some people have reported that demon-possessed individuals have very distinctive odors that alone can send chills up your spine. This would not seem to be explainable by natural causes.

4. Others have reported that demon-possessed individuals have the ability to do things they should not be able to do, like reading your mind and telling you your thoughts.

5. Lastly, it seems that the demons have the ability to speak with their own voice – not always the voice of the person they inhabit. I am told that this can be very frightening to the observer.

As I mentioned I have never been a part of an exorcism. However, my father-in-law has been in several. He does not go looking for them and he is not one of those people who thinks the devil is behind every bush. However, as a well-known pastor, he often gets requests for help. One of the most disturbing experiences of my life occurred on a weekday morning when I just happened to be visiting my in-law's house. I knew my father-in-law was in an office down the hall from where I was. I thought he was doing some typical pastoral counseling but all of a sudden I heard the most terrifying guttural scream that I have ever heard in my life. To this day it sends chills up my spine to remember that scream. I instinctively ducked for cover thinking a curse had been placed on the whole building. I later learned that the scream came from a demon-possessed woman.

Finally, we have to address the matter of Dissociative Identity Disorder (formerly known as Multiple Personality Disorder). This is a disorder in which a person develops two or more personalities as a means of dealing with trauma - usually childhood trauma. The disorder can manifest itself very similarly to demon possession. Individuals can switch personalities, and even though those personalities are in the same body they can be completely unknown to one another. While psychology has developed a theory as to why and how this happens, one could argue that it is still a form of demonic possession. To say that it is 100% not demon possession is like a detective saying he has solved a crime solely because he has established a motive. That alone does not prove anything.

I have never knowingly dealt with anyone with the DID diagnosis so I cannot give an educated opinion. However, it is my feeling that DID and demonic possession are not necessarily mutually exclusive. In other words, a demon-possessed person could accurately be diagnosed with DID and a person with an accurate DID diagnosis could actually be demon possessed.

I would now like to provide some practical advice if you should feel that your child is demon-possessed.

1. Use the guideline I gave above to try to distinguish between medical and mental health conditions versus demon possession.

2. Before you jump to any conclusions, study the matter as much as you can. I have only scratched the surface here. I'm sure there is plenty of information out there.

3. Be careful who you listen to too. There are a lot of crazy people out there who love conspiracy theories and mysterious matters of life. Try to learn from someone who is level-headed.

4. Talk and pray with your pastor or a spiritual mentor. However, realize that this subject matter is something that most pastors have limited experience with.

5. Do a lot of praying. My father-in-law usually does a lot of fasting before he confronts a demonic situation.

DEMONIC OPPRESSION

Now that we have dealt with the matter of demon possession, let us shift to the matter of demonic oppression. This is something you as a VP are more likely to encounter.

I would define demonic oppression as being a cousin to demonic possession. It is not as dramatic but is still mysterious to me. When a person is demonically oppressed they are not likely to exhibit supernatural tendencies but they do seem to be bound and controlled by something beyond what psychology can explain.

In thirty-two years I probably worked with over 1500 young men who had severe behavioral problems. There were only two that I recall who had what I would classify as demonic oppression. Let me be clear, there were numerous kids who were oppressed. They had been so abused and hurt that there seemed to be a cloud hanging over them all the time. However, these two demonstrated something beyond that.

The first was an eleven-year-old boy who had been severely abused in every way imaginable. In addition to several suicide attempts, he seemed to have an air about him that made people feel very strangely uncomfortable. To this day my wife still says her skin crawled every time she was in his presence. She said it just felt like the air around him was thicker than it was in the rest of the room. Ironically, I probably loved this boy as much or more than any kid I ever worked with. Don't get me wrong, he was a handful and was in constant trouble, but God gave me an unexplainable love for him that lasts to this day. However, he creeped out a lot of other people

– particularly women. It was reported to me through the grapevine that an adult from his elementary school had him put on her church's prayer list as a *demon-possessed boy.*

The other boy was as nice of a kid as you would ever want to meet and he tried his best to make something of himself. I really liked the kid but I always felt that he was battling forces beyond his control. As an adult, he still battles his demons and will tell you that they have tried to kill him for years now. Somehow God keeps sparing his life in miraculous ways. It still breaks my heart, but after his most recent suicide attempt, he no longer has the mental faculties to reason properly. There is little I can do. In analyzing these boys I find two common threads:

1. As a person who is not very touchy-feely, I am rather analytical and not prone to superstition. However, with these two boys, there was just something I could not grasp. All I can say is that there was an intuitive feeling I had, and they were dealing with powers beyond the norm. I recall one evening when the younger boy had done something he was not supposed to do. I went into his room with the intention of administering a consequence for his behavior but as I approached him, an overwhelming sense of sadness and compassion came over me. That was the one and only time in my thirty-two-year career that I knelt with a boy and prayed that he would be released from whatever spiritual bondage he was under. Of course, I did not say out loud that I was referring to demonic bondage but in my heart that is exactly what I was saying.

2. Each of these two boys had a mother who was heavily involved in the occult. One of the mothers was a practicing witch. The other practiced some form of mystical naturalism combined with what seemed to me to be new-age teachings.

Demonic oppression can enter via lots of doors. Obviously, it can enter via practicing occult activities like witchcraft but can also gain access through things that most people today don't take seriously; tarot cards, Ouija boards, fortune tellers, and astrology. I can tell you that most kids today think nothing of "playing" with these items. The world of video games and the internet also provides unlimited opportunities to get snatched into occultic activity.

I obviously do not condone the use of the kinds of things I describe in the previous paragraph, but I think we need to be careful with how we deal with them. For some kids in our care, these items and practices are a part of their (birth) family legacy. They are commonplace in their homes. When we carelessly remove these items and practices from their lives, it can be an assault on their birth families which results in rebellion and leads to more of a desire to practice these things. A better approach is to ask your child to explain how these things work and how involved their families are in them. Don't be judgmental. Rationally explain the dangers and kindly ask the kid to remove any occultic items and discontinue any occultic practices. Watch the matter closely.

I would now like to return to the very first case we discussed in this chapter – the case of Saul. I believe that of all the things we've looked at, this one may go the farthest in explaining why we often see some of the things we see in the children we care for.

The Bible says that God himself sent an evil spirit to torment Saul. The most important thing to remember is that God did this because Saul had become too proud and he had decided to do things his own way. Could it be that when the birth parents of our children become proud and arrogant they disregard the need for God? Could this then open the door for spiritual oppression? In my experience that may be the case. We have to attempt to stand in the gap between the children and those adults. This is done only through prayer.

SPIRITUAL OPPRESSION

I would like to discuss one final related thing. Through the years I noticed that some kids have what I call a *spiritual sensitivity* and some kids do not. It has nothing to do with behavior. When I say *spiritual sensitivity*, I mean they are at least open to the concept that there is a God who wants to have a relationship with them. Others have absolutely no interest. I do not wish to offer a theological explanation but I will say that our role is not to bring them to Christ. The Holy Spirit alone can do that. Our job is to show them Christ.

TEN PRACTICAL WAYS TO DEAL WITH DEMONIC POSSESSION AND OPPRESSION.

1. Know what's going on or has gone on in the birth family. If you discover occultic activity, put it on the radar for things to be watched.
2. If your child wants to dabble in occult activity, approach it from the perspective of educating them and showing that you want to protect them. Punitive approaches will likely backfire.
3. If your child seems to have no spiritual sensitivity don't give up. Only the Holy Spirit can bring that into his life.
4. Don't look for the devil behind every bush. There are a lot of psychiatric disorders that manifest themselves in ways that might seem to be demonic.
5. Always remember that exorcism of a demon is a very serious matter which must be dealt with after much prayer.
6. There is a difference between demon possession and demonic oppression. Know the difference (outlined above) and know that the approach to dealing with them may be different.
7. There is a difference between demonic oppression and spiritual insensitivity. Know the difference and understand that each manifests itself differently.
8. Children with severe attachment disorders can be perceived as being oppressed or possessed. They may or may not be. We can usually restrict the disorder to the psychological realm but we also have to realize that the same circumstances that led to them having attachment disorders can be spiritual in nature.

9. It is easy to confuse certain psychiatric disorders (schizophrenia or multiple personality disorder) with demon possession or oppression. However, to do so is a mistake. While many psychiatric disorders can be influenced by environmental factors and sinful actions, not all are. Schizophrenia, for example, is known to creep into the lives of perfectly normal people just like cancer does. There is no spiritual connection.

10. Demonic possession and oppression are real. Some mental health professionals would like to apply a scientific explanation instead of accepting the fact that the spiritual realm exists. These professionals are not in complete balance. By the same token, some spiritual people over-spiritualize everything and think every anomaly has a spiritual basis. Neither side is correct. We all have to realize that there is a spirit world but we also have to realize that not all psychiatric anomalies have a spiritual basis.

FOUNDATION **6**

- *TAKING CARE OF YOURSELF* -

I Love the Kids, The Adults are Driving me Crazy
Boundaries
When Caring Kills You
Living on the Edge
Does it Matter?

CHAPTER 26

- I LOVE THE KIDS, BUT THE ADULTS - ARE DRIVING ME CRAZY

Most of us who have fostered, adopted, or otherwise volunteered to raise our brother's child are doing so because we have a genuine desire to make the world a better place for hurting children. We are not afraid of the hard work, frustrations, or challenges of our calling. We just want to help children and we have given our lives to that cause. Therefore, we prepare well before we go out to save the world. Soon, however, we realize there is a major obstacle to overcome. That obstacle is what we call *adults*.

I have known hundreds of houseparents, foster parents, and others who will quickly tell you they love the kids but the adults are driving them crazy. Adults often get in our way. They create nonsense regulations and have dumb opinions. Adults seem to know how to do things better than we do and they are often full of unsolicited advice and regulation. Most of the good-hearted people I know who are sincere about helping children would function better if not for the adults and all their nonsense. Nevertheless, adults are here to stay and we have to learn to live with them.

In this chapter, I hope to define the categories of these troublesome adults and offer practical advice on getting along with and understanding them. I also want to offer some advice to supervisors and administrators. You can and may already be a major source of frustration for the VPs in your world. It does not have to be that way. Finally, I will give some tips on protecting your most valuable asset – your reputation -and provide some Biblical guidance for dealing with conflict.

ADULTS IN THE WORLD OF A VP

1. OUR OWN FAMILY MEMBERS

Jesus made some rather strong statements about the place of families in relation to following Christ. (Matthew 8:18-22, Matthew 10:21-22, 35-39). In Luke 14:26 he says, "If anyone comes to me but loves his father, mother, wife, children, brothers, or sisters - or even life- more than me, he cannot be my follower."(NCV) If you are one of those people who interpret all scripture literally, you might have a problem here. After all, Jesus spent most of his life with his family and even made arrangements for John to take care of his mother while he was gone. It does not appear that he hated his family. I believe Jesus makes these statements to acknowledge that when we follow him it very well may cause some family strife and we may even have to choose one over the other. The same can be applied any time a person enters a ministry. That ministry may have to take priority over his/her parents, siblings, etc. at least for a time and especially if they reject your calling.

When I decided to open a boys ranch I'm pretty sure my family thought I was crazy. Although they never said so, they must have had private conversations that went something like this, "Well, you know how he is. He's stubborn as a mule. I don't think he knows what he's doing but there is no need to try to stop him." I was very blessed to have a very supportive family. Even my extended family - aunts, uncles, cousins, grandparents, and in-laws - have always been very supportive. They have given their time, money, physical labor, and every other means of support. They have also welcomed my children into their homes and treated them as their own.

A funny thing happened the first time I brought my black child to celebrate Christmas at my PawPaw's house. Back in those days, it was a little unusual, but my PawPaw told me if any family members had a problem they would just have to get over it. Even though PawPaw had lived in Birmingham, Alabama, through the civil rights unrest of the 60s and there had probably not been a black person in his neighborhood for decades, he still supported me and loved my little black boy.

You may not be as fortunate as I was. If you plan to adopt or foster, it is best to get your family on board ahead of time. If they do not support your plans, you may very well have to make a choice between family or children. Sometimes you cannot have both. I have known people who had to forsake their family relationships in order to fulfill their call to help hurting children. It is best to know where everyone stands ahead of time so you can count the costs. Even if you have a supportive family, everyone needs to understand that your time and energy will be limited. It is great when adoptions take place and all the family celebrates together, but we should accept the fact that life has its honeymoons and in a matter of time, things can, and sometimes do, go bad.

Keep in mind, too, that families can be very opinionated. They will want to tell you how to raise your child. Listen and learn, but in the end, know you are the person who knows your child best and will be making the final decisions.

In situations when you are literally raising your brother's child, understand that conflict is almost inevitable. If that child's parents are deceased there will be family members who see it as their calling to be sure you are treating the child well. If the child's parents are still alive don't be surprised when conflict arises. Don't take it personally. Always advocate for the child and don't be afraid to alienate family members in the process. Sometimes we can be too nice to relatives who are not treating their children properly.

2. BIRTH FAMILIES OF OUR CHILDREN

We dealt with this in another chapter, but it is worth repeating.

In many cases when you adopt, foster, or otherwise care for someone else's child, you will know the birth parents or at least know something about them. It can be very easy to get angry with these people for being irresponsible, lazy, or abusive. I always tried to remember three things about birth parents. First, I don't know what the circumstances of their life may have been. They may have been abused or lacked the benefit of having good parenting role models. Secondly, when drugs/alcohol are involved, a person is transformed into something he/she is not created to be. (Yes – they are responsible for their drinking habit). I have worked with parents who were wonderful people until they consumed their chemicals. Thirdly, they are still the child's birth family and the child needs me to love them. As stated in the chapter on families, we have to understand the mysterious dynamic between birth parents and birth children.

Nevertheless, birth parents still need to be held accountable (unless in an adoption scenario in which they are out of the picture). When it comes to advocating for our children, it is ok to be very assertive with birth parents. I once had a birth mother and father tell their two little boys they would visit them at the ranch on Christmas Day. The boys were very excited and could not wait to see them. When the parents failed to show, my attitude quickly changed. My days of being *Mr. Nice Guy* were over. These parents were being self-centered and lazy and their boys were deeply hurt. I did talk to them about the importance of being dependable even as I tried to understand their need for education. By the same token, they absolutely deserved it when I told them to get off their fat, lazy rear-ends and grow up. I do not regret one word of it.

3. SOCIAL WORKERS

In almost every scenario in which you are raising someone else's child, you are going to have to deal with social workers. Some will be great and some will be awful. If the social worker you are dealing with is energetic, competent, compassionate, and communicates well, consider yourself blessed. These people are truly a blessing to all. If you are not blessed with one of these types, I would still urge you to consider a few pieces of background information. First of all, almost all child welfare social workers begin with good motives. They genuinely want to help hurting children. Very few of them go into the field of social work expecting to make a lot of money or to have an easy job. Secondly, most of them thought they would spend their time doing things to make the lives of children better. In many settings, they discover that avoiding lawsuits and keeping good paper trails is their real job and helping children is secondary. Thirdly, they are often blamed for the shortcomings of others. For example, take notice the next time a child gets murdered. The press will typically focus more on the failure of government social workers than on the criminal who committed the crime. Finally, social workers have to deal with multiple difficult situations every day. They are prime targets for experiencing vicarious trauma. Burnout rates are understandably high. Sadly, there are a lot of social workers who know they need to change careers but are too invested. They have spent years getting degrees; they may not have other skills; they have financial obligations, and a career change can be traumatic, so they hang around too long.

While it is important to consider the challenges social workers face, we also have to understand that our children have to become more important than our sympathies. We have to advocate for our children. It may call for some uncomfortable confrontations and may result in broken adult relationships, but we still have to make advocacy our priority.

I have had many situations through the years in which I did not agree with a social worker. I, unfortunately, made a few enemies and was not always well-liked. I learned not to worry too much about it. You have to do what you have to do.

We had one situation in which a social worker was using her position of power to exact vengeance on a birth father who had called her competency into question. He was not the best father in the world, but he had done what was needed to bring his son back home. The social worker was carrying a grudge because the father hired a lawyer to expose some of her shortcomings. Instead of setting aside her legitimate dislike for the man, she decided to exercise her power over him by refusing to let his son return to his home. I was furious, so I requested a meeting. Several lawyers and department heads got involved, I made my case and the boy was returned to live with his father. My relationship with the social worker was dissolved but I feel confident I did the right thing. Children always have to take priority over friendships. There is no room for the *good ole boy* system when it comes to advocating for children.

4. CO-WORKERS

If you serve in a congregate care setting such as a children's home you will have co-workers in the form of other houseparents, social workers, administrators, counselors, and board members. These settings are notorious for creating conflict. It is only natural that this happens. If a husband and wife have disagreements over how to raise children, imagine how many more disagreements occur when you have dozens of adults having input. Do not assume that your co-workers are horrible people or that your organization is in shambles when conflict arises. I have never known a children's home that did not have a fair share of drama and hurt feelings. Don't take it personally. Chances are those people with whom you so often disagree might be your best friend if you did not share in the raising of children. You have to try to remove the personal element and realize that disagreements concerning best childcare practices are common.

Secondly, address disagreements in a kind manner. When children are involved, strong emotions can cause us to lose our kindness. When kindness is gone we tend to be unproductive. Ultimately, our children pay the price. When problems occur, always do your best to be kind.

Thirdly, stay in your lane. Know when a matter is your business and when it is not. Obviously, if a child is being hurt, it is everyone's business. However, many issues arise in which people simply need to keep their opinions to themselves. The fact that you do not agree with a co-worker's actions does not mean you have to confront them.

Finally, know when to confront. If a child is being hurt or his spirit is being crushed, use whatever chain of command is in place to protect that child. If you simply have a difference of opinion regarding the raising of a child for whom you are responsible, it may be time for a heart-to-heart talk with those co-workers. Such talks should occur without totally destroying their relationships. Feelings may be hurt, but usually, time will heal most wounds.

5. SUPERVISORS

It can be very frustrating to answer to a supervisor while trying to raise a child. I can assure you there will be times when you whisper under your breath, "If you're so smart why don't you raise this kid?" I was a supervisor for many years and I can assure you it is not a glamorous job. It is very difficult to correct or discipline adults who have given their lives to the work very few people are willing to do. However, supervisors can be your greatest advocates and supporters. A good supervisor can be more like a teammate than a coach. They may be the quarterback and call the plays, but they can also recognize their value is directly related to their teammates.

If incidents arise in which you suspect illegal or immoral activity with your supervisor, use your reporting procedures immediately – even if you do not have concrete proof. If you do not agree with your supervisor regarding an issue related to childrearing, there is a proper way to express it. Rather than "I don't agree with you," try "Can you help me better understand you?" In the end, there is a chain of authority ordained by God. People in authority have huge responsibilities. If you find yourself in the unfortunate situation of being under an unqualified or undeserving supervisor, you may need to decide if the organization is one you can continue to support. If you cannot respect and trust your supervisor it may be time for you to leave. Otherwise, show them the respect their position deserves, follow their instruction, and understand they will be held accountable for the results of the guidance you followed.

6. NEIGHBORS AND THE GENERAL PUBLIC

If you are confident you are doing what God has called you to

245

do there is no need to concern yourself with the opinions of neighbors and the general public. You can be sure there will be those who think they know a better way and from whom you will receive criticism. Listen for good ideas they may offer and be appreciative when they give encouragement, but otherwise don't pay too much attention. The fact of the matter is that you really will not have the time or energy to worry about other people's opinions. I had to learn this in order to keep my sanity. I hated not being liked. It used to bother me until I realized I was not called to be the homecoming queen nor should I concern myself with popularity contests.

7. THE IVORY TOWER EXPERTS

One of the most frustrating things you will deal with is government rules and regulations. Most of the time these are written by people living in *Ivory Towers* who have no idea about your daily life. It can be extremely frustrating and time-consuming to deal with their nonsense, but you have to remember this goes with the territory. My approach at the ranch was always this: keep the children first and most of the other stuff will fall into place. Do what you have to do to appease the authorities, but when it reaches the point you cannot provide for children because you are so consumed with meeting rules and regulations, it is probably time to quit.

8. CHILD SAVERS

There is a very small segment of the population who seem to believe it is their responsibility to hold others accountable. One time a lady in our town reported me to the child welfare authorities because she thought her son's friend, who lived at our ranch, was being mistreated. She based her opinion solely on the word of a very manipulative child who happened to be mad at me. When the child's social worker called me to do her investigation I suggested she let the boy go live with the lady who had made the report. That ended the investigation and nothing was ever said or done about it from that point forward. My point is we all knew the lady would not take the boy into her home. All she wanted to do was find fault with everybody else. These types rarely offer criticism constructively or in person. They are usually cowards who hide behind anonymity. They are a nuisance to society and need to be either ignored or put in their proper place. It is probably best to ignore them. Use your time more wisely.

PROTECTING YOUR REPUTATION

As a VP you will have your share of critics. You should not worry too much about them. However, being a VP can also put you in vulnerable situations in which your reputation has to be defended. Fortunately, I never had a serious accusation of child abuse made against me. One time I was questioned because a kid had a pet lizard in the house (against health department regulations).

However, I did have a contingency in place to protect against false accusations. I won't go into detail, but I can tell you I would have become extremely aggressive and proactive to protect my reputation. We should defend ourselves against damaging falsehoods.

We did have one instance in which a grandmother accused me of taking advantage of her grandson by selling him an overpriced truck. The story is worth telling. This grandmother had an adult son, an alcoholic, who lived with her along with her grandson. She refused to kick the adult son out of her house so the authorities removed her grandson and placed him at our ranch. The authorities then began withholding whatever welfare check the family had been getting and that money was collected in an account controlled by the welfare agency. When asked what should be done with the money, I suggested we buy the seventeen-year-old a truck, a lawn mower, and a weedeater so he could begin supporting himself. I had a car dealer license, so I found him a great deal on a truck and sold it to him at my cost. I didn't make any money off the deal, but I was wise enough to keep all the paperwork. When the grandmother realized all the welfare money was gone, she told the boy's probation officer I had stolen the boy's money and that I was making money selling overpriced vehicles to kids at the ranch. Instead of calling me personally, the probation officer aided in spreading her lies by suggesting she hire an attorney. Unbeknownst to the grandmother, the attorney she tried to hire was my close friend and he immediately called me. I wasted no time in calling the grandmother and the probation officer to discuss the matter directly. I made it clear that if the lie was repeated, I would take the proper legal path to make them wish they had never met me. I also sent the probation officer a copy of the paperwork. Nothing else was said, but if it had been, I would not have hesitated to file a civil suit against both parties. In fact, criminal charges would have seemed more appropriate. It should be a crime to steal the most valuable possession a man has - his reputation.

On another occasion, I terminated an employee from one of our thrift stores. In retaliation, she went to Facebook and posted a comment suggesting people should avoid shopping at our stores because I was using the money to fund my personal real estate investments. Clearly, that was a lie. Of course, I have true friends and one of them took a screenshot and sent it to me. I immediately sent an email to the former employee giving her twenty minutes to remove the post or face dire consequences. The post was immediately removed but had it not been I would have defended myself publicly and taken legal action against her.

Proverbs 22:1 says, *"Being respected is more important than having great riches. To be well thought of is better than silver or gold"* (NCV). If lies are told about you, you have a right and duty to confront the person who is telling them. Jesus' statement about turning the other cheek does not mean we should accept another's abuse. I challenge you to read Matthew 23:13-17. It seems Jesus got in some people's faces and spoke rather directly. We might all need to follow that example.

TEN PRACTICAL TIPS FOR DEALING WITH ADULTS.

1. Jesus was not always gentle with his interactions. When it came to dealing with the Pharisees he was rather direct. He called them *blind fools* (Matthew 23:17, NCV). Notice that he reserves this sort of rhetoric for people who neglected matters such as justice. When children are not being treated with justice we have to speak up and sometimes have to be very assertive in our advocacy for them.

2. Deal with conflict quickly. There were two reasons I called the grandmother and the probation officer immediately. First, I did not want to give them any more time to spread false rumors. Secondly, I did not want my anger to defile me. The more time I thought about the situation the angrier I would have become. In the Sermon on the Mount Jesus says if we remember that our brother has something against us we should leave worship service and go deal with it. Sounds like he meant we should do it with urgency!

3. Try to settle things one on one. In Matthew 18:15-17 Jesus says, *"If your fellow believer sins against you, go and tell him in private what he did wrong. If he listens to you, you have helped that person to be your brother or sister again"* (NCV). In most situations, it is best to try to handle things one on one. Conflicts do not need to be broadcast any more than necessary. However, just because Jesus gave this instruction does not mean he intended it to be a doctrinal issue and the only way to address conflict. Jesus apparently did not address the Pharisees on a one-to-one basis. There is a time to address things openly but most of the time it is better to begin with one-on-one conversations. Remember that Jesus is specifically referring to a situation in which someone has sinned against you – not simply one in which a disagreement has occurred.

4. Know when to have a witness. Things can get misunderstood very quickly. In Matthew 18 Jesus does address the need for a witness when a private conversation fails. When dealing with conflict it is sometimes good to have a third party. Know when those times are.

5. Keep a good record. I cannot tell you how many times I have seen a misunderstanding get settled by simply presenting a written record of an incident. Written records can also guard against false accusations. When the grandmother, who accused me of taking advantage of boys by selling junk cars, realized I had paperwork regarding every penny spent, she was embarrassed by her accusation and my reputation was protected.

6. Be gentle. Galatians 6:2 instructs those who are spiritual to restore those caught in transgressions with gentleness. I have found that gentleness is a great de-escalator and gives offending parties a chance to admit their fault and make things right. Failure to be gentle can put people on the defensive.

7. Make sure your story is correct. At the time I called the probation officer I was not sure the grandmother had told me the whole story. Therefore, when I called the probation officer I was non-offensive, explained what I had heard, and asked for his side of the story before I concluded what had happened. It is best to assume a misunderstanding and let the offender talk. If they have done wrong, they will likely backtrack and try to defend themselves.

8. Focus on the issue, not the person. Working with children can present issues that can potentially tear us apart. Whether it is with a co-worker, social worker, or someone else, it is wise to begin a conversation with the acknowledgment that you value your relationship with that person. You can then legitimately say you do not want the issue to come between you. If you honestly mean this, a mature person will respond with a spirit of cooperation instead of becoming defensive.

9. Try to see the world through the other person's eyes. They have a different background and set of experiences that have influenced their perception and ideas. You might better understand their position if you first understand those influencers.

10. Listen and think about what the other person is saying. You may decide they have a valid point.

CHAPTER 27

- *BOUNDARIES* -

It was 4:30 in the morning when I heard a frantic banging on the front door of my house. Startled, I ran to the door expecting firemen to tell me the house was on fire. What I saw when I opened the door was more startling than any fireman I could have imagined. There stood a badly beaten fifteen-year-old boy. He had a huge cut above his eye and his nose appeared to be broken. Blood was everywhere. His face was bloody. His clothes were bloody. His hands were bloody. I stood there in shock, needing a minute to allow my heart rate to slow down before I could assess the situation.

Eagle Rock was located on a twenty-three-acre tract of land in a rural area. In the early days, my wife and I lived in a large house with the boys. Eventually, we built a separate residence and moved houseparents into the houses with the boys. Our private house was just a few hundred feet from where the boys lived. On this particular morning, a group of boys had jumped another boy. Houseparents had tried to stop the fight but were too late. By the time they intervened, this poor kid was badly beaten and felt his only escape was to run next door to my house. Needless to say, my day was ruined. After de-escalating the immediate situation, taking care of some medical needs, and explaining the situation to my wife, I was left to carry on with the rest of the day as if it were just another day. I didn't think much of it at the time, but in retrospect, I realize that incidents such as this one took their toll on me emotionally. I eventually had to declare no one was allowed to come to my private residence.

As the years rolled on we not only had a greater number of boys who lived at the ranch, but former residents frequently returned to our house for a visit, often unannounced. I was usually glad to see them and enjoyed their visits, but sometimes it was unnerving. One young man came in the middle of the night and slept in his truck in my driveway. At 7:00 AM he knocked on the door. I let him in but soon realized he was having a psychotic episode. We spent most of the day together, but when he left my house he drove a few miles away and crashed his car in an attempt to kill himself.

We had one former resident spend nine months in prison. The day he was released, using the bus ticket provided by the prison, he found his way to my home. As I had done with numerous other boys, I prepared a place for him to stay at my house. Later that evening, he was riding to church with me when I was stopped by the police due to a blown headlight on my car. When the police saw the young man they recognized him and within minutes we were surrounded by multiple police cars. He had only been out of prison for nine hours and, unknown to me, already had a warrant for his arrest. He was taken into custody and placed in jail. God was protecting me. A few months later he murdered his girlfriend.

In the months just prior to my retirement another of our former residents stopped by our house. This young man had been gone from the ranch for several years. He struggled with alcohol addiction and since he had left the ranch we had picked him up off the streets on several occasions. Sadly, he was ashamed to tell me he was homeless again. Therefore, he pitched a tent behind a building in my backyard and secretly lived there for several weeks. I noticed the tent and assumed it was him but never actually saw him during the day. Eventually, the tent blew away and I figured he had moved on. I was correct. He had died at a hospital.

Unfortunately, I did not have very good boundaries. I cannot honestly say I have regrets. It was part of my calling. I believe sometimes when God calls you to do something you may have to forfeit your boundaries. However, when I retired I knew I could not maintain living the rest of my life under those circumstances. Eagle Rock's Board of Directors bought me a nice house in a secluded area far from the ranch. It is a boundary I felt I had to establish to keep from losing my mind. I jokingly tell people I have joined the witness protection program.

In another chapter, I share more information about our humble beginnings with the ranch. At one point, my wife, two babies, and I lived in a house with five boys. We had only one bathroom. My son and daughter were small, so the four of us shared a bedroom. There was only one door between our bedroom and the kitchen, so privacy was rare and it seemed like the boys were constantly knocking on our bedroom door. One day my wife had just managed to get the little ones to fall asleep and desperately needed a mental health break for herself. Of course, one of the boys knocked on the door, woke up the little ones, and asked a really dumb question. My wife lost it! She had a meltdown and ran to the bathroom – the only place she had any privacy. She sat on the toilet, buried her head in a pillow, and began to scream. We laugh about it today but it was no laughing matter at the time.

We did such a poor job of establishing boundaries in the early days of our ministry that it took a toll on us. Our marriage suffered and we had to seek counseling on two different occasions. Our mental health suffered too. I became depressed to the degree that a doctor prescribed antidepressants for me, even though I never took them. The stress brought on by the lack of boundaries also affected our physical health. Both of us developed serious health issues and we considered closing the ranch. I do not know if it is possible to be in the type of ministry we were in without being stressed. I think it just goes with the territory sometimes. However, when depressed, sick, or dead, we are not worth much in terms of helping others. In the remainder of this chapter, I share some important ideas about boundaries, learned through experience and from personal mistakes.

BOUNDARIES FOR ADOPTIVE PARENTS

As any good parent will tell you, the minute you leave the hospital with your newborn baby your life is forever changed. You have brought a little human into the world and he or she is your total responsibility. You just gave up the rights to your personal space and time! Hopefully, you have some friends and family to give you a break but, otherwise, raising a child is a 24/7 undertaking.

It is no different when you adopt a child. The fact that you did not physically participate in the creation of this child does not excuse you from the responsibility of his/her care. Adopted children deserve the same attention, time, and commitment as birth children.

As with birth children, you need to set boundaries. Set aside time for your spouse and away from the kids. It may have to be late at night or you may need to find a babysitter, but you have to do it. Many couples become so consumed with their children that they forget their marriages. This is not a good idea. You spend approximately eighteen years raising a child. One day that child leaves and you may be left living with a stranger. To avoid this, you need to draw boundary lines around you and your spouse and dare anybody else to cross them.

With adopted children, there can be unique challenges in setting boundaries. Your first line of defense is to make sure you are in agreement before you adopt. This means you both have to be 100% sold on the idea. It might even be a good idea to put it in writing and keep the document in a secure place, just in case one of you decides adoption was not part of your plan to start with.

Regardless of what you have been told, adoption is like a box of chocolates – you never know what you are going to get. You will probably not know the extent or what kind of trauma your child has experienced or what behaviors might manifest as a result. These things can take a toll on your marriage and if you don't set boundaries the challenges can drive you apart.

Setting boundaries to protect your marriage can take many forms. It may take the form of a date night or a designated weekend away. It may mean you have predetermined signals and train the kids to know when you need personal time. For example, put a red flag on the bedroom door and tell them that flag means do not disturb unless the house is on fire.

Men need to understand that wives need time to talk and be heard. From experience, I know that even though my wife may seem to be asking for advice, frequently she really is not looking for me to advise her. She just needs me to listen. If men do not establish boundaries for their wives, there will be no time for listening. When I worked at the ranch, the boys were hungry for my attention and they would take all I would give. On hundreds of occasions I had to say, "Johnny, I need to get home and spend some time with Mrs. Diana. I would love to spend more time with you, but she wants me to spend some time with her also." They were always understanding when I used this approach.

A wife needs to understamd the feelings of her husband. We tend to think of men as being thoughtless brutes who don't have feelings. I recently listened to a TED talk by a female sex worker. She said most of the men who come to her just want to talk, be heard, not be nagged, and not be asked to do anything. Many wives either talk all of the time or devote themselves so much to their children that they neglect the emotional needs of their husbands. Women can become child-centered and forget to be husband-centered. Their husbands may then wrongfully seek that emotional connection elsewhere (in the form of other women). This sex worker explained that physical sex was only a six-minute bi-product of 54 minutes of giving a man her undivided attention.

BOUNDARIES FOR HOUSEPARENTS

Most congregate care settings are staffed by Houseparents. I hate to use the word *staffed* because it implies people are being hired to babysit. Houseparents should not be considered staff because their position is really more of a calling than a job. Whether they are full-time, part-time, or work shifts, they should see themselves as *parents* – not *staff*.

Houseparents face unique challenges. While they should seek to be as much like normal parents as possible, they still have to maintain boundaries. Some of these boundaries are physical. Houseparents need to have separate living quarters that are inaccessible to the children in their care. While this may seem to be a cold and sterile thing to do, it is necessary. The houses I designed at our ranch included separate areas for houseparents and their birth children to live where they had their own bedrooms and bathrooms and no other children were allowed – not even for brief visits. This was done for safety as well as mental health reasons. When I was a houseparent I found it necessary to slip away to my private quarters a few times a day for short mental health breaks. I just needed a moment of silence.

The same applies to the birth children of the houseparents. They need a place to get away as well. Actually, all the children need a place to escape from time to time.

As I stated in the opening paragraph, we did not always have that luxury. In our early days, we did what we had to but it was not healthy.

Houseparents also need time away from their duties. Most of the time they live in the house 24/7 so there is not any off-time. Unfortunately, off-time can seem to be more trouble than it's worth. There was one five-year span during which my wife and I only had six weekends off. It was just too hard to find people who would stay with our boys, and it seemed something bad happened every time we had a weekend away. On those weekends, we simply drove a few miles away, rented a hotel room, and slept for 48 hours. As I noted elsewhere, we burned out and nearly died from the stress. Live-in houseparents need plenty of guilt-free weekends off during which nobody bothers them. It will prolong their lives and make them much more effective.

SETTING BOUNDARIES AROUND YOUR BIRTH CHILDREN

I realize in many adoption situations the adopted child and the birth child are treated the same. That is the way it should be. However, what if you adopt an older child and you have biological children already in your home? Do you treat them differently? I think the answer depends on the situation. Obviously, they are going to be siblings for life, but you cannot afford to let the romance of the situation cause you to be blind. Sometimes adopted children have been sexually or otherwise abused and they may carry with them the effects of that abuse. They may not understand how normal sexual boundaries are supposed to look. The same could be said for a lot of other issues. You have just as much responsibility to protect your biological children as you do to love your adopted children. Set some boundaries regarding unsupervised time.

Carlton was a sixteen-year-old version of Mike Tyson. He had more muscles than any kid I have ever seen. The day I walked him into the high school, the principal called the football coach before he asked for the enrollment papers. Unfortunately, Carlton had anger issues. He would fight a fence post if he thought it had said something about his mother. This very strong and very aggressive boy would be moving into my house where I had two small children – my biological son and daughter. After reading Carlton's social summary and psychological evaluation, I knew I had to set some boundaries. That is when I did something people still laugh about twenty years later. I wrote a contract with Carlton and his Social Worker. The contract clearly stated that if Carlton touched one of my children I reserved the right to physically attack him. The contract further stated that I would serve any jail time necessary and that I would close the ranch after having served my time. Henceforth, my attack was going to be brutal - I was going to make it worth the trouble. I still cannot believe I actually got everyone to sign off on that contract. I loved Carlton and we had a good relationship but he knew I meant business. The fact of the matter is that I had already planned what I would do if he hurt one of my kids. He was a strong boy but I think I could have taken him. Fortunately, Carlton loved my children and they loved him back. He was a gentle giant when it came to babies. You must draw boundaries around your biological children and you must protect them. We lived for twenty-six years at the ranch and not one time during those years was one of my children ever left alone with one of the boys. I trusted many of the boys and would not have expected them to harm my kids in any way, but I was not about to take any chances.

SETTING BOUNDARIES WITH YOUR EXTENDED FAMILY

Again, if you adopt a child into your family, he/she becomes a part of your extended family, too. Before the adoption, there should be an understanding with your extended family (parents, siblings, grandparents, cousins, etc) regarding the adoption. If anyone is not on board with your plans, you probably need to go ahead and exclude them from being a part of normal family activities like holiday celebrations, birthday parties, and family vacations. Hopefully, everyone will be as excited as you are about the adoption. Unfortunately, however, adopted children can come with some curious behaviors which may concern family members. It may be necessary to set up physical boundaries and have friendly but firm discussions with your child. For example, children don't snoop thru bedrooms when they go to the homes of relatives. That is just one of many examples in which adopted children who are not received as infants may need some friendly guidance. This will keep you and your child on good terms with the family.

As for Houseparents, it is common that the children in your care will become acquainted with your extended family. This can be a good thing. My parents, grandparents, and in-laws were always very welcoming to the boys from the ranch. I always had boys with me when we visited for holidays and special occasions. I will forever be grateful that I have such a hospitable family. However, I feel compelled to share one unfortunate experience with you. It is food for thought: When my wife and I were Houseparents we often visited with our boys in the homes of our parents. Sometimes it was the only way we could see our parents. Several years after we had started the ranch I received an unfortunate phone call from my mother late one night. One of the former residents of the ranch, who was now a grown man, had shown up at my parent's house in the middle of the night. He was knocking on her door and asking to come inside. I knew he was not mentally stable so I instructed

Mom to delay him and not let him inside. I rushed to my parents' house in just enough time to keep him from entering. I found him a place to stay for the night and helped him the next day. Several years later he showed up at someone else's house (not related to me) and forced himself inside where he killed them. From that day forward I never took a child to my parent's house. Every situation is different and each person will have to decide for themselves what boundary to set, but that is my story.

SETTING BOUNDARIES WITH FOSTER CHILDREN

If you are a foster parent you can apply the principles noted above. I have also added some practical tips in the Ten Practical Things to Do With Boundaries.

SETTING BOUNDARIES WITH YOUR "BROTHERS CHILD"

When you are literally raising your brother's child or are otherwise raising a child who is not adopted nor in foster care, you will face some unique challenges. Sometimes these children will not use good judgment and will cross boundaries. This can be very upsetting and frustrating. It can even cause you to look forward to the day they leave your house. You can prevent a lot of frustration by being proactive in setting boundaries.

JESUS LOVED BOUNDARIES

I find it interesting that Jesus himself saw the value of setting boundaries. I suppose he, being fully human, knew that if he was going to make it through the three years of his ministry on earth he needed some things to protect himself. Therefore, He set some boundaries. Luke 5:16 indicates Jesus withdrew to lonely places quite often. Have you ever wondered why he went to lonely places? Maybe it was because he was feeling the world caving in on his shoulders. As a VP, you will certainly experience this sometimes. You will be hit by pressures from all directions and feel as if the weight of the world is on your shoulders. If you don't set boundaries you might collapse. Just as Jesus went to lonely places to pray, you will need to do the same thing. Just as he had to get away from the demands of the people, you will have to build boundaries to keep the people in your life from crushing you. One day Jesus had so many people crowding around him that he got in a boat and withdrew to a solitary place (Matthew 14:13). Even the Savior of the world had to set up boundaries to keep his sanity. How much more important it is for you to do the same?

TEN PRACTICAL THINGS TO DO WITH BOUNDARIES.

1. When a child arrives at your home it may be helpful for you to give him/her a full tour of the home and surroundings. This is a good time to establish physical boundaries in a non-threatening, non-personal way. As an added benefit, this can help calm children who have been traumatized. Oftentimes, these children are on high alert for self-preservation. Knowing their surroundings can be calming to them.

2. When you take a child into your home, explain your personal boundaries early on. They will be less likely to take things personally this way. For example, you may explain it this way: "Johnny, on Friday nights mom and dad go out to dinner without the kids. This is our time together. It's not that we don't want you to be with us. Married people are funny sometimes. One day you will understand."

3. If you are a houseparent and have to leave the kids with substitute caretakers, leave plenty of written instructions and set a pre-determined, limited time for a daily phone call. Let it be understood ahead of time that you have boundaries related to phone calls.

4. Know what the boundaries are at specific homes. For example, if a Christmas party is about to be held at a friend's home,

simply call ahead and ask if there are places they will not allow children to go in their homes. With that information, have a brief, clear discussion with your child ahead of time to establish boundaries and avoid having to deal with them being out of bounds later.

5. Know what the boundaries will be with extended family. Will you bring children to their homes? Will children be accepted at all family functions? Plan accordingly.

6. Set boundaries for your personal time with your birth children. This may mean you have to physically get away from home. You do not have to make a public issue of the matter, just do it.

7. If in foster care or congregate care, always set clear boundaries for your birth children. It is not always necessary to be open about boundaries. You don't want to make your non-birth children feel rejected, but they need to know the boundaries. For example, I never left my birth children alone with the other boys at our ranch.

8. Establish some signals to let your kids know when you need time alone. I heard of one mother of a large family who taught her kids that when she laid her head on the kitchen table she was not to be bothered unless the house was on fire. The kids all knew the signal and knew the importance of that boundary.

9. Carve out some personal time in a lonely place for prayer just like Jesus did. You will probably be so tired that you will fall asleep like the disciples, but at least you will regain some of your sanity.

10. Buy a camper or a tent. The best family investment I ever made was a camper. In terms of dollars, it was the most rapidly depreciating item I could have bought, but in terms of maintaining my family, it was the best thing we ever did. As soon as our little ranch was strong enough to hire some help, I made it a point to go camping with my biological family at least four times per year. That is one thing I do not regret.

- WHEN CARING KILLS YOU -

Being a VP can take a mental, physical, and spiritual toll on you. It is a sad fact that many of us who start out with positive attitudes and intentions end up being depressed, cynical, and apathetic about the very things that used to mean so much to us.

In this chapter, I will describe my personal journey and also share what the experts are now saying about burnout, vicarious trauma, and compassion fatigue. You may be an adoptive parent who has a child with attachment issues that manifest in extreme negative behaviors. You may be a foster parent who sees the effects of abuse on child after child after child. You may literally be raising your brother's child due to a death in the family, abuse, or the chemical dependency of relatives. No matter what your situation, the immense challenges and high-stress levels can take you down a road you never thought you would travel, and cause you to become a person you never thought you would be.

Before I share my personal story of how I almost lost my mind, allow me to share three extenuating circumstances that may have made my story unique. I do not want to falsely alarm anyone into thinking everyone will experience what I did.

1. I specialized in working with children and teenagers who already had lots of problems. That was my mission and I stuck to it. I do not want to embarrass any of the boys who lived in our home. In fact, we had three different programs. One was for older youth who were fairly responsible but just needed some guidance before getting out on their own. Another was for boys who, through no fault of their own, became homeless. They were awesome kids whom I admire. These were not troublemakers. The third program, however, was for boys who nobody else would take. They had severe behavior problems and many times came to us from psychiatric hospitals and detention centers. The third group was the group with which I personally invested most of my time.

2. I was very active in the day-to-day life of our boys. In fact, for many years I lived in the house with them. I was the founder/administrator, but for long stretches of time was also the parent. We always had difficulty finding anyone to work directly with those kids, so I had to fill that role quite often. After the initial five years during which my wife and I were live-in Houseparents, there also were many spans of time in which we had to step back into that role temporarily. There was one stretch of nine months when I lived in a house with nine teenage boys on a 24/7 basis. My wife and two small children lived next door in another house. As late as 20 years into my career, my family had to move into a house to serve as houseparents.

3. We had a no expulsion policy. In a lot of foster homes, children's homes, ranches, and even in some adoption situations, there is an option to opt-out if a child gets to be too much trouble. At our ranch, we never kicked anybody out. If a boy became disruptive he had three choices: he could learn to live with us, he could run away, or he could get himself locked up in an institution. Life would definitely have been much easier if we had not had the no-expulsion policy.

Before getting to my story, I wish to acknowledge that a lot of people face much more difficult situations than I did. I visited one children's home in Guatemala where the founder/director lived in the middle of a crowded complex where 300 children resided. Not only did this couple see thousands of horrible cases of abuse each year, but they also had no privacy and very little help. I was deeply humbled and wondered how they managed to survive. In a Mexican orphanage, I witnessed houseparents living full time in a building where 16 children shared a room and there was limited electricity or running water. I certainly have no room to complain but I hope, nevertheless, that my story will be helpful.

I had a very happy childhood and most people would tell you I was a well-adjusted and positive person. I think, for the most part, I was sensitive and kind to others. Even in high school, where I was fairly well-liked and able to hang out with the in-crowd, I still was drawn to the kids who I could see were hurting. For example, we had a boy in our class who was severely handicapped and had few friends. I was the guy who took him for rides in my car after school, just so he could feel like a real person instead of a school freak. I was that kind of kid. As a college student, I started working with troubled boys and found I had great compassion, understanding, and patience. My compassion drove me, at age twenty-seven, to open a home for troubled boys. I sincerely loved those guys and poured out my heart and soul, as well as all my money, to give them a place to call home. Up to that point in my life, anxiety, depression, and hopelessness were foreign concepts to me. Twenty-six years later when I retired I was a very different person and not in a good way.

At the time of this writing, I have been retired and away from social services for almost two years. As my mind and emotions are now recovering, I am able to see more clearly what happened to me during all of those years working with troubled kids.

Initially, within a couple of years of opening our ranch, both my wife and I developed some rather serious health problems that were not common for people our age. Mine were respiratory and hers were digestive. Both of our doctors warned us that we were under too much stress. We knew we needed to hire some help, and

God blessed us with the funds to do so. Otherwise, we would not have survived.

Somewhere along the way, probably seven or eight years into my career, I began to experience mild depression. I attributed it to seasonal depression because it always seemed worse in the winter. I later discovered it was stress related and was magnified by a vitamin D deficiency. The lack of sunlight in the winter months made the vitamin deficiency worse.

About ten years into my career I began to have bizarre dreams on a regular basis. I had always had difficulty sleeping, but these dreams were something new to me. In the dreams, I would become so violent that I actually screamed and hit things while asleep. I constantly woke my wife who would have to shake me and yell at me to get me awake. It became such a problem that I pulled all the slats loose on the headboard of my bed and sometimes would injure my hands and wrist. My wife said I would scream in a guttural sounding voice that reminded her of demons. I eventually went to a sleep lab for evaluation. They said I definitely had some bizarre brain waves while sleeping. At one point they told me it could be a precursor to Parkinson's Disease, but no one seemed to have any idea what to do about it. These dreams went on for many years and it has only been recently that we have discovered a pattern. In all of my dreams, I was fighting bad guys. Having the dream was bad enough, but the real problem was my physical activity during the dream. I actually punched things- I was not just dreaming. In most of my dreams, I got into fights and often wrestled, but I remember few details other than that. My family eventually decided the best thing they could do was learn to laugh at the situation, but it must have been difficult for my wife. Sometimes I even pushed her away when she tried to wake me. Looking back, I now wonder if those dreams were somehow connected to the responsibility I carried for the lives of so many boys who had been placed under my care. Or, it could have been related to the fact that I spent a lot of time fighting "bad guys" who had hurt the boys for whom I cared. I may never know, but perhaps I am not the only person who has experienced this and may be helped by my sharing. Since I have retired the nightmares have gone away.

Looking back, I now realize that I also developed a sense of heightened alertness and awareness of my surroundings. That may seem like a good thing but I know now that it took a toll on my emotions. One night, while on a camping trip with a group of boys, I awoke in the middle of the night with a sense of urgency that something was wrong. It was so urgent that I jumped out of my tent and slammed into a power pole, severing my earlobe. My sense was correct. I caught my three boys stealing cigarettes from a neighboring camper's site. A lot of houseparents have reported having a sixth sense that tells them when something is not right. It happens a lot during sleeping hours and there are countless stories of houseparents waking up in the middle of the night with a feeling that something is wrong. While this may seem like a good thing, when we consider the effect this has on our brains it is not good. When the brain is never at rest it can take a tremendous toll on a person.

I also noticed when I went on vacation with my family, it took me two or three days to settle down enough to enjoy the vacation. When we would return from vacation, I could physically feel the anxiety build about an hour from our ranch. I made it a habit to sneak back to my house after vacation so nobody would know I was home. My mind and body needed some buffer time.

For twenty-six years I slept with a pager or cell phone beside my bed just in case there was an emergency. It rang a lot. To this day I have an aversion to the sound of a cell phone ringing. It still sends shockwaves through me, so I keep the ringer turned off most of the time.

I recall at some point during my career feeling as if a lot of people disliked me very much. This feeling reached the point that I had to determine that I would not be affected either way. I learned to go about my business and tune people's opinions out. Of course, nobody said anything to my face, but I recall feeling like people were talking negatively behind my back. The fact of the matter is that some of what I was feeling was probably true. I realize that I created a few enemies by bringing those kids into neighborhoods and schools. A lot of people were not comfortable with that. However, in retrospect, I realize that my feelings of being disliked were probably exaggerated. I now know that this type of self-perception can be common in people who have experienced an overload of vicarious trauma.

Perhaps the most disturbing thing that happened to me occurred toward the end of my career. I noticed that I was becoming cynical about the boys I had been called to help. I caught myself privately referring to them as *stupid* or *idiotic*. Granted, sometimes they deserved that title, but it was out of character for me to feel that way or to express that feeling so carelessly. I also basically reached a point of giving up hope for some of the boys. This was totally out of character for me. I had always taken the strong stance that there is always hope, no matter how dire the situation is. I found myself increasingly saying things like, "Oh well, let the dumb kid suffer the consequences. We will probably have to bury him too." (I buried more than my fair share of young men who had lived with me. That also contributed to my depression.)

About eight years before I retired I became so overwhelmed with anxiety I wrote in my journal that I did not care whether I lived or died. I was not suicidal, but if God had taken my life at that time I would not have complained. I recall several days when I buried my head in between the cushions of a couch sofa in an attempt to escape the overwhelming anxiety I was feeling. Oddly, I was able to continue operating a ranch and everyone thought I was fine.

I had always accepted speaking engagements and enjoyed them, but toward the end of my career, I quit because I felt so overwhelmed and underqualified. The last one I gave resulted in a standing ovation, but inside I was booing myself. I hated it.

I asked my doctor to refer me to an endocrinologist to determine if I might have some sort of chemical imbalance or possibly a nutritional issue. He found nothing but prescribed an antidepressant. I refused to take it, but I was in a bad place emotionally.

The final signal that confirmed I was too far gone emotionally to do any more good occurred when my daughter was involved in a tragic car crash. She survived, but as a result, I had to move out of town to live near the trauma and rehab center for a couple of months. Fortunately, there was a wonderful person named Belinda Hiti who totally took over the ranch while I was gone. Belinda was already running the day-to-day operations by that time and had worked with me for 13 years. While I was preoccupied with my daughter, I had no choice other than to let Belinda totally take control of the ranch. I put it totally out of my mind, and frankly, I was so concerned for my daughter that thoughts of the ranch were far from my mind. Oddly, it was through this experience I understood just how much pressure I was under and how much it had affected me emotionally and physically. Shortly thereafter I announced my retirement.

In the months following my retirement, I began to experience things that surprised me. I went for a walk one day and, for no apparent reason, experienced a rush of happiness that I had not felt in several years. It was as if my brain had exploded with serotonin. I stopped and looked around. I saw trees that I had never noticed before and heard birds singing that I had never heard before. In the days to come, I caught myself staring at tall trees and admiring their strength. I had never noticed how tall trees really are. Just recently I went for a walk in a park where I saw ducks swimming. I had probably seen them hundreds of times but failed to pay attention to them. This time, I became entranced and sat for hours just watching the beauty of nature. I even forgot to go home for dinner.

While all of this may seem a bit odd, you can only imagine how I feel. I thought I was a well-adjusted individual but did not realize I had become somewhat dysfunctional. I share my story with fear that readers will think I am strange or dramatic, but in the end, I believe someone out there has experienced the same thing and needs to know they are not alone. I now believe I was suffering from burnout, but I also know it went even deeper.

As it turns out, a lot of people in the helping professions (including VPs) have experienced something that now has a name. We call it Vicarious Trauma or Compassion Fatigue. It is generally defined as follows:

> Compassion fatigue is a condition characterized by emotional and physical exhaustion leading to a diminished ability to

empathize or feel compassion for others, often described as the negative cost of caring. It is sometimes referred to as secondary traumatic stress (STS).

It occurs when we go too far in identifying with the traumas of people we help. We take on their traumas and experience them ourselves (vicariously).

Among the signs and symptoms are:
1. Hypervigilance. In my case, I was always on high alert. This manifested itself in my dreams as well as in many other areas of life.
2. Suspicion about people's motives and behaviors. As noted, I began to think people were talking about me. In defense, I developed an attitude of not caring what people thought at all.
3. Difficulty sleeping.
4. Anxiety. As stated, I literally buried my head between the cushions of a sofa in an attempt to escape the overwhelming anxiety I felt.
5. Numbness. People often said I had an uncanny ability to remain calm in a crisis. Part of this was due to personality and training but some of it was from numbness. I reached the point of being utterly numb to a crisis. When we lost a child just before I retired, I was not emotionally affected. When I heard the news I literally said, "Oh well, too bad" and didn't think anything else about it. I never shed a tear.
6. Cynicism.
7. Irritability. Don't ask my wife about this one!
8. Feeling of estrangement. I withdrew from all my friends. I even skipped my high school reunion. It took a full year after my retirement to even begin re-learn how to have friends. My wife says that for 26 years I knew everybody but didn't have any friends. Today, I cherish my friends and have re-learned the skill of friendship.

9. Feeling like the world does not make sense. I personally began to question God and my faith.
10. Shame for not caring anymore. I experienced this manifestation in the latter days of my career when I caught myself referring to some kids as stupid.

Depending on which psychologist you ask, you may find more or fewer symptoms, but it is generally agreed that compassion fatigue happens when we experience too much trauma vicariously and develop a sense of powerlessness. It is also a result of going too far in setting aside our own needs to meet the needs of others. It can also happen sometimes when we do not have enough support or help. My intention here is not to give a psychological presentation or accurate breakdown of the terminology. I just want you, the reader, to know what I wish I had known sooner.

In I Kings 19 we find the story of the prophet Elijah who had been a faithful servant of the Lord. Unfortunately, for Elijah, he had a strained relationship with King Ahab and his wife, Jezebel. They wanted him dead, having already killed all the other prophets. The stress got to Elijah, so he ran away by himself into the wilderness. The scripture says he sat down beside a bush and asked God to take his life. Verse 4 reads, *"I have had enough Lord. Let me die; I am no better than my ancestors"* (NCV).

I think I may know how Elijah felt that day. As I mentioned, I often buried my head between two cushions of a sofa in hopes I might somehow escape reality. I told God that I would be relieved if He would just go ahead and take my life. Thankfully, He did not take me up on my offer.

Next, Elijah laid down under a bush and fell asleep. We don't know how long he slept, but eventually, God woke him and gave him some warm bread and a drink of water. He fell asleep again and once more we don't know for how long, but God woke him up again and sent him on a long journey. At the end of that journey, he went into a cave and slept again. Elijah must have been pretty tired! God then instructed him to anoint Elisha as his successor.

The moral of this story is unclear to me. Perhaps it shows that

God provides us with rest and provision. Perhaps it shows us that when we reach the end of our rope God has someone prepared to take up our cause. Regardless of the point, we should all take comfort in knowing we are not the only people who get tired. We are not the only people who have had thoughts of wishing life was over. We are not the only people who sometimes just want to leave all our troubles behind. These feelings can happen to those of us who care deeply about the needs of others.

TEN PRACTICAL TIPS FOR TAKING CARE OF YOURSELF.

1. Build a support system. You need friends who can relate to your challenges. Don't be afraid to talk to people who are in similar situations. Seek them out. You may be surprised to discover how eager they are to share with you.

2. Reserve some time for adult company. Do not be so wrapped up in your children that you forget to spend some time with adults.

3. Set aside some daily time to pray and meditate. Along with asking God for guidance and hearing his voice, take time to evaluate your life and identify anything that may be contributing to your lack of joy or emotional balance.

4. Develop a backup plan for making a living. You do not want to find yourself in a situation where you have to continue doing a poor job just because you need a paycheck.

5. Set aside vacation time where you can totally get away from the challenges of life. If you have to take children with you, put a moratorium on personal improvement and focus on having some fun.

6. Develop hobbies or interests other than raising children. Find something healthy to distract you from the day-to-day chal-

lenges. Allow your spouse the same opportunity.

7. Have some designated no phone times when you know someone else is taking care of all the emergencies.

8. Keep a written journal of your thoughts, plans, ideas, frustrations, and challenges. Writing is therapeutic for some people and for others is a good way to organize a fragmented thought life.

9. Don't feel like you have to save the world. You are only one person. We all try to think that one person can save the world, but in reality, only God can.

10. Don't count your successes. You are not called to be successful. You are called to be faithful. Trying to help children who have been hurt is difficult work and does not always produce the results you may have dreamed of. Keeping score is not beneficial.

CHAPTER **29**

- *LIVING ON THE EDGE* -

A lot of people live their lives in pursuit of success, security, and peace. The rest of us live on the edge. Jesus, in John 10:10, says, *"I came to give life - life in all its fullness"* (NCV).

I have decided to devote the next two chapters to telling my story. It is the story of how one very ordinary person has lived a very fulfilling life. As a VP, you are probably not one of those people who is satisfied with being average. You probably have within you a deep sense of calling and a desire to do more with your life than just obtain security and peace. It is my hope that this chapter will inspire you and remind you that God does not necessarily choose the most talented nor the most likely candidates to do His work. He chooses people, like yourself, who are willing and faithful.

My story began in the early 1970s in New Orleans, Louisiana. My dad was a seminary student and worked full-time for a trucking company while also pastoring a church. Mom stayed home with me and my baby sister. When people tell you a passport should be required to go to Louisiana, there is a reason. It has a culture all its own. That culture formed part of my personality, and even though we were unaware at the time it would also prepare me for my career. Cajuns are unique people. They have little fear and they like to live life on the edge. Thus the nickname - Ragin Cajuns. My few years in Louisiana instilled a touch of that culture in my personality.

At the age of seven, my family moved to Alabama where my Dad pastored a church. I am told I was basically a good kid with a surplus of energy. My first-grade teacher wrote on my report card, "Scott settled down a little after our talk but he is wearing me out now. I'm having trouble handling him." It was in Alabama that I was tested for the special education program. I still remember the day the special education teacher pulled me out of class and took me to the special room for testing. I recall coming to the realization that something was wrong with me. I began to cry. To this day, that experience helps me empathize with kids who struggle academically and or emotionally in school. There are few things as traumatic as realizing you are *special*. I spent my elementary school years in a regular classroom except for when the special teacher came and got me. In those days they were not very politically correct. She just stuck her head in the door and said, "I need both of my special ed students to come down to the special ed room."

It was also in Alabama that I discovered organized sports. I had never experienced anything like it. In Louisiana, the little boys spent their time romping thru swamps catching lizards and frogs. Football had a lot of rules so it took me a while to catch on. However, once I realized you got points for hitting people it seemed like fun. At age seven I began playing football and baseball and continued through my high school years. Sports formed much of who I became and proved to be a very important part of the preparation for my calling in life.

My parents were the best a boy could possibly have. Momma stayed at home so my sister and I had all the love a kid could want. Daddy was also very active in my life. He was always there for me and we did a lot of things together. He was my coach and my role model. He taught me how to work and when I turned nine, we started mowing lawns together. I always had money. We also spent a lot of time building things together in our garage – something I still enjoy doing with him. Daddy never missed one football game during the entire eleven years I played. There is one notorious story about the night he left a church revival service early so he could attend one of my ball games. It would not have been so extraordinary if he had not been the preacher.

I was blessed with very good coaches all of my life. They were men who invested in me and taught me how to work hard. I excelled in sports and eventually worked my way out of the special education department, too. My high school football team was very successful. Several of the guys earned college scholarships, and by my senior year, major college coaches were attending almost every practice. I was probably the least talented guy on the team, and one of the smallest, but I had a coach who recognized I still had a little bit of a crazy cajun mentality so he found me a spot on the defensive line as a nose guard. This was another of those formative decisions God used to prepare me for the calling he had on my life. Every Friday night I lined up against guys who were twice my size and every Friday night we won. I learned there is no giant too big to defeat – a lesson I would remember for many years to come.

After high school graduation, I decided to attend the same Baptist college my Dad had attended – Samford University. I really was not smart enough to gain admission, but somehow I got in and decided to play football there. On my second day on campus, all the players were required to undergo a physical examination. I had been through plenty of those, so I did not expect any problems. I was surprised when the training staff called me out of a meeting and asked me to go to a special examination room. It was reminiscent of the day I was tested for special ed. However, this was much more serious. I was instructed to lay on a table while five or six doctors examined me. All of them listened to my heart and asked a series of questions. They all had perplexed looks on their faces. I thought I was in phenomenal physical condition. My body fat content was the lowest on the team. However, something was wrong and I soon found myself in the hospital being evaluated by a heart specialist. He too was perplexed, and although he was willing to let me take a chance, I decided my football days were over. In later years, doctors discovered that I have a heart irregularity. I realize now it was God's way of redirecting my life to the place He wanted me to be.

Late one night, three weeks after giving up football, I found myself sitting under a tree on the edge of campus, confused and searching for answers. All I had ever known was sports and it was now taken away from me. I was deeply seeking God's direction when a girl came walking out of the music building. I have always been a little unrefined, so music students seemed weird to me. I hoped she would not see me sitting under the tree, but she did. The next thing I knew we were sitting under the tree together and singing Kumbaya as she strummed a guitar. I was very frustrated and silently asked God why he had allowed this guitar girl to interrupt my quiet time. Before long, several other students joined around the tree and my time with God was thoroughly interrupted. Two guys I had never met were having a conversation and I happened to be sitting between them when one of them asked the other if he was going to volunteer to be a mentor at the *family court*.

The second I heard the words family court I knew God was answering my prayers. I cannot explain why that is the case; I just knew God was speaking to me. The next day, I went to the Campus Ministries office and signed up to be a mentor for the family court. I figured I would be helping families go to court and it would be interesting. I had no idea what I was getting into. The family court turned out to be the juvenile detention center. I showed up for my orientation and was greeted at the door by the biggest man I had ever seen. "My name is Big O. Come on in," he said. He pressed a button and an electronic door lock clicked, then he motioned for me to push the door open. I noticed it did not have a door knob but I was distracted by my concern about whether or not Big O was going to know who I was. He turned out to be very nice and told me they were expecting me. He walked me down a long corridor past two more of the electronic, knobless doors and then into a big room full of teenage boys. Big O said I could let the guards know when I was ready to leave, but he did not introduce me to any guards. They did not even see me come into the big room. The electronic door lock clicked and I was left standing in a room full of self-segregated juvenile delinquents. I just happened to be the only white guy in the room, so it was not like I could hide anywhere. I just stood there for a moment as a couple of dozen boys stared at me. Finally, a boy named Bruce G came over and said, "What are you in for?" I was not sure what he meant, so I just said I thought I was supposed to be a mentor or something. Bruce was kind and took it upon himself to look out for me. I was only four years older than he and we became fast friends. He told me he was awaiting sentencing but would probably be certified as an adult so he was looking at a long time behind bars. When I asked about his family, he told me his dad owned an import/export business and his mom was self-employed.

After a couple of hours with Bruce, I had to convince the guards to let me go. It took some explaining, but I got out and immediately felt I had done the right thing. Visiting the detention center was going to be my new football. I felt very comfortable and even realized I had a gift for getting along with those kids. In retrospect, I now realize God had been forming my personality for many years so I would be ready for this day. I went back to see Bruce and the other boys twice per week for two to four hours at a time. It took discipline and commitment because I was also going to school full time and working to pay my way.

My parents did not have the money to pay for my college. We were not poor, but Samford was not cheap. I worked many jobs and kept a lawnmower in the trunk of my 1968 Plymouth all the time. I mowed so much grass during my college days that all of my shoes were green…. literally. Even though I worked hard, there was never any spending money. Everything I made had to be used for college expenses. I became so cheap that when I was able to afford to come home I would drive my car close behind a big truck on the interstate so that I could draft behind it. I could throw the car into neutral and coast most of the way home (seventy miles). I was crazy. I bought meal tickets from kids who dropped out of school because they would sell them for half price. One year I lived in the crawl space under a friend's house. It was tall enough to stand, but only one wall was made of brick. The rest was dirt. I had to poke a rod into the dirt so I could hang my clothes, but the rent was free so that's all that mattered. God was preparing me for the calling ahead.

After several months of visiting the detention center, Bruce and I built a close bond and he began to speak more freely with me. He admitted he had not exactly told the truth about his family. His dad was, in fact, in the import/export business. He was a drug dealer. Bruce's mom was, in fact, self-employed. She was a prostitute. It was near the end of my freshman year when Bruce revealed this startling information. I vividly remember when I left the detention center that day something strange happened that would forever change my life. As I walked down the sidewalk to leave the center, I looked up through some tall trees and could see the blue sky through an opening in the clouds. I don't think God actually spoke to me audibly, but somehow I heard Him say, "Scott, do you know the difference between you and Bruce?" I thought for a moment. I was a college student with a great family, a good reputation, an awesome girlfriend, and a bright future. Bruce had no family support and was facing a long prison sentence. It seemed like an easy question to answer. Then I had a vision from my childhood of my mother greeting me with a hug one day when I got home from school. I had another vision of me and my dad kicking a football together in the yard across the street from my house. I recalled the day my Dad forfeited watching his favorite college team on TV so he could be the quarterback for a pickup game with my friends and me in our front yard. God said, "Those things are the difference between you and Bruce!" I will never forget that moment in my life. God revealed to me that if I had been born and raised in Bruce's home, I would very likely be facing prison instead of college.

That was the moment God began to unveil His plan for my life. Soon after I declared my major in psychology. Three more difficult years lay ahead. I cannot honestly say college was a great experience. I was a social misfit on campus but felt comfortable at the detention center. I was an academic disaster but not from lack of effort. I never really learned how to read properly so the whole college experience was difficult. I found entry-level employment at a psychiatric hospital and performed well when working with children and adolescents. I just seemed to have a knack for it. Nothing scared me and I was not easily rattled. I had just enough craziness to get along with the setting. I knew God was preparing me to work with troubled boys. I had found my passion.

I graduated from Samford with an undergraduate degree but could not pass the graduate school admissions exam. I had to convince them to let me enter on probation. I keep a copy of my probationary admissions letter as a reminder that God is no respecter of intelligence. When it came time to graduate, I failed the comprehensive examinations, too. I don't remember how many times I re-took them, but I did manage to graduate with a Master's Degree in Counseling. The day after I graduated a company hired me to be an in-home therapist. My boss was one of the most compassionate people I have ever known and was also as crazy as anybody I have ever known. He was a recovering drug addict who had become a licensed counselor and was also a highly ranked martial artist. He had exactly the kind of personality needed to work with troubled kids and I was a good fit as his partner. He did martial arts and I did in-home therapy. Most of my work was with troubled boys. The business was booming for me as a 24-year-old. I earned $500.00 per day working part-time and my boss wanted me to work all the time. I was grateful for the opportunity but had other interests as well. My girlfriend was 2000 miles away so I was frequently on a plane. I had also taken a job as a youth pastor the day after my undergraduate graduation and I loved that ministry.

At this point in life, I was not yet sold on the idea of opening a group home. I knew I wanted to help boys who were in trouble but I was not exactly sure how that would look. I bought a piece of land and my dad and I built a little house. Once again, I was a cheapskate. I bought used plywood from a guy who had torn down an aircraft hanger to build my house. I was twenty-four years old and making $500.00 per day, but still too cheap to pay full price for a piece of plywood.

One day I stopped by my Dad's house and found him working in his garage. He shared with me some devastating news. One of the boys I had previously worked with had shot and killed himself. I took the news in stride, but it made me wonder what would have happened if I could have provided that boy with a better home environment. At about the same time, I was dealing with a 14-year-old boy as part of my counseling practice. We had built a good rapport and I felt good about his progress, but every time I visited his home he begged me to take him home with me. I was a single man in a small house. I saw no way to do as he had asked. He finally told me that his mom's boyfriend had been raping him. That's why he wanted to live with me. At around that same time another boy confessed his plans to kill his parents with an ax handle. When he shared the reason for his rage, I could not say I blamed him. I had to scramble to find him a place to live. Another of my clients was expelled from a boys ranch so I also had to help him find a new home. It did not turn out well. He soon resorted to crime and committed a murder. During this time I had also begun to talk to my girlfriend about the possibility of us getting married and opening a boys ranch for troubled kids. There was already a very good boys' ranch nearby, but they would not consider accepting the kind of kids I wanted to take. She agreed and we soon got engaged. She had no idea what this agreement would mean!

One day I was riding my bike down a country road when I noticed an empty building on an abandoned recreation complex in a rural area. I went to take a look and discovered it was being used as a *crack house*. To make a long story short, I acquired a lease on the building, kicked out the drug users, and started readying the building to house my little group home. I had been married for six months when we received our first six boys. I used all of the money I had saved and had all my earnings from the counseling practice deposited directly to the new non-profit I had formed. I hired a friend to live in the building with the boys while I continued to work in the counseling practice. Our only source of income was what I was making in counseling.

Our mission was to only take boys who were not suitable for traditional foster homes or had been kicked out of other boys' ranches. In other words, we took boys nobody else would take. Eventually, my helper got married and tried to bring his new wife to live in the rec center. This did not last long but nobody can blame her. They soon moved out and he became a guard at the jail – a job for which he was now well prepared. My new wife and I moved into the rec center with the boys. Not long after, during a winter storm, all the pipes in the ceiling burst, and everything was flooded. The rec center was beyond repair so we moved six boys into our one-bedroom, one-bath house with us. I enclosed a porch but we still had boys sleeping on sofas in the living room. We had been taking care of kids for three years by now and God had blessed us with some supporters. After a few months in the tiny house, we bought an old farmhouse from one of my former high school teammates.

The coming years proved very difficult. My wife and I had two babies and we lived in an old farmhouse with five boys. For a long time, we only had one bathroom, and the boys had to come through our bedroom to get there. Although we were able to pay cash for the house and twenty-three acres, I was still a cheapskate. A lumber yard gave me all the poor-grade lumber I could haul in my Toyota pickup. I spent my days, while the boys were in school and with my little girl in a car carrier in the front seat of my truck, running back and forth to the lumber yard, picking up lumber so we could build an addition to the house. A group of students from the community college volunteered to do the construction. My wife got a job so we could have insurance and I continued to do counseling to support our little operation.

There is not enough room to describe everything that happened over the next twenty-three years. We built three houses on that property and then bought another thirty-two acres where we built three additional houses. During that time, we also opened two thrift stores to help raise funds. We only borrowed money on two brief occasions to invest in profit-making equipment.

When we began we had five boys with a budget of $70,000.00 per year. My compensation consisted of food and utilities, but no salary. Our only reliable source of income was what I earned through the counseling practice. Everything I earned went directly to the non-profit I had formed. The organization owned one piece of property – a van that I had paid $300.00 for. When I retired twenty-six years later, we had twenty boys in three different programs and had cared for over 300 over the years. Our budget was over one million dollars per year and we had thirty employees working at four locations. We were totally debt free. I do not think our numbers are that impressive. A lot of ministries can boast numbers much larger. What is impressive, though, is how God took a former special ed kid who had no special talents, no remarkable accomplishments, no celebrity status, no money, and no wealthy contacts, and used him to build a ministry that positively impacted hundreds of people.

I wish there was room to tell our whole story. There were truly some remarkable and miraculous things that happened along the way. A lot of people talk about what they would like to do and many speak of what the world really needs. Very few people take action and even fewer are willing to pay the steep price to accomplish great things. It is my prayer that as a VP you will be one of those people who just does it – that you will learn to live on the edge and experience the abundant life as a follower of Christ. I hope you will always remember God is not concerned with who you know, what you know, what you have, or how talented you are. He just wants you to be faithful to His calling on your life.

TEN PRACTICAL TIPS FOR STARTING AND MAINTAINING A MINISTRY FOR CHILDREN.

1. Understand the difference between a calling and a liking. With a liking, you know of something you think you would like to do and you think you would be capable of doing. With a calling you know in your heart that you will not be happy unless you do this particular thing.

2. Count the cost before announcing the call. Once you go public with your calling you will be ashamed to back out when you

discover it had some unexpected challenges. Do your due diligence before telling anyone you have been called.

3. Talk to as many people as possible who have done similar things. Learn all you can from the mistakes and good decisions of others.

4. Prepare yourself. You may still need years of training and education. You may need more patience than you ever dreamed. If you are truly called to do something, training and waiting may be part of the process of fulfilling that calling.

5. Once you set your mind to do something, don't look back. Be determined, persistent, and stubborn. It may be the only way you will accomplish the goal. Success is rarely easy or quick.

6. If you have a spouse, make sure they are on board with your calling. If they are not, don't do it. This does not mean they have to fully understand everything or that they even need to like your plans. You just have to know that they are willing to go on the journey with you.

7. Get rid of all financial debt. Starting and maintaining a ministry might mean you go without money for long periods of time. You cannot focus on your ministry while worrying about debt.

8. Check your lifestyle. There is nothing wrong with nice clothes, nice cars, and nice houses, but most of the time when we start a ministry there will not be financial resources to support those things. Learn to be happy driving old cars, shopping in thrift stores, and living in less desirable neighborhoods.

9. Scrap the office when you are getting started. A lot of people think they have to have a nice office with a secretary and all the latest technology. In reality, those things come much later in the process, if at all. Most successful ministries, or businesses for that matter, started with some poor guy working out of a closet with a notebook and a few ink pins.

10. Don't expect anybody to jump on board and help you just because you think you have a good idea. Use your own money to get started. Don't quit your day job. Do something tangible and people will slowly begin to help.

CHAPTER 30

- *DOES IT MATTER?* -

The following story, like all of the stories in this book, may be difficult to believe but it is true. Much of what I present is taken from the personal, hand-written diary of the now deceased Ora Gladys Detwiler. I was fortunate to obtain a copy of the diary which started in 1920. The focus of this story is her little brother, Arvel.

Ora was seven years old and lived in a small town called Riceton, Alabama where her father, Arthur Detwiler, worked in a coal mine. Her mother, Ada Detwiler, was a fine Christian lady who enjoyed being a mother to six children. Clarence, the oldest, was followed by Floyd, then Flora May, Ora, and two little brothers Arvel and Leon. The family enjoyed a happy life despite the fact that a couple of the children had a mean streak, including little Arvel who reportedly started getting into fights when he was old enough to walk.

In December of 1923 tragedy struck the happy family. Ada, who was five months pregnant, caught pneumonia and struggled to recover. As a result, she had a miscarriage - her unborn baby died. Consequently, a few days later, Ada also passed away. She was buried on Christmas day 1923.

Ora, in her diary, wrote, "We were a sad bunch. The bottom fell out of all our lives. My dad almost lost his mind." In fact, Mr. Detwiler, in great pain over the loss of his wife, resorted to alcohol and the family completely fell apart. By this time Clarence, the oldest had moved out on his own but Mr. Detwiler was left alone to raise five children ages one, five, seven, twelve, and fifteen. With no other family to lean on and desperately needing to go back to work, he hired a young lady to help care for the children. The children, however, were mean to her and, probably due to their state of frustration, were not well behaved. When the young lady quit the job Mr. Detwiler found another babysitter but she was mean to the children and she eventually quit too. In the process, Arthur was missing a lot of work and the family was short on resources so the children nearly starved to death. According to one account, little Arvel was reduced to skin and bones and although five years old could be held in the palm of one's hand.

Members of the community noticed Arthur was struggling so a family friend, Adeline Massey, offered to take one-year-old Leon into her home. Arthur gladly gave him to her but he still had four hungry and frustrated children to raise by himself.

For Arthur the pressures of life were overwhelming and his children were starving so he made a desperate decision. He decided to abandon his family and escape to another state. However, before he could do so he made a decision that has always been difficult for me to understand. He decided to throw his four remaining children in the warrior river and end their lives. It is unclear whether he had lost his mind or if he was under the influence of alcohol but, whatever the case, it would be a horrible decision.

In researching to tell this story, I personally went to the little town of Sayre, Alabama, and found the old abandoned bridge thought to be the place where Mr. Detwiler planned to throw his children off into the Warrior River. It was a chilling experience to walk down that path where these four children had walked almost one hundred years ago.

As they walked to the bridge a chain of events took place that would affect the course of history for literally thousands of people. Ora's diary reads, "Dad gathered us up and told us he was going to throw us in the warrior river. We walked to the river and there was

Mrs. Conner... She wanted me." Ora went home with the Conner family but did not know what happened to her siblings. They are not mentioned again in her diary.

That was 1923 and it would be decades before the remaining facts of that fateful day emerged.

My source of information was my grandmother who had lived near Sayre where the incident occurred. Arvel survived the incident and later told her the rest of his story.

Arvel recalled that as his dad was walking him to the bridge an old black lady happened to be working in the yard outside her little "shack" that sat near the dirt road. She noticed how skinny he was so she stopped them and offered to give him something to eat. When Arvel went inside to eat with the lady, his Dad continued walking. It would be several years before he would see him again. The old lady did not have much food but she made biscuits for him and he recalled her putting syrup on those biscuits. That would be their meal together. That night, and for many nights to come, she made for him a small pallet on the floor in front of her fireplace. At just five years old he was confused and afraid but had one comfort, the love, and attention of the old black lady - a lady whose name he never knew.

Arvel was not sure how long he stayed with the lady. It could have been several weeks or months but he remembers she nursed him back to health and treated him kindly until finally a young couple, Mr. and Mrs. Roy Fason, heard about him and went to find him at the old lady's shack. The couple decided to adopt him and took him home with them. This changed his life. They changed his name from "Arvel" to "Ted." He became Ted Fason.

Ted grew up as a member of the Fason family. He loved them and they loved him. Unfortunately, his adoptive father was killed in an accident at the Republic Steel plant in Gadsden, AL. His passing placed abnormal responsibility on Ted's shoulders.

At the age of 15, he lied in order to get a job with the Civilian Conservation Corp; a group created as part of Roosevelt's plan to lift the country out of the great depression. He worked to help support his family and eventually met the love of his life – Dura Mae

McDonald. Ted eventually got a good job as a train car inspector for the steel plant and also opened a small plumbing business. He and Dura married and built a house in Pleasant Grove, Alabama. They had four daughters.

By all accounts, Ted became a wonderful father to his four girls. He was always gentle and tender-hearted with them, and they all adored him. Just as he had been a fighter as a child, he was a fighter as a grown man - though not in a bad way. He fought hard to overcome his own childhood traumas and to give his girls the love and security he had so often lived without following the loss of his mother.

Ted also became the proud grandfather of eleven grandchildren. The two oldest grandboys were particularly blessed with his attention because Ted considered them to be the sons he never had. He took them camping, fishing, and boating on a regular basis, and is said to have spoiled them with fun outings.

I had the privilege of meeting and getting to know Ted, so when he passed away in 1996, I attended the funeral. I still have a visual image of the eleven grandchildren circled around his casket, laughing, telling stories, and remembering what a wonderful grandfather he had been. I recall seeing his four daughters and wife mourn the loss of the man who had become their hero. I could not stop thinking about the little old lady who had saved his life as a little boy. None of this would have been possible without her - the lady whose name nobody knows. She is a living testimony to the fact that even those who seem to have little to give can give in abundance when they give all they have. She reminds me that it is most often those whose names are forgotten who have the most impact on our world. She reminds me that we may never know if it is worth it or not - at least not in our lifetime. She may be lost to history, buried in an unmarked grave, and forgotten but her impact will live on.

As a VP, you may very well be called to be the little ole black lady whose name is now forgotten, but please never forget that the work you are doing may very well impact thousands of people in generations yet to come. As you shall see, this is not the end of Ted's story!

Fast forward almost 100 years, I am settled into a comfortable lawn chair at the side of the pool. My 32 years of pouring out my life to others have come to an end. I am emotionally spent and desperately need a break. It was a Sunday afternoon and eight little children splashed around in the pool, each of them with their own personality. One little boy sat alone and tried to dismantle a toy. Another little boy ran wildly around the edge of the pool before diving in. A little girl was busy gathering all the beach balls and trying her best to hold them all at one time. The smallest baby cuddled in his mother's arms as she gently introduced him to the warm water. Four beautiful young wives tended to the children while sharing motherhood stories and laughing about funny things their husbands had done. Gathered around the grill stood four grown men - all of them in their early thirties – each of them the father of two, each of them a committed husband, each of them successful in his career, and each of them with a story. I knew each story intimately. A decade and a half earlier, I combed through their social summaries and psychological evaluations and made a decision to take those four boys into our little ranch. They had all grown up there. None of them had the benefit of having a stable birth family. Their early lives had been filled with trauma and instability. None of them had a father to spend time with them or teach them how to be a man. Each of them had seen more than his fair share of the sadness of life. Through the years they had become like brothers. The other men at the ranch and I felt like fathers to them. I had the good fortune of sharing my life with them and, likewise, they shared theirs with my family. I had the good fortune of trying to be a role model, teacher, and encourager for them. I was there with them through hard times and good times. Life with these guys was not always easy. It was often filled with heartaches, disappointments, and even tragedies. All those years I wondered if they would make it.

Would they do what had to be done to turn things around and grow up to be the husbands and dads God intended them to be? Finally, now, I could see that they were going to make it. It is common to reflect on our experiences and wonder if we did anything that really matters. As I sat poolside that day and watched those happy little children, a warm sense of peace came over me. I realized that my efforts really mattered. Eight little children would have a stable, happy home with a loving father and mother. Eight little children would not have to grow up with the same trauma and challenges their dads had faced. Four men had made a decision to break the cycles of dysfunction and step up to be responsible men. That made me very proud. While I cannot take responsibility for the success of these young men, I can take joy in knowing that I had a small part in creating an atmosphere in which they became men who would make any father proud. Sometimes, God gives us a glimpse of heaven. That day as we sat by the poolside I believe I had a glimpse. I knew that my life mattered. Nothing can be more fulfilling.

Before opening Eagle Rock, I provided counseling at a shelter for runaway youth. One night I received a phone call asking me to come to the shelter. A young man to whom I had grown close had received some bad news and had become suicidal as a result. He had requested my visit. This is not the type of call you like to receive at midnight on a stormy night, but I got dressed and drove to the shelter. I found the boy outside in the middle of the storm, shooting basketball. I joined him and for about two hours he shot baskets and I caught rebounds and tossed them back to him. The entire time he was talking about his situation and I simply listened. At about 2:00 in the morning, another storm began to brew and it started to rain again. Neither of us paid any attention; he needed to talk and a little rain was not going to stop us. The wind was blowing and rain was pouring sideways, but the boy continued to shoot baskets and I continued to catch rebounds. We were both soaked, but he was feeling a little better and I knew my time was being well spent. Unfortunately, at about the time I started feeling good about the situation, a tragedy struck. The heavy metal basketball rim and backboard, under the pressure of the high winds, broke loose from the pole and came crashing down on top of me. The boy saw it happening but there was no time to save me. He watched as it slammed into the top of my head, knocking me senseless. I immediately collapsed to the ground in a state of semi-consciousness while he ran to get help. Not realizing I was seriously hurt, the boy came back and began to laugh hysterically. It must have been a funny sight to see. Eventually, I stood to my feet. We then realized I was bleeding badly, so he helped me inside the house. The corner of the backboard had gashed my head open. I was rushed to the hospital where I spent the rest of the night getting stitches and being evaluated.

The next day I went by the shelter to check on the boy. Once we knew I was going to be ok, we both shared a huge laugh. We had built a great memory together and he had forgotten about his troubles for a while. A few weeks later I had a clean bill of health and the stitches were removed but I did have a big scar. Things worked out well for the boy and eventually he was adopted by a great family. I mostly forgot about the incident, but occasionally my barber would ask about the scar and I would retell the story. I lost all contact with the young man. Twenty years passed since the incident when one evening I opened an email from someone I did not recognize. I normally do not do that, but something told me I needed to open this one. It began, "Are you the Scott Hilton who used to work at a runaway shelter about 20 years ago?" I replied that I was. The person replied, "Do you recall a basketball goal falling on your head at the shelter in the middle of the night?" I replied, "Yes."

Within a few minutes, I received the following email. It came to mean a lot to me. (For confidentiality reasons I have changed the name).

> My name is Tim. You and I share a very important part of my history. I was taken to the runaway shelter because I accused my stepfather of being sexually involved with some young girls. Whenever I would try to report it I was beaten pretty badly, sometimes hospitalized. Once I got to the shelter I was treated well. Most people I know have horror stories about group homes but my story was good. You played a very large part in that. A young local couple offered to take me into their home for Christmas and so I did. We became very attached, and we tried to make that move permanent. My parents did not want that and went to court. I was told by staff that I would

be sent home, which was frightening for me. I remember being out back, in the rain, trying to play basketball by myself to get my mind off of it. You came out, and played with me, in the rain, until the goal broke, and landed on your head. You had to get stitched. Your level of personal involvement during the time that I was there, had a huge impact on me. I lived in a survivor mentality. I could not trust or depend on anyone, and that could have stayed with me for the rest of my life, and I certainly would not be where I am today. I did not graduate high school. I did go to college and served almost ten years in the Army. I have two children of my own, a wife, and her son. I have what some would consider a very successful career in IT and currently work at the headquarters of (a nationally recognized government agency). I had to fight to get where I am because of the disadvantages I grew up with. I never would have gotten where I am on my own and that I attribute directly to you. If I could convince you of anything it would be this: My ability to get where I am in life, and the efforts I have to volunteer and give back as much as I can, can all be traced back to you, and I wanted to say thank you.

Occasionally I still touch that little scar on the top of my head and I am reminded of Tim and many other young men who God brought into my life. I, maybe like you, made a lot of mistakes and there are things I wish I had done differently. However, I was present. Sometimes the greatest successes in life come by simply being there when someone needs us.

The scar on my head reminds me that if I never take a risk, never step out on a limb, and never go out into the storm, I will never have a scar.

I choose to live my life in the storm, but it is through those storms that life is truly lived. My challenge to you, V.P., is to continue living in the storm. I love the words of Amy Carmichael:

Hast thou no scar?
No hidden scar on foot, or side, or hand?

I hear thee sung as mighty in the land,
I hear them hail thy bright ascendant star,
Hast thou no scar?
Hast thou no wound?
Yet, I was wounded by the archers, spent.
Leaned me against the tree to die, and rent
By ravening beasts that compassed me, I swooned:
Hast thou no wound?
No wound? No scar?
Yet as the Master shall the servant be,
And pierced are the feet that follow Me;
But thine are whole. Can he have followed far
Who has no wound nor scar?

....

I began this chapter with a story about a boy who was almost thrown off a bridge. I would like to dedicate this book to the poor old black lady who took little Ted in and nursed him back to health. She represents every VP who does the hard work, day in and day out, to help those among us who are most vulnerable.

Finally, as promised I will now provide the rest of the story about little Ted and the bridge:

Ted was my Grandfather.

Heart of the Project.

Scott Hilton retired from Executive Director of Eagle Rock Boys Home in 2019, where he served in the trenches with at-risk boys for over 32 years. Upon his retirement, his heart was still beating for the fatherless and was eager to use his decades of experience to continue to make a difference in the lives of fathers and children.

In 2021, Scott founded the **That's My Dad Project** - a comprehensive project aimed at breaking cycles of generational fatherlessness and inspiring fathers to become great dads.

Through his podcast, books, speaking engagements, fatherhood seminars, and coaching sessions, Scott's mission is to inspire these men to become the best dads they can be and "flip the script" in their family tree. Generations will be better because of it.

To learn more about the That's My Dad Project,
you can visit their website:
www.thatsmydadproject.com

You can view the latest episodes on YouTube
by scanning the QR Code.

breaking cycles of generational fatherlessness
and inspiring fathers to become great dads

social platforms:

YouTube: That's My Dad Podcast
Instagram: @podcast.thatsmydad
Facebook: That's My Dad Podcast
TikTok: @podcast.thatsmydad

Interested in having Scott come and speak?

Reach out to him at:
thatsmydadproject.com

At the age of 27, Scott Hilton left a successful counseling practice to open a home for disadvantaged boys in Alabama - Eagle Rock Boys Home. Over the past 27 years, Eagle Rock has grown into a vibrant ministry that continues to serve society's most vulnerable. Along the way, over 300 boys have called Eagle Rock home, and generations have been greatly impacted because of it.

Eagle Rock Boys Home is a place where boys are empowered to overcome. Eagle Rock empowers these at-risk boys by helping them find healing, experience family, and prepare for the future. In many cases, this journey takes years simply because of the trauma these boys have endured. But, each day, the staff and leadership get to watch in awe as God moves in miraculous ways, and leads these boys towards a better future.

Today, led by Belinda Hiti, Eagle Rock continues to serve boys through their Boys Home, Independent Living Program, and Connector Mentoring Program. Their mission remains the same - empowering boys to overcome.

If you'd like to learn more about Eagle Rock Boys Home, you can visit the website:

eaglerockfamily.org

Eagle Rock International Kids (ERIK) is the international branch of our efforts to reach and help hurting children. ERIK seeks to provide the tools necessary for orphanages in developing countries to become self-supporting. We primarily build farms which will become self-supporting and provide perpetual sources of food and income for the orphanages we partner with. ERIK's second area of focus is to assure that infants and children receive adequate physical and emotional contact with caring adults during critical bonding periods. ERIK does not own nor operate these orphanages. We leave that up to the experts who are already there doing the hard work. We are simply a support system.

The funds used for these projects comes from real estate investments and other businesses created by the Eagle Rock family inside the United States. Donations to these projects are accepted but not actively sought after.

ERIK was launched in 2019.

CPSIA information can be obtained
at www.ICGtesting.com
Printed in the USA
BVHW090524031122
651016BV00005B/23